ASCAP

COPYRIGHT LAW SYMPOSIUM

Number Fifteen

NATHAN BURKAN
1878–1936

COPYRIGHT LAW SYMPOSIUM

Number Fifteen

NATHAN BURKAN
MEMORIAL COMPETITION

SPONSORED BY THE

*American Society of Composers
Authors and Publishers*

COLUMBIA UNIVERSITY PRESS

NEW YORK AND LONDON

1967

© *Copyright 1967*
American Society of Composers,
Authors and Publishers
575 Madison Avenue, New York

Library of Congress Catalog Card Number: 40-8341

Printed in the United States of America

Preface

A PREFACE TO THIS volume seems superfluous in view of the splendid foreword of Judge Bergan and Judge Kiley. We can add only the gratitude of the men and women who write and publish the music of America to those who have participated in and encouraged the Nathan Burkan Memorial Competition—judges, deans, law professors, and students.

The Copyright Law Symposium series, in which the best papers submitted in this Competition are published, has become a standard work of reference in the field of Copyright Law. This reflects great credit on the high standards of legal education in America. Indeed, the scholarship and literary quality of the papers have invariably won commendation from the national judges of the Competition, who have given so much time and patient study, reading and selecting the papers to receive National Awards.

Judge Kiley and Judge Bergan, as their Foreword and the papers in this volume indicate, have done much to carry on the "fruitful program cultivating and maintaining the interest of teachers and students in an important field of law." It is hardly necessary to add a biographical note about these eminent judges, but we cannot omit a reference to the striking parallels in their respective careers and their devotion to the public interest.

Both Judge Bergan and Judge Kiley earned their LL.B.'s in 1923, Judge Bergan at Union and Judge Kiley at Notre Dame. Both were admitted to the bar in 1924, Judge Bergan in New York and Judge Kiley in Illinois. Both had interesting careers in fields other than law before turning to the "jealous mistress"; Judge Bergan was a newspaper reporter from 1919 to 1932, and Judge Kiley, an All-American protégé of Knute Rockne, was player and then an assistant football coach at Notre Dame while in law school. Until 1932, Judge Kiley also coached university football on a seasonal basis while engaged in private law practice.

In their experience on the bench, too, the careers of Judge Kiley and Judge Bergan have much in common. Judge Kiley was elected as a judge of the Superior Court of Cook County, Illinois, in 1940, then served as Justice of the Appellate Court of Illinois, First District, from 1941 until his appointment to the United States Court of Appeals for the Seventh Circuit in 1961, the post he now holds. Judge Bergan was elected Justice of the Albany (New York) City Court in 1929 and as Justice of the New York Supreme Court in 1935. He served as an associate justice of the Appellate Division of that court from 1940 to 1960, and as Presiding Justice from 1960 to 1963, when he was elected as a judge of the New York Court of Appeals.

Judge Bergan and Judge Kiley have both found time for civic activities. A former alderman of Chicago's 37th Ward, from 1933 to 1940, Judge Kiley is a member of the Advisory Council of the University of Notre Dame Law School, a director of Great Books Foundation, Inc., of the St. Thomas More Association, Inc., and of Catholic Charities. His professional memberships include the American, Illinois, and Chicago Bar Associations.

Judge Bergan is a member of the American Law Institute, has been a member of the board of directors of Jacob's Pillow Dance Festival, and trustee of Dudley Observatory, the Albany Hospital, and the Albany Medical College. He also received a citation of merit as library trustee from the American Library Association in 1959, served as Chairman of the New York State Commissioner of Education's Commission on Public Library Service and is president of the board of trustees of the Albany Public Library. Judge Bergan has

Preface

served on the New York State Constitutitonal Convention Commissions of 1938 and 1956–58.

In addition to their numerous scholarly opinions from the bench, Judge Bergan and Judge Kiley have been frequent contributors to law reviews.

The three winners of National Awards whose papers are published here were members of the law reviews at their respective law schools—two of them heading their editorial boards. The achievements of all five authors show an earnestness and devotion that foretell outstanding careers at the bar.

Ciro Gamboni, author of the National First Prize essay, was a member of Order of the Coif, on the *Law Review*, and on the Dean's List at New York University Law School. Mr. Gamboni is now serving as a lieutenant in the United States Army.

The Second Prize winner, Matthew Nimetz, a Rhodes Scholar before entering Harvard Law School, was president of the *Harvard Law Review* and winner of the Fay Diploma for being first in his graduating class. Mr. Nimetz was a teaching fellow in social science at Harvard College and is presently law clerk to United States Supreme Court Justice John M. Harlan.

Third National winner, Michael E. Mecsas, was editor-in-chief of the *Cornell Law Quarterly*. He is associated with the Buffalo, New York, law firm of Saperston, Wiltse, Duke, Day, and Wilson.

In addition to these winners, the essays of Gary D. Ordway and Daniel E. Nester received Honorable Mention. Mr. Ordway received awards for excellence in Taxation Law and Pleadings at Drake University Law School. Mr. Nester, who was graduated from Seton Hall University School of Law, is at present on the patent staff of Bell Telephone Laboratories, Inc.

These outstanding young men are carrying forward the

tradition of excellence in Nathan Burkan Memorial Competition winners. The views they express are, of course, their own and in no way reflect the opinions of the judges or sponsor of the Competition.

Again we express our gratitude to Judge Kiley and Judge Bergan for their enthusiastic participation in the Competition, which has played such a great role in the development of Copyright Law in America.

STANLEY ADAMS,
PRESIDENT

HERMAN FINKELSTEIN,
GENERAL COUNSEL

AMERICAN SOCIETY OF COMPOSERS, AUTHORS AND PUBLISHERS

HONORABLE FRANCIS BERGAN
JUDGE, NEW YORK COURT OF APPEALS

HONORABLE ROGER J. KILEY
JUDGE, UNITED STATES COURT
OF APPEALS FOR THE SEVENTH CIRCUIT

Foreword

FIVE ESSAYS WERE CHOSEN as the best of forty-eight written by law students throughout the country in this the Twenty-Seventh Nathan Burkan Memorial Competition conducted by the American Society of Composers, Authors and Publishers (ASCAP). The forty-eight essays had previously been selected as the first and second prize winners in their respective school competitions. The five chosen for this Fifteenth ASCAP Copyright Law Symposium are the winners of the first, second, and third Competition prizes of $1,000, $500, and $250, and two additional essays selected as next best.

The forty-eight essays reflect the continuing interest stirred by the Competition, its sharp impact on our law schools, and its stimulating influence toward original, imaginative expression in copyright law. The essay subject matter ranges from the need of copyright for modern dance choreography to the problem of attaching liability for infringement in relay of television programs beamed to communication satellites. Within the range are other interesting subjects: the history of copyright law; the copyrightability of pornographic materials and of computer programs; and copyright protection for architectural principles and for corporate symbols, such as "3M." There are imaginative titles: "The Hapless Licensee"; " 'Old Soldiers Never Die . . . They Just Fade Away' or *Common Law Copyright v. H.R. 4347.*" There are essays upon current problems: the effects of the Supreme Court *Sears-Compco* decisions; the protection of varied interests in Community Antenna Television (CATV). Even the copyright royalty implications for the lowly jukebox were not overlooked. There are many suggestions to improve and modernize the 1909 Copyright Act.

The forty-eight essays presented many close problems of selection to the judges. The differences in quality separating the essays were in a number of instances very close. But using as well as they could standards of good writing, persuasive and lawyerlike argument, originality, and significance to legal science, the judges by carefully reading and rereading made the choices they thought pointed to the highest merit.

The essay of Ciro A. Gamboni, of New York University School of Law, "Unfair Competition Protection after *Sears* and *Compco*," was recommended for first prize. It is the most lawyerlike. It has a professional touch and an academic breadth, and should enrich one's library. And it hits a current problem that is vexing judges and lawyers alike, i.e., the extent to which *Sears* and *Compco* have preempted states from power over unfair competition litigation. This essay stood out from the rest.

"Design Protection," by Matthew Nimetz, of Harvard University Law School, was chosen for second prize. Here is an advocate's product, written in depth and urging limited design protection in the garment industry. The essay discloses a mature knowledge, not only of copyright and related law, but of the economics of the industry and the garment-making process.

For third prize, the judges selected the essay of Michael E. Mecsas, of Cornell Law School, "The Effect of the Copyright Act and the Proposed Revision on Educators as Users of Copyrighted Materials." This thorough essay hits its mark squarely, is tightly written, has persuasive and original arguments, and critically analyzes the proposed revision of the copyright statute. The proliferation of educational materials in a "publish or perish" academic world poses many difficulties for authors, educators, and publishers. This essay should stimulate further thought on how to overcome these difficulties. The difficulties were noted in a recent article,

"Our 'Model T' Copyright Law," in *The Reporter*, March 10, 1966.

The choice of a fourth essay for rounding out the Symposium is that of David E. Nester, of Seton Hall University School of Law, "Is CATV Infringing Proprietary Rights in Television Broadcasts?" His thesis is that the copyright law should recognize CATV programs as public performance for profit and should afford adequate protection to broadcasters for the CATV replaying of the original programs. It is well written and shows a competent grasp of the operation of CATV systems, their relationship to the television programs upon which CATV feeds, and the relevant copyright law as it is and as it ought to be. The subject is of great importance today, and the essay's contribution to solution of a pressing problem was a considerable factor in the decision to give it a place in the Symposium.

Gary D. Ordway, of Drake University Law School, wrote a highly imaginative and delightful essay, "Choreography and Copyright," urging copyright protection for modern dance, which tells no story but communicates an emotion. This is a little known area of the entertainment world. In fact, the area was too little known to make a significant contribution to the development of copyright law. The essay was difficult to exclude from a prize. It has been selected for the Symposium to add a refreshing fillip.

The judges gladly accepted ASCAP General Counsel Herman Finkelstein's flattering invitation to serve in the roles filled by the distinguished men who served in preceding Competitions, and we are grateful for his amiable and thoughtful solicitude during the work. The assignment has been a challenge, and an enriching experience. As in all results of the decisional process, the choices made were not entirely free of doubt. The Nathan Burkan Memorial Competition is a most worthy idea in the development of law, and

ASCAP deserves generous commendation upon a fruitful program cultivating and maintaining the interest of teachers and students in an important field of law.

> ROGER J. KILEY
> JUDGE, UNITED STATES COURT OF APPEALS
> FOR THE SEVENTH CIRCUIT
>
> FRANCIS BERGAN
> JUDGE, NEW YORK COURT OF APPEALS

Rules Governing the Competition

1. *Participating Law Schools:* All accredited law schools are invited to participate in the Competition.
2. *Eligible Students:* Third-year students. In the discretion of the dean, second-year students may also be eligible.
3. *Subject Matter:* Any phase of *Copyright Law.*
4. *Determination of Awards:* The prizes will be awarded to the students who shall, in the sole judgment of the dean—or such other person or committee as he may delegate—prepare the two best papers. The dean may in his discretion withhold the awards entirely, if in his opinion no worthy paper is submitted, or may award only the first or second prize.
5. *Prizes:* A *first prize of $250* and a *second prize of $100*, to be paid through the dean, upon his written certification.
6. *Formal Requirements, Right of Publication, etc.:*
   (a) Manuscript must be typewritten (double-spaced) on 8½" × 11" paper, 1" margin all around; indent and single space all quotations exceeding four lines.
   (b) Manuscript must not exceed 50 pages.
   (c) Citations must be in approved law review form.
   (d) Submit *two* copies of manuscript.
   (e) Cover for manuscript: any standard form stiff cover with label on outside showing title of paper, your name, and permanent *home address.*
   (f) Two copies of the winning papers will be forwarded by the dean to the Society, which may authorize publication.
   (g) Papers may appear in law reviews, provided their entry in the Nathan Burkan Memorial Competition is duly noted.
7. As papers are presumed to represent individual study, collaboration with others in their preparation is not permitted.
8. *Closing Date:* August 15th—or any earlier date the dean may specify. Winning papers must be certified to the Society not later than August 31st.
9. *National Awards:* The best papers certified to the Society will be selected for National Awards of *$1,500, $1,000, $750, $500* and

$250, respectively. The award papers selected by the judges will be printed in the form of a "Copyright Law Symposium".

Questions concerning the Competition may be addressed to the Society's General Counsel, Herman Finkelstein, 575 Madison Avenue, New York, N.Y. 10022.

Contents

Preface v
BY STANLEY ADAMS, President, and HERMAN FINKLESTEIN, General Counsel, American Society of Composers, Authors, and Publishers

Foreword ix
BY ROGER J. KILEY, Judge, United States Court of Appeals for the Seventh Circuit, and FRANCIS BERGAN, Judge, New York Court of Appeals

Rules Governing the Competition xiii

NATIONAL FIRST PRIZE, 1965

Unfair Competition after Sears *and* Compco 1
BY CIRO A. GAMBONI, New York University School of Law

NATIONAL SECOND PRIZE, 1965

Design Protection 79
BY MATTHEW NIMETZ, Harvard University Law School

NATIONAL THIRD PRIZE, 1965

The Effect of the Copyright Act and the Proposed Revision on Educators as Users of Copyrighted Materials 134
BY MICHAEL E. MECSAS, Cornell Law School

Contents

HONORABLE MENTION, 1965

Is CATV Infringing Proprietary Rights in Television Broadcasts?   153
BY DANIEL E. NESTER, Seton Hall University School of Law

HONORABLE MENTION, 1965

Choreography and Copyright   172
BY GARY D. ORDWAY, Drake University School of Law

Panels of Judges   191

Papers Appearing in Copyright Law Symposia Numbers One through Fourteen   195

Law Schools Contributing Papers to Previous Copyright Law Symposia   203

Statutes and Cases   211

Works Cited   227

Index   237

NATIONAL FIRST PRIZE, 1965

Unfair Competition Protection after Sears and Compco

By CIRO A. GAMBONI

NEW YORK UNIVERSITY SCHOOL OF LAW

INTRODUCTION

JUDICIAL PROTECTION against simulation of product design developed to compensate for the limited protection afforded by the federal patent and copyright acts. The Design Patent Act's [1] grant of protection for a maximum of fourteen years to those nonmechanical elements which enhance an article's distinctive or artistic appearance rather than affect its purpose, action, or performance,[2] represents an ambitious statutory attempt to protect the design of commercial products.[3] Nevertheless, the statute confers limited relief,[4] since the occasion is rare when the requisite purely original design is created.[5] Most creative ideas are only slight modifications of known ideas. Consequently, most designs fail to qualify for patent protection,[6] although they are often of tremendous

---
[1] 35 U.S.C. §§ 171–73 (1958).

[2] West Point Mfg. Co. v. Detroit Stamping Co., 222 F.2d 581 (6th Cir.), cert. denied, 350 U.S. 840 (1955).

[3] See generally Comment, *Trade Regulation: Legal Protection of Commercial Design*, 1959 WIS. L. REV. 652. For a discussion of the historical development of the design patent law, see Hudson, *A Brief History of the Development of Design Patent Protection in the United States*, 30 J. PAT. OFF. SOC'Y 380 (1948).

[4] See GOTSHAL, TODAY'S FIGHT FOR DESIGN PROTECTION (1957); Note, 26 U. CIN. L. REV. 86 (1957); Note, 49 YALE L.J. 1290 (1940).

[5] 1 CALLMANN, UNFAIR COMPETITION AND TRADE-MARKS § 16.3, at 254 (2d ed. 1950).

[6] See Vacheron & Constantin-LeCoultre Watches, Inc. v. Benrus Watch Co.,

commercial value. In addition, rigorous procedural requirements make design patent protection impractical for many who may meet the strict standards.[7]

To obtain statutory copyright protection, three-dimensional articles of commercial utility must qualify as "works of art."[8] Since the Supreme Court held a lamp base statuette copyrightable as a "work of art" notwithstanding its utilitarian function,[9] a toy animal,[10] a necklace,[11] and a fabric pattern design [12] have been held copyrightable; but it is improbable that the design of a can opener, or of a steam iron, or of the vast majority of commercial products, would constitute a "work of art."[13]

The originator unable to obtain either patent or copyright looked to state courts of equity for protection against competitors who appropriated his creation to their own commercial advantage. Although the originator's decision to incur the expenses of creation was presumably made with an awareness of the risks involved, the argument was made that federal patent and copyright enactments to promote the progress of science and the useful arts [14] do not necessarily evidence an intent to prevent states from protecting commercial investments against business practices regarded as unfair. The limited scope of federal protection was, in fact, urged as aggravating the need for state protection.

---

260 F.2d 637, 642–43 (2d Cir. 1958) (Clark, C.J., dissenting). One ten-year survey of design patent litigation showed a mortality rate of about 80%. Walter, *A Ten Year Survey of Design Patent Litigation*, 35 J. PAT. OFF. SOC'Y 389 (1953).

[7] Note, *Protecting the Artistic Aspects of Articles of Utility: Copyright or Design Patent?*, 66 HARV. L. REV. 877 (1953).

[8] 17 U.S.C. § 5(g) (1958). [9] Mazer v. Stein, 347 U.S. 201 (1954).

[10] Rushton v. Vitale, 218 F.2d 434 (2d Cir. 1955).

[11] Trifari, Krussman & Fishel, Inc. v. Charel Co., 134 F. Supp. 551 (S.D.N.Y. 1955).

[12] Peter Pan Fabrics, Inc. v. Brenda Fabrics, Inc., 169 F. Supp. 142 (S.D.N.Y. 1959).

[13] See Comment, 1959 WIS. L. REV. 652.

[14] The patent and copyright clause of the Constitution empowers Congress "To promote the Progress of Science and useful Arts, by securing for limited Times to Authors and Inventors the exclusive Right to their respective Writings and Discoveries." U.S. CONST. art. I, § 8, cl. 8.

Unfair Competition Protection

Any ethical code, however, necessarily conflicts with the ideal of free competition.[15] Yet courts apparently reacted with repugnance to the "slavish copying" of unpatented and uncopyrighted products with the intention of passing off the copy as the original.[16] The interests of the honest businessman in the fruits of his creation and of the public in knowing the true source of a product, outweighed the interest in maintaining the ideal of free competition.[17] To enjoin inordinate imitation of minor embellishments was not thought to create common law patents or to provide an incentive and reward for invention,[18] but to prevent public deception,[19] improper diversion of trade,[20] and loss of good will.[21]

The result was the law of unfair competition, the "book of rules of the business game," [22] with its criteria for the granting

[15] See Chas. D. Briddell, Inc. v. Alglobe Trading Corp., 194 F.2d 416, 418 (2d Cir. 1952) ("it is of the essence of competition that competitors copy and undersell the product of an originator"). *But see* Sell, *The Doctrine of Misappropriation in Unfair Competition*, 11 VAND. L. REV. 483, 497 (1958) ("free competition impels honest, fair conduct by the parties").

[16] Courts which have refused protection have admitted that such a result is harsh. Even Judge Hand, who traditionally denied relief in such situations, spoke in terms of a "hiatus in completed justice," Cheney Bros. v. Doris Silk Corp., 35 F.2d 279, 281 (2d Cir. 1929), *cert. denied*, 281 U.S. 728 (1930). But copyists consider the question of ethics irrelevant because, they contend, their conduct is beneficial both to the industry and to the consumer, and therefore justified. See Hutchinson, *Design Piracy*, 18 HARV. BUS. REV. 191 (1940).

[17] Judge Frank, however, considered that the public's interest in encouraging "honesty" and "fair dealing in business," in procuring "the security of the fruits of individual enterprise," and in "safeguarding consumers from being deceived" is outweighed by the "basic public policy" that "social welfare is best advanced by free competition." Eastern Wine Corp. v. Winslow-Warren, Ltd., 137 F.2d 955, 958 (2d Cir.), *cert. denied*, 320 U.S. 758 (1943) (trade names). See also Standard Brands, Inc. v. Smidler, 151 F.2d 34, 37 (2d Cir. 1945) (concurring opinion) (trade names).

[18] Cf. International News Serv. v. Associated Press, 248 U.S. 215 (1918). *But see* Cheney Bros. v. Doris Silk Corp., 35 F.2d 279 (2d Cir. 1929) (L. Hand, J.), *cert. denied*, 281 U.S. 728 (1930).

[19] See, *e.g.*, Norwich Pharmacal Co. v. Sterling Drug, Inc., 271 F.2d 569, 570-71 (2d Cir. 1959), *cert. denied*, 362 U.S. 919 (1960).

[20] See, *e.g.*, American Safety Table Co. v. Schreiber, 269 F.2d 255, 271-72 (2d Cir.), *cert. denied*, 361 U.S. 915 (1959).

[21] See, *e.g.*, Insect-O-Lite Co. v. Hagemeyer, 151 F. Supp. 829, 833 (E.D. Ky. 1957).

[22] NIMS, Foreward to UNFAIR COMPETITION AND TRADE-MARKS, at viii (3d ed. 1929).

of injunctions proscribing copying.[23] Realizing that "imitation is the life blood of competition,"[24] the judiciary formulated a dual test to avoid creating perpetual monopolies and to determine whether imitation of product features should be enjoined.[25] First, it was necessary to determine whether the imitated features were functional or nonfunctional. If they were nonfunctional, it then became necessary to see whether the first entrant established a secondary meaning so that the product of the later entrant created a likelihood of public confusion as to source. Injunctive relief was confined to nonfunctional aesthetic features of the original product to assure that the later competitor was left able to compete,[26] thereby assuring the public healthful competition between similar functional devices.[27] The judiciary assumed that wrongful intent was properly inferred from the copying of nonfunctional parts,[28] even though overall product simulation could be motivated by an intent to offer fair and vigorous competition.[29]

[23] For an analysis of the economic consequences of unfair competition protection, see Treece, *Protectability of Product Differentiation: Is and Ought Compared*, 18 RUTGERS L. REV. 1019 (1964).

[24] American Safety Table Co. v. Schreiber, 269 F.2d 255, 272 (2d Cir.), *cert. denied*, 361 U.S. 915 (1959); see SAMUELSON, ECONOMICS 440 (1961); Handler, *Unfair Competition*, 21 IOWA L. REV. 175, 189 (1936). Long-term policy considerations, including the destruction of incentive to maintain quality because of inevitable imitation by seemingly identical inferior products at lower prices, have led some economists to a contrary view. See CHAMBERLAIN, THE THEORY OF MONOPOLISTIC COMPETITION 273 (7th ed. 1960); GALBRAITH, AMERICAN CAPITALISM 89–99 (1952).

[25] See generally Pollack, *Unfair Trading by Product Simulation: Rule or Rankle?*, 23 OHIO ST. L.J. 74 (1962); Note, *Unfair Competition and the Doctrine of Functionality*, 64 COLUM. L. REV. 544 (1964).

[26] The judiciary recognized that injunctions against overall product simulation made competition much more difficult than those preventing the copying of trademarks, labels, or packages. See, *e.g.*, Shredded Wheat Co. v. Humphrey Cornell Co., 250 Fed. 960 (2d Cir. 1918) (L. Hand, J.); Flagg Mfg. Co. v. Holway, 178 Mass. 83, 59 N.E. 667 (1901) (Holmes, C.J.).

[27] See, *e.g.*, Wesson v. Galef, 286 Fed. 621 (S.D.N.Y. 1922). A competitor was thought to suffer nothing by abandoning nonfunctional features since they are likely to be for beauty, decoration, and identity. Huston v. Buckeye Bait Corp., 145 F. Supp. 600 (S.D. Ohio 1956).

[28] Harold F. Ritchie, Inc. v. Chesebrough-Pond's, Inc., 281 F.2d 755, 760 (2d Cir. 1960).

[29] See Note, 64 COLUM. L. REV. 544, 551 (1964).

Nevertheless, discordant judicial attitudes militated against the establishment of an immutable definition of functional features.[30] Some courts restrictively interpreted functional features as those absolutely necessary to a product's use—the cutting edge of a knife as distinguished from its color or shape.[31] Others expanded the definition to include anything which contributed to consumer appeal—a feature which gives the consumer a substantial reason for purchasing the goods as distinguished from merely differentiating them.[32] In general, however, courts used the functionality requirement to limit any effect unfair trade protection had upon free competition.[33]

If, in addition to being nonfunctional, a product had established a secondary meaning, a competitor was forbidden to incorporate the embellishments into the design of his wares. This occurred when the product's embellishments were found to signify origin in the minds of buyers, thereby accumulating good will similar to that obtained by formal trademarks. Because buyers often remember products by their distinctive appearance and are likely to purchase by that appearance alone,[34] the chance that simulation would deflect buyers who otherwise would buy the products of the originator cancelled the second entrant's privilege of duplicating, which he had in common with the world at large.[35]

Consistent with the theory of state unfair competition protection that relief was not designed to lessen the strain placed upon the originator, the private litigant was allowed

[30] See generally, Netterville, *California Law of Unfair Competition: Unprivileged Imitation*, 28 So. CAL. L. REV. 240 (1955).
[31] See, e.g., Haeger Potteries v. Gilner Potteries, 123 F. Supp. 261 (S.D. Cal. 1954).
[32] See, e.g., Pagliero v. Wallace China Co., 198 F.2d 339 (9th Cir. 1952); Zippo Mfg. Co. v. Rogers Imports, Inc., 216 F. Supp. 670 (S.D.N.Y. 1963); Note, *Developments in the Law—Trade-Marks and Unfair Competition*, 68 HARV. L. REV. 814, 856 (1955).
[33] See, e.g., West Point Mfg. Co. v. Detroit Stamping Co., 222 F.2d 581 (6th Cir.), cert. denied, 350 U.S. 840 (1955).
[34] See Derenberg, in *Symposium—Product Simulation: A Right or a Wrong?*, 64 COLUM. L. REV. 1192, 1206 (1964).
[35] American-Marietta Co. v. Krigsman, 275 F.2d 287, 289 (2d Cir. 1960).

to bring suit only to vindicate the public interest, not to redress his private griefs.[36] The relief granted a plaintiff was deemed incidental to the main purpose of redressing injuries to the competitive process. Under traditional rules, therefore, an originator was allowed to protect his market position only if the second entrant had misled the public into buying his goods by palming them off as those of his rival; anyone had the right to copy nonfunctional features which had not become associated solely with the original manufacturer.[37] For example, the original manufacturer of a lamp may have created public demand for one of two things—for his lamps above the lamps of all other makers, or for lamps made in a particular form, regardless of who makes them. The law of unfair competition was interested only in the first of these conditions —the one attaching to personality.[38] The mere fact that a demand for lamps of a particular form was created by a plaintiff did not give him any greater rights to the design than the copier. Once secondary meaning was established, the plaintiff had to show that the second entrant's imitation would confuse the public. It was not necessary to prove instances of actual confusion; rather it was necessary only to demonstrate a likelihood of confusion.[39]

Application of the secondary meaning doctrine was by no means uniform. A growing number of courts believed that the law should protect the originator against any loss of trade to an imitator seeking a "free ride," and should do so without regard to the presence or absence of secondary meaning or public deception.[40] Dramatic attacks on the barrier of second-

[36] Stern & Hoffman, *Public Injury and the Public Interest: Secondary Meaning in the Law of Unfair Competition*, 110 U. PA. L. REV. 935 (1962).
[37] See Callmann, *Style and Design Piracy*, 22 J. PAT. OFF. SOC'Y 557 (1940).
[38] *E.g.*, Crescent Tool Co. v. Kilborn & Bishop Co., 247 Fed. 299 (2d Cir. 1917).
[39] Zippo Mfg. Co. v. Manners Jewelers, Inc., 180 F. Supp. 845 (E.D. La. 1960).
[40] *E.g.*, Flint v. Oleet Jewelry Mfg. Co., 133 F. Supp. 459 (S.D.N.Y. 1955); see 3 CALLMANN, *supra* note 5, at 1371.

Unfair Competition Protection

ary meaning were made in New York [41] and California.[42] The act of copying itself was held sufficient evidence of secondary meaning where the court could find no logical reason for precise simulation other than an attempt to capitalize upon existing consumer familiarity.[43] Other courts expanded the rights of originators by judging imitation to be actionable whether or not consumers cared about source.[44] They simply required a likelihood of confusion between goods rather than source, and deception in accordance with a plan to that end. The question was not whether a secondary meaning had been established, but whether the acts of a defendant were fair or unfair according to principles recognized in equity rather than by "the morals of the market place." [45] But despite these departures from traditional doctrine, rules minimizing anticompetitive effect generally prevailed.

It now seems clear, however, that the attempts to restrict infringements upon competition were not enough. *Sears, Roebuck & Co. v. Stiffel Co.*[46] and *Compco Corp. v. Day-Brite Lighting, Inc.*[47] make clear that state injunctions against product simulation result in an unconstitutional conflict with federal patent and copyright policy, and that the public interest in free competition outweighs the interests which gave rise to the law of unfair competition.[48]

---

[41] *E.g.*, Santa's Workshop, Inc. v. Sterling, 282 App. Div. 328, 122 N.Y.S.2d 488 (3d Dep't 1953), *aff'd*, 3 N.Y.2d 757, 143 N.E.2d 529, 163 N.Y.S.2d 986 (1957); see Note, 70 YALE L.J. 406, 418–21, 426–30 (1961).
[42] Audio Fidelity, Inc. v. High Fidelity Recordings, Inc., 283 F.2d 551 (9th Cir. 1960); Grant v. California Bench Co., 76 Cal. App. 2d 706, 173 P.2d 818 (Dist. Ct. App. 1956).
[43] Audio Fidelity, Inc. v. High Fidelity Recordings, Inc., *supra* note 42.
[44] See Santa's Workshop, Inc. v. Sterling, 282 App. Div. 328, 122 N.Y.S.2d 488 (3d Dep't 1953), *aff'd*, 3 N.Y.2d 757, 143 N.E.2d 529, 163 N.Y.S.2d 986 (1957).
[45] Oneida, Ltd. v. National Silver Co., 25 N.Y.S.2d 271, 276 (Sup. Ct. 1940).
[46] 376 U.S. 225 (1964). [47] 376 U.S. 234 (1964).
[48] See also Treece, *supra* note 23.

FEDERAL PREEMPTION

In *Compco Corp v. Day-Brite Lighting, Inc.*,[49] after holding Day-Brite's design patent invalid for lack of invention, the district court nevertheless enjoined Compco from selling flourescent lighting fixtures identical or confusingly similar to those made by Day-Brite, finding that the overall appearance of Compco's fixture was the same to the ordinary observer as Day-Brite's reflector, that the appearance of Day-Brite's design identified Day-Brite to the trade, and that the concurrent sale of the two fixtures caused actual confusion among customers.[50] In affirming the decision, the court of appeals observed that Compco chose precisely the same design used by Day-Brite, despite the apparent availability of several alternative designs to meet the functional needs of the product.[51] The court held that a design identifying its maker to the trade is protectable although unpatentable.

In *Sears, Roebuck & Co. v. Stiffel Co.*,[52] just as in *Compco*, the district court held plaintiff's design patent invalid for lack of invention, but nevertheless enjoined Sears from selling pole lamps identical or confusingly similar to Stiffel's lamps, after finding that Sears had caused confusion by producing a copy of Stiffel's lamp almost identical to the original both in appearance and functional detail.[53] The Seventh Circuit affirmed,[54] holding that to prove a case of unfair competition under Illinois law there was no need to show that Sears had been palming off its lamps as Stiffel lamps; rather, Stiffel

---

[49] 376 U.S. 234 (1964).
[50] The unreported opinion of the District Court for the Northern District of Illinois is summarized in Day-Brite Lighting, Inc. v. Compco Corp., 311 F.2d 26, 27–28 (7th Cir. 1962).
[51] 311 F.2d 26 (7th Cir. 1962). [52] 376 U.S. 225 (1964).
[53] The unreported opinion of the District Court for the Northern District of Illinois is summarized in Stiffel Co. v. Sears, Roebuck & Co., 313 F.2d 115, 116–17 (7th Cir. 1963).
[54] 313 F.2d 115 (7th Cir. 1963).

had only to show that the two articles were so alike that customers could not identify their manufacturers.

The *Compco* court's decision was in accord with both state and federal precedent. In *Sears*, however, no finding was made that the features copied were nonfunctional or that they had acquired a secondary meaning. The Supreme Court, therefore, could have reversed *Sears* and affirmed *Compco* under existing law, giving recognition both to the interest in vindicating federal patent policy, and to the state interest in protecting businessmen and consumers from the evils subsumed under the recognized tort of unfair competition.[55] Instead, the Court issued a sweeping pronouncement: protection based upon state unfair competition laws in any case of product simulation results in an unconstitutional encroachment upon the federal patent and copyright policies of granting monopolies only for true inventions and limited in time. No article unprotected by a patent or copyright may be immunized by state law from being copied. "Just as a state cannot encroach upon the federal patent laws directly," the Court stated, "it cannot, under some other law, such as that forbidding unfair competition, give protection of a kind that clashes with the objectives of the federal patent laws." [56]

Constitutional and statutory limitations upon patent grants

---

[55] See Derenberg, *The Seventeenth Year of Administration of the Lanham Trademark Act of 1946*, 54 TRADEMARK REP. 655, 701 (1964); Brief for the United States as Amicus Curiae, pp. 11-12, Compco Corp. v. Day-Brite Lighting, Inc., 376 U.S. 234 (1964).

[56] 376 U.S. at 231. Unfair competition proscriptions may be defended as consistent with the policies of free competition on the ground that they stimulate innovation by forcing businessmen to innovate around their rivals' products, and thus benefit the public by producing a greater diversity of innovations directed to the same end. See James P. Marsh Corp. v. United States Gauge Co., 129 F.2d 161, 165 (7th Cir. 1942); Stedman, *Invention and Public Policy*, 12 LAW & CONTEMP. PROB. 649, 653 (1947); cf. Frost, *The Patent System and the Modern Economy*, S. Doc. No. 22, 85th Cong., 1st Sess. 6 (1957). However, it has been questioned whether, with regard to any specific product, this type of competition is a satisfactory substitute for the hard competition in marketing which is reflected by lower prices to the public. Stern & Hoffman, *supra* note 36, at 940 n.23.

reflect the same basic premise which underlies the antitrust laws—that the unrestrained interaction of competitive forces will yield the best allocation of our economic resources, the lowest prices, the highest quality, and the greatest progress.[57] To further these goals, authors and inventors are encouraged to make their writings and discoveries available to the public by the grant of the exclusive right for a limited term to market their innovations.[58]

To minimize inroads upon our competitive economy, it is argued that the policy of rewarding new ideas with a grant of monopoly enjoyment should be limited to those cases in which society feels that the gain in inventiveness outweighs the restriction upon competition,[59] and that the duration of the monopolistic enjoyment should be limited to that period of time which will serve as an adequate reward or stimulus to prospective innovators.[60] *Sears* and *Compco* conclude that this process of selection and limitation has already been accomplished by the patent and copyright acts.[61] Thus, the composite thesis of *Sears* and *Compco* seems an authoritative embodiment of Judge Learned Hand's persistent view that in the absence of a federal statutory right a man's property is limited to the chattels which embody his invention.[62] To create a form of common law patent or copyright for reasons

[57] Stern & Hoffman, *supra* note 36, at 950; see Northern Pac. Ry. v. United States, 356 U.S. 1, 4 (1958).

[58] U.S. CONST. art. I, § 8, cl. 8; 17 U.S.C. §§ 1, 101 (1958); 35 U.S.C. §§ 154, 271(a) (1958). See generally Frost, *supra* note 56, at 1-19; Oppenheim, *The Public Interest in Legal Protection of Industrial and Intellectual Property*, 40 TRADEMARK REP. 613 (1950). As to the same theory behind the copyright grant, see G. Ricordi & Co. v. Haendler, 194 F.2d 914 (2d Cir. 1952) (L. Hand, J.); *cf.*, Scott Paper Co. v. Marcalus Mfg. Co., 326 U.S. 249 (1945).

[59] See Great Atl. & Pac. Tea Co. v. Supermarket Equip. Corp., 340 U.S. 147, 152 (1950); Note, 70 YALE L.J. 406 (1961).

[60] See Kellogg Co. v. National Biscuit Co., 305 U.S. 111 (1938).

[61] *Accord*, Chafee, *Unfair Competition*, 53 HARV. L. REV. 1289, 1318 (1940). See also Comment, *Product Appearance in the Law of Unfair Competition—Preemption or Protection?*, 73 YALE L.J. 389 (1963).

[62] Cheney Bros. v. Doris Silk Corp., 35 F.2d 279 (2d Cir. 1929), *cert. denied*, 281 U.S. 728 (1930).

of fair play "would flagrantly conflict with the scheme which Congress has for more than a century devised to cover the subject matter," [63] by undermining the federal requirement of originality, and by substituting a perpetual grant for the limited terms of the federal patent and copyright laws.[64]

Of greater significance than the immediate impact of federal preemption is the Court's explicit sealing off of the main avenues through which inroads could have been made upon the *Sears* and *Compco* doctrine. That an article copied from an unpatented product could be made in some other way, that the design is nonfunctional and nonessential to the use of either article, that the configuration of the article copied has a secondary meaning identifying its maker to the trade, or that confusion exists among purchasers over the identity of the articles or the makers may, according to the Court, be relevant in applying a state's law requiring such precautions as labeling; but neither these facts nor any others can now furnish a basis for prohibiting or punishing the actual acts of copying and selling, "regardless of the copier's motives." [65]

These decisions have generated considerable comment, both favorable and unfavorable.[66] Some comment, however, ap-

[63] Id. at 280.
[64] See, *e.g.,* Capitol Records Inc. v. Mercury Records Corp., 221 F.2d 657, 664 (2d Cir. 1955) (dissenting opinion); Fashion Originators Guild of America, Inc. v. FTC, 114 F.2d 80 (2d Cir. 1940), *aff'd on other grounds,* 312 U.S. 457 (1941).
[65] Compco Corp. v. Day-Brite Lighting, Inc., 376 U.S. 234, 238 (1964). Brown, in *Symposium—Product Simulation: A Right or a Wrong?*, 64 COLUM. L. REV. 1216, 1222 (1964), suggests that in enunciating such strong *dicta* Justice Black may have had in mind the excessive reliance on supposed bad motives in American Safety Table Co. v. Schreiber, 269 F.2d 255 (2d Cir.), *cert. denied,* 361 U.S. 915 (1959). See the dissenting opinion of Judge Clark, 269 F.2d at 277.
[66] Andrew, *Domestic Protection of Commercial Designs: The Federal-State Conflict,* 39 ST. JOHN'S L. REV. 23 (1964); Chapman, *The Supreme Court and Federal Law of Unfair Competition,* 54 TRADEMARK REP. 573 (1964); Derenberg, *supra* note 55, at 658–63, 699–706; Hearings on H.R. 4651 Before the Subcommittee on Commerce and Finance of the House Committee on Interstate and Foreign Commerce, 88th Cong., 2d Sess. *passim* (1964); Kunin, *The Lindsay Bill Before and After the Stiffel Case,* 54 TRADEMARK REP. 731 (1964); Marks,

pears not to give due weight to the Court's explicit pronouncements.[67] Thus, one commentator theorizes in a manner which would nullify the sweeping scope of the decisions. By reading the Court's statements as simply underscoring the principle that mere copying of overall product appearance does not constitute unfair competition, the commentator concludes that *Sears* and *Compco* preclude neither restraints on palming off the copy, nor restraints on copying source-identifying nonfunctional features which create customer confusion.[68]

This theory appears untenable, however, in light of Mr. Justice Harlan's concurring opinion, which would carve out of the Court's proscription an exception allowing states to impose reasonable restrictions on "copying itself" if such copying had been undertaken with the dominant purpose and effect of palming off one's goods as those of another or of confusing customers as to source. The inference seems unassailable that the seven Justices joining in Mr. Justice Black's opinion were aware of the consequences of a literal interpretation of his words proscribing state injunctions against copying unpatented articles.

Manifestly, the more comprehensive the application of the Court's ruling, the more extensive will be the repercussions in the law of torts as it affects the market place.[69] Indeed, the prospect of a literal application of Mr. Justice Black's unqualified language may well stimulate the Bar and the courts to salvage, where possible, the principles and prec-

---

Copying an Article of Commerce not Necessarily Unfair Competition, 55 TRADEMARK REP. 47 (1965); Smith, *"In Vino (Mogen David Brand) Veritas"?*, 54 TRADEMARK REP. 581 (1964); *Symposium—Product Simulation: A Right or a Wrong?*, 64 COLUM. L. REV. 1178 (1964); Treece, *Patent Policy and Preemption: The Stiffel and Compco Cases*, 32 U. CHI. L. REV. 80 (1964); Treece, *supra* note 23, at 1059–68.

[67] See Bender, in *Symposium—Product Simulation: A Right or a Wrong?*, 64 COLUM. L. REV. 1228 (1964); Leeds, in *Symposium—Product Simulation: A Right or a Wrong?*, 64 COLUM. L. REV. 1179 (1964); Smith, *supra* note 66.

[68] Leeds, *supra* note 67, at 1182.

[69] See also Treece, *supra* note 23, at 1059–68.

edents of the law of unfair competition. It is not to be expected or desired, however, that courts will ignore the Court's pronouncements where they are clearly applicable.[70] Indeed, little purpose is served in further attempts to work outside the context of the opinions themselves. Moreover, it would seem more sensible for attorneys, as advisors to clients and legislators contemplating changes in the law, to investigate and be cognizant of the broadest potential scope these decisions might have. It is the purpose of this paper to begin this investigation in as neutral a manner as possible.

LABELING

Although the Court in *Sears* held the states powerless to proscribe copying, it explicitly preserved state power to "require that goods, whether patented or unpatented, be labeled, or that other precautionary steps be taken to prevent customers from being misled as to the source." [71] This reservation of power to the states makes significant, as never before, the area of labeling. Because a producer could secure an injunction against the competing product itself prior to *Sears* and *Compco*, product simulation was all-important. Injunctions to require labeling were seldom, if ever, sought. As a consequence, little discussion of the area exists.[72] Now, labeling, as the only relief explicitly available, assumes greater prominence. An exposition of the principles and philosophy

[70] A number of courts have adhered to the letter of the decisions. Aerosol Research Co. v. Scovill Mfg. Co., 334 F.2d 751 (7th Cir. 1964); Kingsway, Inc. v. Werner, 233 F. Supp. 102 (E.D. Mo. 1964); Jerrold Stephens Co., Inc. v. Alladin Plastics, Inc., 229 F. Supp. 536 (S.D. Cal. 1964); Duplex Straw Dispenser Co. v. Harold Leonard & Co., 229 F. Supp. 401 (S.D. Cal. 1964); Wolf & Vine, Inc. v. Pioneer Display Fixture Co., 142 U.S.P.Q. 112 (N.Y. Sup. Ct. 1964). In Jerrold Stephens Co. v. Alladin Plastics, Inc., *supra*, where injunctive relief against copying was sought on the ground of interference with customers, the court held that *Sears* and *Compco* preclude relief in any suit based on common-law unfair competition, no matter how it may be described.
[71] 376 U.S. at 232.
[72] See Note, *Developments in the Law—Competitive Torts*, 77 HARV. L. REV. 888, 914–15 (1964); Comment, 1957 U. ILL. L.F. 677.

of labeling law and a re-evaluation in light of *Sears* and *Compco* therefore appears in order.

TRADITIONAL RULES

Labeling, as the term is used in the law of unfair competition, encompasses trade dress, wrappers, packages, and containers including both boxes and bottles. A dichotomy exists, however, between affirmative and negative labeling injunctions. The affirmative injunction deals with simulation of product configuration, and the subsequent marketing of such products without adequate source indicia so that the product configuration causes confusion. The negative injunction deals with simulation of trade dress, wrappers, packages, and containers—with confusion caused by the identifying covering rather than by product appearance.

Affirmative Requirements. Under traditional concepts of labeling law, a rival manufacturer may seek to benefit from the public's desire to have goods in a particular form, even if that desire was created by another.[73] He has no right, however, to capitalize upon the good will attaching to the originator's personality—the public's desire to have goods manufactured by the originator.[74] Two interests motivate protection: the originator's interest in the reputation his product configuration has acquired, and the public's need for a means of distinguishing between similar goods.[75] The second entrant's right to copy is therefore conditional upon his selling his goods as his own, thereby eliminating confusion caused by his counterfeit.[76] The new competitor is not an insurer against all possible confusion. Nor is he obligated to protect against confusion resulting from consumer indifference or negligence. He is required only to mark or designate his prod-

---

[73] Flagg Mfg. Co. v. Holway, 178 Mass. 83, 59 N.E. 667 (1901) (Holmes, C.J.).
[74] *Ibid.*
[75] William R. Warner & Co. v. Eli Lilly & Co., 265 U.S. 526 (1924).
[76] *E.g.,* Neely v. Boland Mfg. Co., 274 F.2d 195 (8th Cir. 1960).

uct so purchasers exercising ordinary care to discover whose products they are buying will not become confused or mistaken.[77] A prominent and unmistakable indication of the manufacturer's name will usually constitute sufficient explanation and notice.[78]

Immutable rules do not exist, however, for determining what are reasonable means of identification. Under traditional doctrine, courts may require that the means of distinction imposed be reasonable under the circumstances, bearing in mind the nature and cost of the product, the type of customers generally involved, the negotiations and care usually employed prior to making the purchase, and the likelihood that the mark will be seen.[79] Thus, considering that purchasers of phonograph cabinets ordinarily would not buy from advertisements or from hasty glances at display models, but would carefully examine the product, a second entrant was held to have satisfied his duty to identify by placing his name inside the cabinet door, although the originator placed his name on the front.[80]

Negative Requirements. A copier not only bears an affirmative duty clearly to label his imitation to avoid confusion created by product design, he must also avoid presenting and packaging his copy in a manner which confuses the public as to source.[81] In the latter situation it is not the originator's product configuration which has taken on a secondary meaning, identifying him in the minds of the public as the product's

[77] *E.g.,* West Point Mfg. Co. v. Detroit Stamping Co., 222 F.2d 581 (6th Cir.), *cert. denied,* 350 U.S. 840 (1955).

[78] J. C. Penney Co. v. H. D. Lee Mercantile Co., 120 F.2d 949 (8th Cir. 1941); Zippo Mfg. Co. v. Manners Jewelers, Inc., 180 F. Supp. 845 (E.D. La. 1960); Winston & Newell Co. v. Piggly Wiggly Northwest, Inc., 221 Minn. 287, 22 N.W.2d 11 (1946).

[79] American Safety Table Co. v. Schreiber, 269 F.2d 255, 274–75 (2d Cir.), *cert. denied,* 361 U.S. 915 (1959).

[80] Estate Stove Co. v. Gray & Dudley, 41 F.2d 462 (6th Cir. 1930), *vacated on other grounds,* 50 F.2d 413 (1931).

[81] Ronson Art Metal Works, Inc. v. Gibson Lighter Mfg. Co., 3 App. Div. 2d 227, 159 N.Y.S.2d 606 (1st Dep't 1957).

source; rather, it is the originator's distinctive, original, and ornamental style of dress, label, wrapper, package, or container which readily distinguishes his product from those of other manufacturers.[82]

The primary purpose of labels and trade dress is to identify merchandise and give directions for use.[83] Unless they are protected by patent or copyright no one may obtain exclusive rights to their use; competitors may copy all details which contribute to beauty, attractiveness, and utility.[84] But trade dress may become the sign or symbol by which the originator's products are known in the market. Typically, under modern merchandising methods, an originator may have expended large sums for advertising, and managed to establish thereby a substantial market for his product, identified to the consuming public by its familiar trade dress.[85]

Technically, such dress cannot be called a trademark, but because it serves substantially the same purpose, protection is afforded for the same reason and in the same manner as for trademarks.[86] The trademark has no significance other than to identify a particular manufacturer. Therefore, a product simulator who copies a trademark can have no purpose

[82] F. W. Fitch Co. v. Camille, Inc., 106 F.2d 635 (8th Cir. 1939).
[83] 1 NIMS, UNFAIR COMPETITION AND TRADE-MARKS 330 (4th ed. 1947).
[84] *Ibid.*
[85] See, *e.g.*, Kitchens of Sara Lee, Inc. v. Nifty Foods Corp., 266 F.2d 541 (2d Cir. 1959); Colgate-Palmolive Co. v. North American Chem. Corp., 238 F. Supp. 81 (S.D.N.Y. 1964). In Galbally, *Unfair Trade in the Simulation of Rival Goods—the Test of Commercial Necessity*, 3 VILL. L. REV. 333 (1958), the author demonstrates that the personality of goods—imparted by an eye-catching package, an oddly shaped container, or an exotic wrapper—plays a vital role in the art of merchandising. This personality prompts the prospective buyer to recall on second meeting that the article is a familiar one, thereby breaking down sales resistance to the unknown. "In short," the author states, "personality sells." The trend of the last decade toward serve-yourself merchandising, with its consequent increase in purchasing by sight, has set the stage for passing off without the necessity of overt deception on the part of the retail merchant. The author concludes that when an imitation of familiar trade dress is simply placed in the usual display case "serve yourself becomes deceive yourself."
[86] Wirtz v. Eagle Bottling Co., 50 N.J. Eq. 164, 24 Atl. 658 (1892).

other than to cause source confusion. Good will is protected by preventing use of the mark by copiers. The package or label, distinctive and not common to the trade, likewise destroys any reasons for its use by another.[87] Both the interests which motivate labeling protection to prevent confusion caused by configuration—the originator's right to benefit from his own reputation and the public's interest in being able to determine source—apply with equal force when confusion is caused by similar dress.

Under traditional rules it is generally held that actual confusion need not be proved if the second entrant has sufficiently plagiarized his rival's package that confusion is likely.[88] An intent to derive benefit from the reputation of another is sufficient to justify an inference that confusion is likely.[89] With practically an unlimited field of distinctive designs, shapes, and colors available, the later entrant who deliberately copies the dress of a competitor is required at least to prove his attempt to cause confusion failed to achieve its intended result.[90] Moreover, because he was intimately concerned with probable consumer reaction, his judgment, manifested prior to suit, that confusion would result, is highly persuasive.[91]

In approaching a style of dress, however, the designer typically is careful to stop short of complete identity except in the use of color. Consequently, it is easier to point out specific differences than to show specific likenesses.[92] Obviously, a producer cannot acquire proprietary rights in the color or

[87] Rogers, GOODWILL, TRADE-MARKS AND UNFAIR COMPETITION 84 (1914).

[88] *E.g.*, American Chicle Co. v. Topps Chewing Gum, Inc., 208 F.2d 560 (2d Cir. 1953); Bostitch, Inc. v. King Fastener Co., 87 R.I. 274, 288, 140 A.2d 274, 282 (1958).

[89] RESTATEMENT (SECOND), TORTS § 729, comment *i* (Tent. Draft No. 8, 1963). In Harold F. Ritchie, Inc. v. Chesebrough-Pond's, Inc., 281 F.2d 755 (2d Cir. 1960), the court recognized that reliable evidence of actual instances of confusion is almost impossible to secure.

[90] My-T-Fine Corp. v. Samuels, 69 F.2d 76 (2d Cir. 1934); Bostitch, Inc. v. King Fastener Co., 87 R.I. 274, 140 A.2d 274 (1958).

[91] American Chicle Co. v. Topps Chewing Gum, Inc., 208 F.2d 560 (2d Cir. 1953); Socony-Vacuum Oil Co., Inc. v. Rosen, 108 F.2d 632 (6th Cir. 1940).

[92] N. K. Fairbank Co. v. R. W. Bell Mfg. Co., 77 Fed. 869 (2d Cir. 1896).

colors used on its packages and labels, as the list of colors would soon run out; [93] but simulation amounting to unfair competition resides neither in single features of dress nor in indistinguishability when articles are set side by side.[94] Rather, it is tested by the general impression made upon the eye of the ordinary purchaser, even though upon close examination differences can be found.[95] In making purchases, the consumer often depends upon his recollection of the appearance of the product. Most cases recognize that the ordinary buyer exercises much less caution in buying a package of chewing gum or a bottle of beer than in buying a hat or a coat; [96] hence, defendant's name on the carton may be insufficient to prevent confusion.[97]

Although a producer who markets a product causing confusion by virtue of its design alone need only protect the ordinary prudent purchaser,[98] a more severe burden is borne by one who causes confusion by virtue of trade dress.[99] It is thought that businessmen of ordinary acuteness, wishing to establish a distinctive reputation for their goods, seek to array their wares so they will always be unmistakably recognized.[100] When it is found that large sums have been expended for advertising, the inference has been held conclusive that

[93] Campbell Soup Co. v. Armour & Co., 175 F.2d 795 (3d Cir. 1949).
[94] Martini & Rossi, Societa Anonima v. Consumers'-People's Products, 57 F.2d 599 (E.D.N.Y. 1931), aff'd, 57 F.2d 600 (2d Cir. 1932); Pharmaceuticals, Inc. v. United Whelan Corp., 197 N.Y.S.2d 22 (Sup. Ct. 1959).
[95] Chesebrough Mfg. Co. v. Old Gold Chem. Co., 70 F.2d 383 (6th Cir.), cert. denied, 293 U.S. 599 (1934); Hi-Land Dairyman's Ass'n v. Cloverleaf Dairy, 107 Utah 68, 151 P.2d 710 (1944).
[96] E.g., J. N. Collins Co. v. F. M. Paist Co., 14 F.2d 614 (E.D. Pa. 1926); Wirtz v. Eagle Bottling Co., 50 N.J. Eq. 164, 24 Atl. 658 (1892).
[97] Tas-T-Nut Co. v. Variety Nut & Date Co., 245 F.2d 3 (6th Cir. 1957); Hi-Land Dairyman's Ass'n v. Cloverleaf Dairy, 107 Utah 68, 151 P.2d 710 (1944).
[98] West Point Mfg. Co. v. Detroit Stamping Co., 222 F.2d 581 (6th Cir.), cert. denied, 350 U.S. 840 (1955)
[99] See Florence Mfg. Co. v. J. C. Dowd & Co.. 178 Fed. 73 (2d Cir. 1910).
[100] See J. N. Collins Co. v. F. M. Paist Co., 14 F.2d 614 (E.D. Pa. 1926); H. A. Metz Labs., Inc. v. Blackman, 153 Misc. 171, 275 N.Y. Supp. 407 (Sup. Ct. 1934).

the second entrant's sole motive was to encroach upon the originator's established reputation.[101] Moreover, the level of proof of secondary meaning is generally lower in trade-dress cases than in product-simulation cases.[102] Source association is typically the most stringent demand imposed.[103] Thus, even though plaintiff cannot sustain the burden of proving that consumers in fact desire to purchase his product, relief will be granted if he can show that consumers believe products identified by similar trade dress emanate from one source.

IMPLICATIONS OF THE SEARS-COMPCO THESIS

SECONDARY MEANING. The above discussion demonstrates that labeling law is based upon the protection of two interests: the public's and the originator's. *Sears* and *Compco*, however, explicitly allow protection only of the public's interest in source identification: "A state . . . has power to impose liability upon those who, knowing that the public is relying upon an original manufacturer's reputation for quality and integrity, deceive the public by palming off their copies as the original." [104] It could be inferred from this explicit language that secondary meaning is prerequisite to relief: No possibility of customer source confusion can exist before secondary meaning has been established. In addition, if *Sears* and *Compco* are read as intending to provide affirmative protection for all copying until actual source confusion occurs, then secondary meaning, as the measure of possible customer confusion, is essential, and the opinions would abrogate existing labeling protection under state law founded upon the originator's interest alone. Thus, it is arguable that evidence of customer confusion may no longer be founded upon infer-

---

[101] Wm. Wrigley, Jr. Co. v. Colker, 245 Fed. 907 (E.D. Ky. 1914); N.K. Fairbank Co. v. R.W. Bell Mfg. Co., 77 Fed. 869 (2d Cir. 1896).
[102] See Tas-T-Nut Co. v. Variety Nut & Date Co., 245 F.2d 3 (6th Cir. 1957); Bostitch, Inc. v. King Fastener Co., 87 R.I. 274, 140 A.2d 274 (1958).
[103] *E.g.*, Socony-Vacuum Oil Co. v. Rosen, 108 F.2d 632 (6th Cir. 1940).
[104] Compco Corp. v. Day-Brite Lighting, Inc., 376 U.S. 234, 238 (1964).

ences drawn solely from the mere act of copying, and that the states, in the administration of a federal right, must now demand evidence of actual confusion rather than rely upon inferences drawn from copying now authorized by federal law.[105]

That such a literal reading of these opinions is not improbable is amply illustrated by post-*Sears* and *Compco* cases. One court, quoting from *Compco*, stated that the secondary meaning test remains relevant for labeling relief, and then denied such relief on the ground that plaintiff could not prove that customers purchased his product because of its source and not because of its appearance.[106] Another court merely noted that although evidence supported a finding of deliberate copying of plaintiff's unpatented device, no unfair competition existed under the *Sears-Compco* thesis, absent evidence of attempted or actual customer deception with regard to the product's origin.[107]

Any wholesale application of the secondary meaning requirement, whether the standard be source association or source motivation, requires the result that, regardless of the unique external elements an originator combines to give his goods or packages personality, he is easy prey to the copyist unless the buying public has become so familiar with the appearance of his wares that all articles or packages of that appearance are identified with him as their source.[108] Labeling protection would therefore depend upon the speed with which the public and the copier react to the new product.[109] An entrepreneur must consider that, in the introductory stage

---

[105] *Cf.* Bender, *supra* note 67, at 1241.
[106] Kingsway, Inc. v. Werner, 233 F. Supp. 102 (E.D. Mo. 1964).
[107] Aerosol Research Co. v. Scovill Mfg. Co., 334 F.2d 751 (7th Cir. 1964). *Accord*, Spangler Candy Co. v. Crystal Pure Candy Co., 235 F. Supp. 18 (N.D. Ill. 1964), *aff'd*, 147 U.S.P.Q. 434 (7th Cir. 1965) (defendant admitted attempt to imitate plaintiff's package as closely as possible).
[108] See Galbally, *supra* note 85.
[109] See Netterville, *California Law of Unfair Competition: Unprivileged Imitation*, 28 So. CAL. L. REV. 240, 277 (1955).

of a promotion, when costs are heaviest and returns leanest, when protection is most needed against sales diversion, no protection exists.[110] The secondary meaning requirement is by no means immune to criticism.[111] Even prior to *Sears* and *Compco*, when injunctive relief was available, it had been argued that courts ought to recognize that few plaintiffs are interested in adjudicating the rights of the public; they spend their time and money to protect their own interests.[112] Granting or denying protection on the basis of criteria essentially foreign to a plaintiff's case seemed incongruous.[113] Moreover, proving secondary meaning is often difficult,[114] since some courts are unwilling to infer source identification from extensive advertising [115] or instances of consumer confusion.[116]

It might further be observed that the most significant function the doctrine served—to limit the scope of unfair competition protection—may now amply be served by the *Sears-Compco* thesis. Gone with the abolition of state injunctions

[110] Galbally, *supra* note 85. [111] See generally *ibid*.
[112] Netterville, *supra* note 109; see Callmann, *What is Unfair Competition?*, 28 GEO. L.J. 585 (1940).
[113] See Callmann, *supra* note 112.
[114] Note, *Developments in the Law—Competitive Torts*, 77 HARV. L. REV. 888, 916 (1964). Zippo Mfg. Co. v. Rogers Imports, Inc., 216 F. Supp. 670, 682–84 (S.D.N.Y. 1963), indicates that if proper polling techniques are used, plaintiff can establish source association and source motivation by exclusive reliance on consumer surveys. See also Eastman Kodak Co. v. Royal-Pioneer Paper Box Mfg. Co., 197 F. Supp. 132 (E.D. Pa. 1961) (successful use of a poll as evidence establishing source association). *But see* American Luggage Works, Inc. v. United States Trunk Co., 158 F. Supp. 50 (D. Mass. 1957), *aff'd sub nom*. Hawley Prods. Co. v. United States Trunk Co., 259 F.2d 69 (1st Cir. 1958) (poll unpersuasive since small sample was selected from a universe designed by experts inadequately informed of the problem and hence arbitrarily making exclusions and inclusions).
[115] *E.g.*, Chas. D. Briddell, Inc. v. Alglobe Trading Corp., 194 F.2d 416 (2d Cir. 1952); General Time Instruments Corp. v. United States Time Corp., 165 F.2d 853 (2d Cir.), *cert. denied*, 334 U.S. 846 (1948).
[116] See Norwich Pharmacal Co. v. Sterling Drug, Inc., 271 F.2d 569 (2d Cir. 1959), *cert. denied*, 362 U.S. 919 (1960) (public opinion survey); C. S. Hammond & Co. v. International College Globe, Inc., 210 F. Supp. 206, 219 (S.D.N.Y. 1962) (letters from purchasers).

is the paramount argument against creation of perpetual monopolies which are "immunities from competition." [117] Since *Sears* and *Compco*, no strong policy supports allowing a seller to hide his identity; in fact, it has been contended that a copier's reluctance to identify himself suggests that he would not mind being confused with a preferred source.[118]

Sears and *Compco* do not explicitly require the retention of secondary meaning as a condition to court-imposed labeling. This would appear to leave to analysis the question whether a court's rejection of the doctrine would be compatible with the rationale of those decisions. The principal objection to such protection is that the Supreme Court specifically proscribes judicial consideration of the originator's interest in copying protection, and specifically authorizes protection only of the public's interest in avoiding source confusion in labeling protection. This might imply that of the two interests traditionally protected in the labeling area, only the public's interest remains significant.

If the opinions are read as a Magna Carta for all forms of unfair competition,[119] as being motivated by a desire to protect the copier and not simply to protect the public's interest in free competition, the copier's interest must prevail over the originator's interest in labeling. But the holdings provide no basis for the conclusion that the Court was attempting to protect copiers. Rather, the rationale is that the public has the right to benefit from free competition in areas not explicitly encompassed by the patent and copyright laws. Protection of the copier is ancillary to the Court's main purpose of benefiting the consumer. This is supported by the Court's reservation to the states of the power to impose adequate label-

---

[117] See, *e.g.*, Eastern Wine Corp. v. Winslow-Warren, Ltd., 137 F.2d 955, 957 (2d Cir.) (Frank, J.), *cert. denied*, 320 U.S. 758 (1943).

[118] Brown, in *Symposium—Product Simulation: A Right or a Wrong?*, 64 COLUM. L. REV. 1216, 1224 (1964).

[119] See generally Derenberg, *The Seventeenth Year of Administration of the Lanham Trademark Act of 1946*, 54 TRADEMARK REP. 655, 702 (1964).

ing requirements to prevent consumer confusion. Freedom from labeling would assist a copier in his attempt to benefit from the originator's reputation, so if the Court had the copier's interest in mind it would have permitted copying *carte blanche*.

It therefore seems wholly consistent with *Sears* and *Compco* to protect the interest of the originator as against the interest of the copier, when the public interest is not prejudiced. So long as no infringement upon competition is created, so long as state labeling requirements do not place the copier at a competitive disadvantage, the public interest will presumably be vindicated. Subject to this free-competition condition, the criteria employed to determine when labeling relief will be granted despite the absence of secondary meaning seems a matter for each state to resolve as it sees fit. The focus of inquiry will no doubt be the originator's and the copier's interests. Where the essence of relief is related to protection of the public from deception, source identification is fundamental; but where relief is designed to protect the originator, source association is less important.[120] Protection will depend on the particular state's view of the need to enforce higher standards of business morality, and upon the court's reaction to the particular facts of each case.

One significant extension of protection that becomes possible concerns the measure of proof of confusion which a plaintiff must establish before protection will be granted. It would be impossible for a plaintiff to establish actual confusion as to source if no secondary meaning exists. And if a plaintiff may obtain relief despite the absence of secondary meaning, and therefore without establishing actual confusion, there appears to be no reason to require him to prove actual confusion exists even when secondary meaning has been established. The

[120] Pollack, *Unfair Trading by Product Simulation: Rule or Rankle?*, 23 OHIO ST. L.J. 74 (1962). See also Stern & Hoffman, *Public Injury and the Public Interest: Secondary Meaning in the Law of Unfair Competition*, 110 U. PA. L. REV. 935 (1962).

proper standard is probably a judicial determination that there is a likelihood of confusion, established by a visual comparison of the products involved.[121]

The question arises as to why a producer would desire labeling relief in the absence of secondary meaning, since he has no reputation to protect, and since such relief could never place the copier at a competitive disadvantage. If A were the originator and C the copier, no immediate benefits would insure to A should he manage to compel C to label his product because, assuming the nonexistence of secondary meaning, the public cannot distinguish between the products. A significant benefit could, however, be derived from this protection: the opportunity for A to establish his own reputation. Copiers are notorious for products of inferior quality,[122] and if A could require C to distinguish his product in some clear and unmistakable manner, consumers will relate their reactions—satisfaction or dissatisfaction—to the appropriate producer. In this way, protection based on the originator's interest alone would enhance competition, since the copier would be compelled to compete on a par with an originator who intends to establish his own reputation. It is significant in this regard to note the possible invalidity in the assumption that there necessarily exists in all situations a difference between the interests of the public and the originator. The explicit reservation to the states in *Sears* and *Compco* of the power to require labeling to avoid source confusion is based on the assumption that the public has an interest in exercising its choice. It would seem to follow that the public must therefore gain when producers are given an opportunity to establish secondary meaning, for if they are not given such an opportunity the public's choice will tend to be limited.

The argument that adequate source indicia are present

[121] See Brown, *supra* note 118, at 1224.
[122] See Capitol Records, Inc. v. Greatest Records, Inc., 43 Misc. 2d 878, 252 N.Y.S.2d 553 (Sup. Ct. 1964); H.R. REP. No. 1758, 87th Cong., 2d Sess. 1–2 (1962) (phonograph records).

Unfair Competition Protection

when the originator labels his own product,[123] flounders upon an inaccurate factual assumption. Unmarked products may easily be substituted in a line of commerce for marked products. For example, in *Zippo Mfg. Co. v. Rogers Imports, Inc.*,[124] a substantial number of consumers who had purchased Rogers cigarette lighters sent them to Zippo for repairs, thinking they had been made by Zippo. Moreover, unless courts require the copier to label, customers will be far less able to relate differences in quality to the respective producers.[125]

Even where the copy is in all respects equal to the original, labeling relief may benefit an originator who has not established a reputation by serving effectively to inform the public that he in fact originated the product involved. Certainly, an originator has the right to label his product as "The original . . . ." The above analysis relating to the need for two products to be presented to consumers with distinguishable labels applies here as well, and if the originator legitimately indicates that he is the originator, a state, absent anticompetitive effect, should arguably be able to make effective this legitimate desire by requiring the copier to label his product.

ANTICOMPETITIVE EFFECT. While proof of secondary meaning may be unnecessary to legitimize state efforts to protect the interests of the originator, any relief granted must ultimately be tested against possible interference with free competition. This same test, derived from the rationale of *Sears* and *Compco*, must also apply where the public interest rather than the originator's is being protected. Although the Court allows states to "protect businesses in the use of their trademarks, labels, or distinctive dress in the packaging of goods,"[126] states may not "give protection of a kind that

---

[123] Parker Pen Co. v. Finstone, 7 F.2d 753 (S.D.N.Y. 1925).
[124] 216 F. Supp. 670 (S.D.N.Y. 1963).
[125] See also C. S. Hammond & Co. v. International College Globe Inc., 210 F. Supp. 206, 219 (S.D.N.Y. 1962); Art Metal Works, Inc. v. Cunningham Prods. Corp., 137 Misc. 429, 242 N.Y. Supp. 294 (Sup. Ct. 1930).
[126] Sears, Roebuck & Co. v. Stiffel Co., 376 U.S. 225, 232 (1964).

clashes with the objectives of the federal patent laws."[127] State labeling relief must not impinge upon free competition. This means, of course, that states must accord full exploitation of the originator's work to the copier, and that court-imposed precautions must be consonant with the imitator's fundamental right to make and sell what he chooses.

Cases in which plaintiffs seek to compel copiers to mark their imitations of product configurations fall into at least three basic categories: (1) where the copier is compelled to identify himself to the same extent as the originator, (2) where the copier must identify himself more clearly than the originator, and (3) where the copier must affirmatively distinguish his product from the originator's.

Certainly, when secondary meaning is present, and the originator clearly identifies himself as manufacturer, the least states may require after *Sears* and *Compco* is that the copier clearly and unmistakably reveal his product's origin by label. Moreover, if *Sears* and *Compco* leave room for states to protect the originator as against the copier when competition is not restricted, then the copier may also be required to label clearly in the absence of secondary meaning. By allowing states to require such labeling, *Sears* and *Compco* implicitly confirm the conclusion that equal labeling will not, in general, result in a lessening of competition.

Under traditional rules, marking the imitation in the same manner as the originator, though in small and inconspicuous type, is normally deemed reasonable, since the originator's own practice indicates the mark's sufficiency to inform the public of origin.[128] There have been cases, however, that go further and impose higher standards on the copier than those observed by the originator.[129] Thus, in the case of an un-

---

[127] *Id.* at 231.
[128] Vaughan Novelty Mfg. Co. v. G. G. Greene Mfg. Corp., 202 F.2d 172 (3d Cir. 1953).
[129] In Zippo Mfg. Co. v. Rogers Imports, Inc., 216 F. Supp. 670 (S.D.N.Y. 1963), for instance, although defendant imprinted both its name and the words

Unfair Competition Protection 27

marked product identified to the consuming public only by its distinctive shape, the copier is sometimes required to label his imitation to dissipate customer confusion, although the originator leaves his product unmarked.[130] In such a case, secondary meaning would appear to be essential to relief, since the product's distinctive configuration would in effect be the label by which the public identified the product as emanating from the originator. If no secondary meaning exists and the public had made no such identification, the originator should have the burden of initially distinguishing between the products by first labeling himself. Then, he may be entitled to require the copier to label to inform the public that the products of two distinct manufacturers are on the market. When secondary meaning is absent, the originator cannot claim that the product configuration is serving as his label, since by definition no relationship has been established among the public between the configuration and the product's source.

Thus, where secondary meaning had been established and where identical unidentified shredded wheat biscuits reached ultimate consumers in restaurant plates, defendant was required to impress a mark upon the surface of his biscuit as the only practicable method of dispelling deception and distinguishing his biscuit from plaintiff's well-recognized product.[131] Similarly, an imitator was required to stamp its name clearly and indelibly in shoes made to the shape and contour of human feet, where the court deemed the stamp necessary to prevent source confusion.[132]

"Made in Japan" on the bottom of cigarette lighters sold from display cards bearing its name, the high likelihood of confusion between the competing lighters required that defendant's display cards be altered so that the name "Rogers" would appear more prominently.

[130] *E.g.*, Smith, Kline & French Labs. v. Clark & Clark, 157 F.2d 725 (3d Cir. 1946).

[131] Shredded Wheat Co. v. Humphrey Cornell Co., 250 Fed. 960 (2d Cir. 1918).

[132] Murray v. Miller, 3 App. Div. 2d 1008, 164 N.Y.S.2d 257 (1st Dep't 1957) (*per curiam*).

Court-imposed indelible stamping of source indicia may well conflict with the policy of encouraging free and open competition. Superficially, it might appear that such relief will in no way hamper the copier's enjoyment of the full benefits of his right to copy whatever is in the public domain, since the relief is designed to protect the originator's reputation or right to acquire one, not to prevent the copier from marketing his product. Nevertheless, relief may impose a handicap by preventing or making more difficult any diversion of the originator's trade.[133] Thus, a court directive such as that requiring Rogers Imports, despite its lack of fraud, to take steps to prevent retailers from selling Rogers lighters in Zippo boxes or without Rogers display cards,[134] may unduly restrict Rogers' right to derive profits from Zippo's design. Significantly, the court in the shredded wheat case, aware of the possibility that its decree might infringe upon defendant's right to compete, stated that defendant might apply at the end of six months to the district court to be relieved of the requirement if he could prove himself unable to comply with the court's decree except at an expense which would make continued competition impossible.[135]

Not all courts, however, when formulating their decrees to adjust the conflicting interests of the parties before them, have given sufficient weight to the public's interest in free competition. In view of the *Sears* and *Compco* limitations on state relief, traditional methods of resolving recurring problems may no longer be valid. For example, the drug industry, a prolific source of unfair competition litigation, is notorious for marketing tablets, capsules, and pills without source indicia because some members of the medical profession want their patients to believe that prescriptions are prepared specially for

---

[133] See Shredded Wheat Co. v. Humphrey Cornell Co., 250 Fed. 960 (2d Cir. 1918).
[134] Zippo Mfg. Co. v. Rogers Imports, Inc., 216 F. Supp. 670 (S.D.N.Y. 1963).
[135] Shredded Wheat Co. v. Humphrey Cornell Co., 250 Fed. 960, 967 (2d Cir. 1918).

them, an allusion which would be destroyed if the patient received tablets stamped with a manufacturer's initials.[136] In this industry, therefore, requiring a company to stamp its product to distinguish it from another well-recognized product may well create a competitive disadvantage.

Smith, Kline & French Labs. v. Clark & Clark,[137] was just such a case. Because defendant's salesman induced unscrupulous druggists to fill prescriptions calling for plaintiff's uniquely shaped amphetamine sulphate tablets with defendant's identical tablets, the court ordered defendant to stamp the initials "C & C" on each of its tablets. Here, the legal wrong was not in the use of plaintiff's unique tablet design but in the unfair and fraudulent advantage taken of such use.[138] Therefore, it might be argued that plaintiff, being entitled to relief, was entitled to effective protection against the fraudulent passing off of defendant's product as his. But this argument ignores the overriding consideration that an originator is not entitled to a decree which assists, creates, or supports a monopoly in a product or design that everyone is free to copy and sell.[139] Owing to a peculiarity of the medical profession the relief granted may conceivably impose a commercial handicap that could eventually dissipate the imitator's right to copy and compete, since the presence of stamped initials might prevent physicians from prescribing defendant's product on its own merit. The likelihood that such a result would ensue from the relief granted in *Smith, Kline & French* makes the decision questionable under the *Sears* and *Campco* free competition philosophy.

A plaintiff in the situation of *Smith, Kline & French*, however, need not be without remedy. Obviously, adequate labeling of a defendant's cartons sold to retail druggists will not

---

[136] Smith, Kline & French Labs. v. Clark & Clark, 157 F.2d 725, 730 n.15 (3d Cir. 1946).
[137] 157 F.2d 725 (3d Cir. 1946).
[138] See William R. Warner & Co. v. Eli Lilly Co., 265 U.S. 526 (1924).
[139] *Ibid.*

help: It is the druggist who intentionally substitutes products when filling a prescription. But a more extreme type of relief than making the copier identify himself more clearly than the originator is possible. Some courts have seen fit to require defendants to attach to all cartons sold to retailers a warning that the preparation is not to be dispensed as the product of the plaintiff.[140] This would normally violate *Sears* and *Compco*, since requiring a copier to call attention to the originator's product may put the copier at a competitive disadvantage by providing, in effect, free advertising of the original, and by raising doubts about the copier's product in the minds of consumers. In the drug area, however, when the fraud of the defendant's salesmen is weighed against the fact that the warning is seen only by druggists who might participate in the fraud and not by ultimate consumers, the originator's right to negate the components of fraudulent deception may well outweigh any possible infringement upon competition.

A different problem would arise if such a warning were directed to ultimate consumers. Traditionally, it has not been an answer to a charge of inadequate labeling that the manufacturer's name is imprinted on the product;[141] the duty of adequate labeling is not satisfied if the plan of labeling in its entirety indicates an attention to conceal notice.[142] In *Ronson Art Metal Works, Inc. v. Gibson Lighter Mfg. Co.*,[143] for example, defendant impressed the name "Gibson" on each exact replica of plaintiff's well-known pocket lighter. The court noted that, although this might be an infallible means of distinguishing competing lighters, the name was stamped so im-

[140] *Ibid.*; Upjohn Co. v. Schwartz, 246 F.2d 254 (2d Cir. 1957).
[141] *E.g.*, Swanson Mfg. Co. v. Feinberg-Henry Mfg. Co., 54 F. Supp. 805 (S.D.N.Y. 1943), *modified*, 147 F.2d 500 (2d Cir. 1945).
[142] *E.g.*, R. H. Macy & Co. v. Colorado Clothing Mfg. Co., 68 F.2d 690 (10th Cir. 1934).
[143] 205 Misc. 155, 127 N.Y.S.2d 786 (Sup. Ct. 1953), *modified per curiam*, 283 App. Div. 937, 130 N.Y.S.2d 814 (1st Dep't), *aff'd mem.*, 283 App. Div. 1050, 131 N.Y.S.2d 891 (1st Dep't 1954).

perfectly and was so small and inconspicuous as hardly to be visible even on close inspection. In fact, at times the "son" was easier to see than the "Gib." This case might fall into the first category mentioned above since defendant failed to meet the originator's standard of labeling. Adequate labeling therefore might be found in a clear and unmistakable stamping of the name "Gibson" or a paper label containing that name glued to each lighter. As the court stated, however, "the name selected indicated not an attempt to distinguish source but an attempt to assert as the source of manufacture a name as similar to plaintiff's name as anyone short of a desperately reckless thief would dare to attempt." [144] Adequate labeling in view of the artifices employed required a specification on all lighters and advertising material that such lighters were not the product of plaintiff. While this decision might have been correct under prior law, after *Sears* and *Compco* a court would at least be required to condition such extreme relief upon the defendant's refusal to change its name.

But the *Ronson* case and the drug industry situation are both very special. Normally, a requirement that the copier distinguish his product by indicating the source of his inspiration, will interfere with his ability to compete. For example, in one case, although anyone had the right to publish a "Webster's dictionary" and to call it by that name because its copyright had expired, the court found that "Webster's dictionary" in the mind of the public meant a Merriam book and enjoined a second publisher from marketing a "Webster's dictionary" without clearly indicating upon the title page and in its advertising that *"this dictionary is not published by the original publishers of Webster's dictionary."* [145]

It has been suggested since *Sears* and *Compco* that requiring such disparaging language would hinder competition.[146]

[144] 205 Misc. at 162, 127 N.Y.S.2d at 793.
[145] G. & C. Merriam Co. v. Saalfield, 198 Fed. 369, 378 (6th Cir. 1912). (Emphasis added.)
[146] Brown, *supra* note 118, at 1225.

Since the imitator infringes no patent or copyright in unfair competition cases and since it is now essential that he be allowed freely to market his product, the court-imposed self-abasement in the *Ronson* and *Webster* cases could not stand as it assists the originator in retaining a monopoly over the sale of a product protected by neither patent nor copyright.[147] Gibson would now have a federally protected right to copy the shape of Ronson's lighter. Of course, requiring him to place his name on his lighter does not infringe upon that right; but requiring him to tell the public that his lighter is a copy, is a possible obstruction to free copying. Similarly, requiring a publisher to call attention to the fact that his "Webster's dictionary" is not marketed by the original publisher effectively destroys his right to identify his book by a name known to the public and in the public domain. (Merriam, of course, can identify its volume as "The Original Webster's Dictionary.") It should be apparent, therefore, after *Sears* and *Compco*, that labels may no longer "be the vehicle for state courts to award prizes to minor innovators who, we should recall, have not advanced the progress of useful arts enough to merit a patent." [148]

POSSIBLE CONFLICT WITH FEDERAL STATUTES. While court-imposed labeling of simulated product configurations raises the possibility of infringement upon free competition, a cognate possibility of state encroachment upon the federal Patent and Copyright Acts is generated when courts enjoin producers from using labels and trade dress similar to those of rival manufacturers. Here, customer confusion is not created by deceptively similar designs, since the articles are usually sold in completely enclosed packages. Nor need complainant be the originator of the products involved. Typically, complainant has established sufficient source motivation or source association that his rival finds it remunerative to imi-

---

[147] *Cf.* Feathercombs, Inc. v. Solo Prods. Corp., 306 F.2d 251 (2d Cir. 1962).
[148] Brown, *supra* note 118, at 1225.

tate the lettering, color, design, size, or shape of complainant's labels, trade dress, and packages, affirmatively attempting to palm off his enclosed product through customer confusion.[149]

Labels. "[L]abels . . . [for] articles of merchandise" are specifically enumerated as subjects of copyright protection.[150] Not every label is copyrightable, however; to deserve federal protection a label must contain an appreciable amount of original text or pictorial material.[151] Logically, whatever *Sears* and *Compco* say about products within the Copyright Act would seem to apply to labels, thereby dedicating noncopyrighted labels into the public domain. Copiers, under this view, would be allowed freely to imitate the labels of any producer, since *Sears* and *Compco* maintain that anything in the public domain is not to be protected. The Court explicitly stated, however, that states may require labeling to prevent consumers from being misled as to source. This would appear to present somewhat of a dilemma; for if a producer is free to copy the label of his rival it would be impossible for a state to exercise effectively its power to prevent customer confusion. But it would be contrary to the Court's opinion to read its statement any other way than as an exception to the *Sears* and *Compco* proscription. The clear case is where a copier simulates not only an unpatented product, but also the accompanying uncopyrighted label. State relief equal to that available under the federal Copyright Act is essential to give vitality to the Court's allowance of adequate labeling requirements, which in this case would entail power to enjoin use of any deceptively similar label.

Presumably, the Court felt that this exception to its ruling against copying product configuration would not appreciably affect its free competition objective, since relief typically will

[149] See Ronson Art Metal Works, Inc. v. Gibson Lighter Mfg. Co., 3 App. Div. 2d 227, 231–32, 159, N.Y.S.2d 606, 610–11 (1st Dep't 1957).
[150] 17 U.S.C. § 5(k) (1958).
[151] Kitchens of Sara Lee, Inc. v. Nifty Foods Corp., 266 F.2d 541 (2d Cir. 1959).

be less burdensome than in product simulation cases. The costs for changes in label design are less onerous than for changes in product configuration.[152] True, a copier's right to use a label's elements is curtailed, but his interest is apparently less compelling than the public's interest in being able to distinguish between competing products in a line of commerce, and, if the earlier analysis is correct, the originator's interest in establishing a reputation.[153]

Extent of Relief. One who places a simulated configuration on the market need not protect the negligent customer.[154] A prominent disclosure of source will usually suffice.[155] The rival manufacturer's name usually appears on his label, but in cases of label simulation the overall appearance is such that a consumer familiar with complainant's label is likely to pick up the copier's product thinking it to be the originator's.[156] Therefore, courts must mold relief with the average purchaser in mind, a person probably careless and unanalytical, who is governed by appearance and general impression.[157] The injunction should not enumerate particular features, but should be aimed at dissipating the general effect of the combination;[158] this will enable copiers to use similar colors and shapes if their labels differ adequately in general appearance.[159]

[152] Note, 77 HARV. L. REV., *supra* note 114, at 913.
[153] See Caron Corp. v. V. Vivaudou, Inc., 4 F.2d 995 (2d Cir. 1925).
[154] West Point Mfg. Co. v. Detroit Stamping Co., 222 F.2d 581 (6th Cir.), *cert. denied*, 350 U.S. 840 (1955).
[155] J. C. Penney Co. v. H. D. Lee Mercantile Co., 120 F.2d 949 (8th Cir. 1941).
[156] See Tas-T-Nut Co. v. Variety Nut & Date Co., 245 F.2d 3 (6th Cir. 1957).
[157] See Florence Mfg. Co. v. J. C. Dowd & Co., 178 Fed. 73 (2d Cir. 1910); H. A. Metz Labs., Inc. v. Blackman, 153 Misc. 171, 275 N.Y. Supp. 407 (Sup. Ct. 1934); Hi-Land Dairyman's Ass'n v. Cloverleaf Dairy, 107 Utah 68, 151 P.2d 710 (1944).
[158] See Howard Dustless Duster Co. v. Carleton, 219 Fed. 913 (D. Conn. 1915); Fisher v. Blank, 138 N.Y. 244, 33 N.E. 1040 (1893).
[159] N. K. Fairbank Co. v. R. W. Bell Mfg. Co., 77 Fed. 869 (2d Cir. 1896); National Biscuit Co. v. Pacific Coast Biscuit Co., 83 N.J. Eq. 369, 91 Atl. 126 (1914).

The issue whether a court should enjoin the use of confusingly similar labels can arise in four conceivable situations, in all of which complainant need not be the originator of the product involved. The marketing of a similar product combined with the copying of a label having secondary meaning would present the clear case triggering injunctive relief. Seldom would a later competitor in a given line of commerce simulate the collocation of complainant's label design in the absence of secondary meaning. When this does occur, however, the inference would seem strong that defendant's use of a confusingly similar label on an identical product was motivated by an attempt to benefit in the future from an evolving reputation through source confusion. If it can be shown, however, that the copier was motivated by a desire to use an attractive label, simply because of its inherent beauty, the originator would have to change labels himself if he wished to establish his own reputation. If the copier once again changed labels, the inference that he was attempting to capitalize on an evolving reputation would become even stronger.

A situation closer to the line of proscribed injunctions would be the use on a product in a different line of commerce of confusingly similar labels having secondary meaning. Nevertheless, if plaintiff has a reputation upon which consumers rely, protection should be afforded. A higher standard for confusion should be demanded, however, when complainant's label has no secondary meaning and he is seeking to enjoin the use of a similar one on a product in a different line of commerce. If courts are willing to provide a producer with an opportunity to establish his reputation, relief may be appropriate here as well. Corporate producers often market diverse products in unrelated lines of commerce, and consumers naturally transpose good will associated with familiar labels to new articles bearing similar labels. It seems true, however, that the inference in the absence of secondary meaning that copying was designed to capitalize on an established or developing reputation in another field is not so strong as where both products are in the same line of commerce.

Trade Dress. The Court also allows states to "protect businesses in the use of . . . distinctive dress in the packaging of goods so as to prevent others . . . from misleading purchasers as to the source of the goods." [160] The same considerations apply here as in the consideration of labels, the only significant issue being what the Court means by trade dress. Normally, in addition to the coloring and printing scheme on a wrapper or package, trade dress is thought to include packages, boxes, and bottles, and this would seem to include within the Court's exception the many cases concerning the configuration of packages which hold products. A federal act covers these items also, and here too, it seems justifiable to conclude that in general the opinions except these items from their purview.

Cases involving packaging may arise in the same four situations as in labeling, but considerations here involved differ substantially. Normally, producers do not market their goods in bare containers or packages without other source indicia. Hence, it is difficult to adduce a secondary meaning to the contour of a container or package.[161] Nevertheless, there are shapes and forms of containers and packages which are so unique or distinctive that through long utilization they become associated with a particular product.[162] The most common situation arises when a producer in the same line of commerce simulates complainant's distinctive box or bottle

---

[160] Sears, Roebuck & Co. v. Stiffel Co., 376 U.S. 225, 232 (1964).

[161] *Cf. In re* Hillerich & Bradsby Co., 40 C.C.P.A. (Patents) 990, 204 F.2d 287 (1953). See also Note, 27 GEO. WASH. L. REV. 104, 118 (1958).

[162] *E.g.,* the shape of the Haig & Haig "pinch bottle" indicates to some shoppers the source of its contents without the need of a label. *Ex parte* Haig & Haig, Ltd., 118 U.S.P.Q. 229 (Comm'r 1958); see Moxie Co. v. Daoust, 206 Fed. 434 (1st Cir. 1913); Charles E. Hires Co. v. Consumers' Co., 100 Fed. 809 (7th Cir. 1900). See also Note, *Principal Registration of Contours of Packages and Containers under the Trademark Act of* 1946, 27 GEO. WASH. L. REV. 104 (1958).

that has become a primary means of source identification. Thus, a plaintiff who was the first to manufacture gum in round tin lithographed boxes was held entitled to an injunction even though the prudent purchaser would not be misled, because the conspicuous characteristic in the minds of many purchasers was the "round gum in the tin box," and because most purchasers would not be likely to observe differences in coloring or lettering.[163] In another case, although any bottler could purchase "Mount Vernon" whiskey in bulk, bottle it, and sell it as such, only plaintiff was franchised to bottle "Mount Vernon" whiskey on the premises of its distiller, thereby acquiring a wide reputation for marketing a superior and purer product.[164] Because purchasers of whiskey relied on the unique square-shaped "bottle with the bulging neck" to differentiate plaintiff's "Mount Vernon" whiskey from all others, defendant's use of the exact bottle was enjoined as an unfair diversion of plaintiff's customers. Similarly, where plaintiff's globular based, long-necked cologne bottle, subject of an expired design patent, became fixed in the minds of cosmetic patrons through extensive advertising, defendant could not eliminate source confusion merely by placing a different tag on the bottle since the bottle configuration remained the dominant indicator of source.[165]

Because the physical contours of the boxes and bottles involved in these three cases fall within the scope of "invention" under the design patent statute,[166] a corridor of possible conflict with *Sears* and *Compco* is presented. The fact that a design patent on a bottle or package is invalid [167] or has expired [168] has been held not to destroy the right of its user to

[163] H. E. Winterton Gum Co. v. Autosales Gum & Chocolate Co., 211 Fed. 612, 617 (6th Cir. 1914).
[164] Cook & Bernheimer Co. v. Ross, 73 Fed. 203 (C.C.S.D.N.Y. 1896).
[165] Lucien Lelong, Inc. v. George W. Button Corp., 50 F. Supp. 708 (S.D. N.Y. 1943).
[166] 35 U.S.C. § 171 (1958).
[167] Krem-Ko Co. v. R. G. Miller & Sons, 68 F.2d 872, 873 (2d Cir. 1934).
[168] Tas-T-Nut Co. v. Variety Nut & Date Co., 245 F.2d 3 (6th Cir. 1957).

protection under the law of unfair competition. *Sears* and *Compco*, however, recognize that a constitutional question is involved in any attempt to assert a monopoly in a product without reliance on either the patent or copyright laws,[169] "regardless of the copier's motives."[170] Hence, granting protection to the subject of an invalid or expired design patent appears to be in direct contravention with the *Sears-Compco* declaration that a court cannot consistently with the supremacy clause of the Constitution extend the life of a design patent beyond its expiration date or give patent protection to an article which lacks the invention required for a federal patent. Such protection also seems to negate the constitutional limitation that exclusive rights shall exist only for "limited times." It is arguable, therefore, that the Court's proscriptions should be applied literally so that no patentee or originator may claim rights under unfair competition laws because such protection deprives the public of a part of its right to utilize freely a configuration in the public domain.

Consistent with this view, another court considering the Lucien Lelong cologne bottle stated that plaintiff's formal dedication of the design upon expiration of its patent precluded any injunction, however necessary, based on the exclusive right to that form.[171] Where a patent has expired it would appear that plaintiff has had his protection for the statutory period and can no longer enjoy his monopoly on the design patented.[172] It must be determined, therefore, whether the concept of dedication, stemming from the constitutional provision restricting exclusive rights to true inventions for

---

Contra, Lucien Lelong, Inc. v. Lander Co., 164 F.2d 395 (2d Cir. 1947) (the court distinguished cases which granted unfair competition protection to subjects of invalid design patents).

[169] Smith, *"In Vino (Mogen David Brand) Veritas"?*, 54 TRADEMARK REP. 581, 587 (1964).

[170] Compco Corp. v. Day-Brite Lighting, Inc., 376 U.S. 234, 238 (1964).

[171] Lucien Lelong, Inc. v. Lander, 164 F.2d 395 (2d Cir. 1947).

[172] *Cf. Ex parte* Metals & Controls Corp., 110 U.S.P.Q. 62, 64 (Comm'r 1956).

limited times, operates to limit unfair competition protection of package and container configurations.

The Design Patent Act provides the design patentee with a remedy against anyone who "applies the patented design, or any colorable imitation thereof, to any article of manufacture for the purpose of sale." [173] The scope of protection afforded the design patentee is broad.[174] Infringement has been found where a design for a general purpose braid was applied to a hat that was not specified in plaintiff's patents,[175] and where a design for sterling silver was applied to plated spoons.[176] The test for design patent infringement—whether the infringing article has the same appearance to the general observer as the appearance of the design disclosed in the patent [177]—indicates that the design patentee may exclude others from employing his design regardless of the nature of the infringing article.[178] This is a true negative monopoly under which every use of the validly patented design is prohibited.

Unfair competition, in contrast, provides a remedy only against a manufacturer who attempts to deceive purchasers as to source of origin. Manifestly, the use of a source-identifying package or container in conjunction with the sale of any article is not automatically unfair competition. For example, the use of Lucien Lelong's distinctive cologne bottle to market ketchup would not constitute unfair competition.[179] Where

[173] 35 U.S.C. § 289 (1958).

[174] See Law & Junkins, *Registrability of Packages and Configurations of Goods on the Supplemental Register: Design Patent vs. Trademark Registration*, 45 TRADEMARK REP. 22, 33–35 (1955); Note, 27 GEO. WASH. L. REV., supra note 162, at 120.

[175] Jacob Elishewitz & Sons Co. v. Bronston Bros. & Co., 40 F.2d 434 (2d Cir. 1930).

[176] Dominick & Haff v. R. Wallace & Sons Mfg. Co., 209 Fed. 223 (2d Cir. 1913).

[177] Gorham Co. v. White, 81 U.S. (14 Wall.) 511, 528 (1871); Man-Sew Pinking Attachment Corp. v. Chandler Mach. Co., 33 F. Supp. 950, 954–55 (D. Mass. 1940).

[178] Law & Junkins, supra note 174, at 34.

[179] See Derenberg, *The Seventeenth Year of Administration of the Lanham Trademark Act of 1946*, 54 TRADEMARK REP. 655, 661–63 (1964).

the bottle's shape functions as its label, the right to prevent a competitor's simulation of the bottle grows out of actual use and consumer identification with the user. It is clear, therefore, that unfair competition and design patent protection have distinct purposes.[180] Rights under the patent grant attach to the bottle irrespective of its label and contents. While the purpose of the design patent is to encourage creation and disclosure of inventions, the purpose of unfair competition protection is to ensure that customers are not confused or deceived as to source, and, absent an anticompetitive effect, to preserve good will symbolized by a distinctive container.[181] It therefore seems possible to distinguish, at least in certain instances, the protection accorded distinctive containers, packages, and bottles from a mere substitution or extension of design patent protection.[182]

Insofar as packages and bottles can themselves be considered "products," the rule of law expressed in *Sears* and *Compco* gives complete freedom to copy with impunity, provided only that the competitor clearly affix his own name.[183] Nevertheless, unfair competition protection of bottles and packages when used in a given line of commerce may not necessarily conflict with the *Sears-Compco* rationale, since the public policy which permits imitation of an article of commerce is often without relevance to the package or container in which the article is marketed.[184] Arguably, the package may be thought to be simply a nonfunctional feature of the product, and if protection is afforded it, protection might just

[180] 1 NIMS, UNFAIR COMPETITION AND TRADE-MARKS 350 (4th ed. 1947).
[181] *Cf.* 1 SEIDEL, DUBROFF & GONDA, TRADEMARK LAW AND PRACTICE § 1.09(2) (1963).
[182] *Cf.* Law & Junkins, *supra* note 174; Note, 27 GEO. WASH. L. REV., *supra* note 162.
[183] Spangler Candy Co. v. Crystal Pure Candy Co., 235 F. Supp. 18 (N.D. Ill. 1964), *aff'd*, 147 U.S.P.Q. 434 (7th Cir. 1965).
[184] See Bostitch, Inc. v. King Fastener Co., 87 R.I. 274, 286, 140 A.2d 274, 280 (1958). *But see* Treece, *Copying Methods of Product Differentiation: Fair or Unfair Competition?*, 38 NOTRE DAME LAW. 244, 262 (1963).

as well be afforded the nonfunctional parts of Day-Brite's fixture. This argument fails to recognize, however, that in the typical case the package is not a part of, and has no relation to, the product itself. Consumers may identify the enclosed product by its distinctive package, but after purchase or upon consumption the package, having served its purpose, is discarded. While an article will almost invariably be simulated because of a supposed or established public desire for that article, the simulation of a bottle, container, or package configuration which identifies source is more likely to be motivated by an intent to deceive. A plaintiff in such a situation, therefore, is not complaining of defendant's making or selling a bottle, but of his using a bottle in a particular trade to gull the public. Consonant with this view, a court has held that *Sears* and *Compco* do not preclude an injunction to prevent the use of a polyethylene lollipop bag.[185] The court noted that *Sears* and *Compco* proscribe protection of property interests of the first entrant as property interests, so that a polyethylene bag manufacturer could not prevent the bag's manufacture by a rival producer. On the other hand, the court felt a lollipop bag manufacturer could request an injunction on behalf of his customers who have become accustomed to a certain form of packaging in order to protect against their being deceived through deceptive imitation of that format.

Even if valid, this theory points to the essentiality of secondary meaning as a prerequisite to relief when the dispute concerns a package configuration rather than the coloring and lettering on a label, wrapper, or package itself. In its absence no inference of deception would be possible; a rival may want to copy a bottle merely because he likes it, which he is perfectly entitled to do. Since the bottle has at no time been associated with any manufacturer, customers might assume that this was the typical bottle used in the line of

[185] Spangler Candy Co. v. Crystal Pure Candy Co., 235 F. Supp. 18 (N.D. Ill. 1964), aff'd, 353 F.2d.641 (7th Cir. 1965).

commerce, but they would make no assumptions as to source. The only protection possible in the absence of secondary meaning, therefore, is probably that of adequate labeling; protection of the bottle itself would appear to be proscribed by the *Sears-Compco* thesis. There is, of course, the same interest here, as in labeling, in protecting the originator's right to establish secondary meaning. But the likelihood that a package will be copied for its attractiveness is probably substantially greater than it is with labels. It seems only consistent, however, to enjoin the copying even of packaging if the plaintiff is able to demonstrate that the copying was motivated exclusively by a desire to capitalize on the plaintiff's attempts to establish his reputation.

Other problems occur when a source-identifying bottle is copied and used by a producer in another line of commerce. Here, a question of fact is created as to whether consumer confusion as to source exists. If closely analogous products are involved such confusion may well be created, but it is doubtful whether consumer association of a bottle with a particular perfume manufacturer would cause consumers to believe he was also the manufacturer of ketchup marketed in the same bottle. A strict standard of proof would appear to be a necessity in this instance in view of the possible anticompetitive effect of removing a container shape from the business community. When no secondary meaning exists and when the copied bottle is used in a different line of commerce, relief would appear to be entirely precluded. It is highly unlikely that a plaintiff could ever establish that a producer in another line of commerce copied his package exclusively for the purpose of capitalizing on the plaintiff's efforts to gain a reputation.

While in labeling situations an anticompetitive effect is seldom, if ever, created by an injunction, this is not the case with certain types of packaging. The package may be so distinctive, attractive, or useful that it might become an

Unfair Competition Protection 43

essential selling feature of the article. In such a situation, the rationale used to justify an injunction against use of any source-identifying package in a similar line of commerce can no longer be relied upon to overcome the *Sears-Compco* thesis.

A wine bottle that substitutes as a fine decanter illustrates the problem. Although it may be an arbitrary embellishment or form of dress primarily adopted for purposes of individuality and source identification, it is not completely unrelated to basic consumer demands; the wine may be purchased in part because of the dual purpose bottle. Therefore, to avoid any possible anticompetitive effect, the *Sears* and *Compco* trade-dress exception should apply only to the extent that the container or bottle is intended primarily to indicate origin. Thus, prior to *Sears* and *Compco*, where plaintiff's tubular package displaying a rear view picture of a girl wearing one of plaintiff's girdles was imitated, an injunction was issued only to enjoin imitation of the picture.[186] The tubular container was allowed to be imitated freely because its utility as a self-service unit, facilitating display in counter dispensers, necessarily dedicated it to the business community.[187] Other courts prior to *Sears* and *Compco* refused to apply the doctrine of secondary meaning to functional features, features common to the trade,[188] and features using common shapes appropriate to the size and kind of goods sold.[189] The true basis of these holdings, it has been said,

---

[186] International Latex Corp. v. Flexees, Inc., 281 App. Div. 363, 119 N.Y.S.2d 409 (1st Dep't 1953).

[187] See also National Biscuit Co. v. Pacific Coast Biscuit Co., 83 N.J. Eq. 369, 91 Atl. 126 (1914) (no monopoly in shape, size, or capacity of cracker box, lined with paraffin paper capable of interfolding at the ends, since such a system must necessarily be common to all bakers).

[188] See Seven Up Co. v. Sheer Up Sales Co., 148 F.2d 909 (8th Cir.), cert. denied, 326 U.S. 727 (1945); Coca-Cola Co. v. Glee-Nol Bottling Co., 221 Fed. 61 (5th Cir. 1915); Industrial Rayon Corp. v. Dutchess Underwear Corp., 17 F. Supp. 783 (S.D.N.Y.), rev'd on other grounds, 92 F.2d 33 (2d Cir. 1937); United States Tobacco Co. v. McGreenery, 144 Fed. 531 (C.C. Mass.), aff'd per curiam, 144 Fed. 1022 (1st Cir. 1906).

[189] See William Faehndrich, Inc. v. Wheeler Riddle Cheese Co., 34 F.2d 43

is not that such features do not indicate source to the purchasing public, but that there is an overriding public policy in preventing their monopolization.[190] Similarly, under the *Sears-Compco* labeling exception, it is arguable that a certain amount of purchaser confusion must be tolerated to insure the public the advantages of free competition.[191]

It may be, however, that a unique container or bottle, though it contributes to consumer demand, should not be considered functional, as that term has been restrictively applied, where in fact the configuration has come to identify source. Nevertheless, whether competition has in fact been hindered is the crux of the problem. As has been suggested, the merchant who begins to package frozen vegetables or toothbrushes or cereals should expect that his packaging method will be imitated as the convenience and standardization of a prepackaged display becomes accepted by consumers.[192] Still, the argument has also been made that any demand for wine in decanter type bottles, for example, can be met without the right to copy a specific design. It is true that, even if there is an aesthetic value in a particular design, its use is not essential for a fully functioning decanter bottle, and depriving the public of its right to purchase copies of the particular configuration involved is arguably insignificant when weighed against the public's and the producer's right to protection from confusion.[193] But *Sears* and *Compco* seem

---

(E.D.N.Y. 1929); Oakite Prods., Inc. v. Boritz, 161 Misc. 807, 293 N.Y. Supp. 399 (Sup. Ct. 1936).

[190] *In re* Deister Concentrator Co., 48 C.C.P.A. (Patents) 952, 966, 289 F.2d 496, 504 (1961).

[191] See National Biscuit Co. v. Pacific Coast Biscuit Co., 83 N.J. Eq. 369, 91 Atl. 126 (1914), where the court refused to restrain the use of a package that was necessarily dedicated to the trade, even though its use was part of a general plan of imitation.

[192] International Latex Corp. v. Flexees, Inc., 281 App. Div. 363, 119 N.Y.S.2d 409 (1st Dep't 1953).

[193] See Application of Mogen David Wine Corp., 328 F.2d 925, 932 (C.C.P.A. (Patents) 1964) (concurring opinion).

clearly to preclude the balancing of a producer's interest when the result is anticompetitive. And while the public may gain in source identification if a particular design is disallowed, where a package is treated as part of a product the anticompetitive effect is likely to be too significant to justify state protection. The first entrant, by using a bottle that has a commercial impact on the sale of his product, has probably precluded protection for his bottle on the basis of its labeling function.

TRADEMARKS

Although *Sears* and *Compco* deal only with state law, the decisions may have as yet unexplored repercussions in the federal law of trademarks. The question before the Court was whether a state's unfair competition law could, consistent with federal patent laws, prohibit the copying of an article protected by neither a federal patent nor copyright. It seems clear that when the subject of an invalid or expired design patent becomes public property no further right to exclude the public from its use may be claimed merely because it has acquired secondary meaning or trademark significance even if confusion as to source would result. Yet, uncertainty exists as to whether the opinions create an absolute right in the public to copy an article or feature in the absence of a valid subsisting patent or copyright.

This in turn raises the issue whether the subject of an invalid or expired design patent, admittedly dedicated to the public, can be withdrawn from the public domain to give its proprietor a perpetual monopoly on the design merely because he succeeds in registering it as a trademark under the Lanham Trademark Act of 1946.[194] Should the article's con-

---

[194] For a detailed discussion of the significant Patent Office and Court of Customs and Patent Appeals decisions that have created perpetual federal pro-

figuration meet all the standards required of trademarks under the act, copying can be prohibited by a suit for trademark infringement. The Supreme Court in *Sears* and *Compco*, however, did not determine whether Congress, as distinguished from the states, can enact legislation such as the Lanham Act under the commerce clause of the Constitution, providing for the recognition and protection of the subject matter of a design patent as a trademark.

"Configurations of goods" which are "capable of distinguishing" the proprietor's goods may be registered on the Supplemental Register established by Section 23 of the Trademark Act of 1946.[195] This section originally attempted to insure protection for United States nationals against design and trademark piracy in various countries in which trademark rights are based solely upon registration and in which a foreign applicant must prove that his mark is registered in his home country to succeed in obtaining registration.[196] Today, this registration serves as a preliminary step to obtaining registration on the Principal Register. Registration on the Supplemental Register, therefore, constitutes recognition that the configuration is capable of indicating origin [197] and capable of distinguishing the applicant's product from the like products of others,[198] but it affords the registrant no presumptive right to exclusive use.[199]

It is possible, however, to obtain registration for arbitrary or nonessential features of an article on the Principal Register

---

tection for originators of successful commercial designs, see Andrew, *Domestic Protection of Commercial Designs: The Federal-State Conflict*, 39 ST. JOHN'S L. REV. 23, 29–38 (1964).

[195] 60 Stat. 435 (1946), as amended, 15 U.S.C. § 1091 (1958), as amended, 15 U.S.C. § 1091 (Supp. V, 1964).

[196] 1 SEIDEL, DUBROFF & GONDA, TRADEMARK LAW AND PRACTICE § 15.01 (1963).

[197] *Ex parte* Caron Corp., 100 U.S.P.Q. 356 (Comm'r 1954).

[198] Wehringer, *Two for One: Trademarks and Design Patents*, 50 TRADEMARK REP. 1158 (1960).

[199] 1 SEIDEL, DUBROFF & GONDA, *supra* note 196, § 15.01; see *Ex parte* Caron Corp., 100 U.S.P.Q. 356 (Comm'r 1954).

under section 2(f),[200] provided the registrant can establish that such features have acquired a secondary meaning.[201] In contrast to the Supplemental Register, this registration constitutes prima facie evidence of registrant's exclusive right to use the mark in commerce on the goods specified in the certificate.[202] Accordingly, the originator of a design which might otherwise be freely copied may seek to enjoin such copying by bringing suit for infringement of the trademark right which the originator has acquired in the design.[203] The protection granted, based upon congressional enactment under the "commerce clause" rather than under the "patent and copyright clause," is tantamount to protection under the law of unfair competition where secondary meaning has been established. Both packages and configurations of goods are not registrable, however, unless intended primarily to indicate origin and unless they are of such a nature that the ordinary purchaser would be likely to consider that they indicate origin.[204] Still, the fact that the design is recognizable is not sufficient to make it registrable, for if this were the criterion every unpatentable utilitarian article somewhat different from others of like kind would be granted a perpetual monopoly as an alleged trademark.[205] Hence, functional shapes, though they may have adduced a secondary meaning, are not entitled to trademark registration, since such a monopoly would be contrary to the "socio-economic policy . . . [of] the encouragement of competition . . . [which] encompasses the right to copy."[206] Nevertheless, where an article

[200] 60 Stat. 429 (1946), 15 U.S.C. § 1052(f) (1958).
[201] 4 CALLMANN, UNFAIR COMPETITION AND TRADE-MARKS § 98.4(d) (2d ed. 1950).
[202] Trademark Act § 7(b), 60 Stat. 430 (1946), 15 U.S.C. § 1057(b) (1958).
[203] Andrew, supra note 194, at 30.
[204] In re Bourns, 45 C.C.P.A. (Patents) 821, 824, 252 F.2d 582, 584 (1958).
[205] Ex parte Alan Wood Steel Co., 101 U.S.P.Q. 209 (Examiner in Chief 1954), aff'd, Alan Wood Steel Co. v. Watson, 150 F. Supp. 861 (D.D.C. 1957).
[206] In re Deister Concentrator Co., 48 C.C.P.A. (Patents) 952, 961, 289 F.2d 496, 501 (1961). Accord, In re Shenango Ceramics, Inc., 143 U.S.P.Q. 48 (Trademark Trial & Appeal Board Sept. 23, 1964).

is "in its concept arbitrary," the fact that its shape is utilitarian will not deprive it of trademark protection.[207]

If the analysis of the preceding section is correct, possible conflict with *Sears* and *Compco* will arise only when an entire product configuration or a distinctive part, as distinguished from its package or container, is registered as a trademark.[208] While a distinctive bottle or container may acquire trademark significance for the enclosed product, it generally, if not always, remains free for use by producers of unrelated products.[209] Trademark registration of the product, however, results in a theoretically perpetual monopoly of a configuration that *Sears* and *Compco* seem to assign to the public domain in the absence of a valid design patent.[210]

Prior to *Sears* and *Compco* it was thought a fundamental principle of the law of trademark ownership that functional features and utilitarian shapes be denied registration not because they failed to meet trademark requirements, but rather because nothing which the public had a right to copy under traditional unfair competition doctrine could be the subject of a valid trademark registration irrespective of its use as an indicator of source.[211] Because *Sears* and *Compco* have abrogated the dichotomy between functional shapes incapable of being monopolized and those shapes which might be monopolized because they are of such an arbitrary nature that the law does not recognize a right in the public to copy them, it has been stated that no other conclusion seems compatible with these opinions than that product configura-

[207] *In re* Deister Concentrator Co., 48 C.C.P.A. (Patents) 952, 968, 289 F.2d 496, 506 (1961) (dictum).
[208] See Derenberg, in *Symposium—Product Simulation: A Right or a Wrong?*, 64 COLUM. L. REV. 1192, 1201 (1964).
[209] See Derenberg, *The Seventeenth Year of Administration of the Lanham Trademark Act of 1946*, 54 TRADEMARK REP. 655, 661–63 (1964).
[210] *Cf.* Arnold *A Philosophy on the Protection Afforded by Patent, Trademark, Copyright and Unfair Competition Law: The Sources and Nature of Product Simulation Law*, 54 TRADEMARK REP. 413 (1964).
[211] *In re* Pollack Steel Co., 50 C.C.P.A. (Patents) 1045, 314 F.2d 566 (1963).

tions, other than distinctive containers, should be considered incapable of "trademark" significance as a matter of law.[212]

Justice Black, in generalizing about what may be copied, stated: "But if the design is not entitled to a design patent *or other federal statutory protection*, then it can be copied at will." [213] While the reference to "other statutory protection" may, from the tenor and context of the opinions, appear to relate to a mechanical patent or copyright, the Trademark Trial and Appeal Board in *Electric Storage Battery Co. v. Mine Safety Appliances Co.*[214] could not be sure, and it therefore denied a motion opposing registration on the Principal Register of a design impressed upon the crown of applicant's safety helmets. The Board noted that if it were to rule that an article's configuration is, by virtue of the Supreme Court's rulings, per se unregistrable as a trademark, it would in effect be ruling that Section 23 of the Trademark Act of 1946, which expressly provides for the registration of configurations of goods on the Supplemental Register, is unconstitutional.

It is significant that in two cases prior to *Electric Storage Battery Co.* the Court of Customs and Patent Appeals, without mentioning *Sears* and *Compco*, held that an overall product configuration adopted primarily to indicate origin was "capable of distinguishing" as a "mark" under Section 23 of the Trademark Act so long as the shape was nonfunctional in purpose,[215] and also held that a wine decanter, subject of an existing design patent, could be registered on the Principal Register.[216] Because the patent and trademark law are federal laws distinct in purpose and philosophy, the court in the latter

---

[212] Derenberg, *supra* note 208, at 1202.

[213] Compco Corp. v. Day-Brite Lighting, Inc., 376 U.S. 234, 238 (1964). (Emphasis added.)

[214] 143 U.S.P.Q. 163 (Patent Office Trademark Trial & Appeal Board 1964).

[215] *In re* Minnesota Mining & Mfg. Co., 335 F.2d 836, 839–40 (C.C.P.A. (Patents) 1964).

[216] Application of Mogen David Wine Corp., 328 F.2d 925 (C.C.P.A. (Patents) 1964).

case, *Application of Mogen David Wine Corp.*, felt that trademark registration was not inimical to the rights of others, conditioned under the patent grant, to make fair use of the subject matter after expiration of the patent, and would not thereby effectually extend the patent monopoly, contrary to the intent and purpose of the patent law.[217] Under this rationale, it has been concluded that if the designs involved in *Sears* and *Compco* were in fact capable of serving as indicators of origin, the producers might have been successful in their efforts to protect their designs had they sought the protection of the federal trademark statute rather than that of state common law in a federally preempted area.[218] The Trademark Trial and Appeal Board is of the opinion that what the Supreme Court struck down is state prohibition of mere copying of an article unprotected by either a patent or copyright, because such prohibitions are contrary to federal constitutional and patent policies;[219] but under the rationale of the *Deister*[220] and *Mogen David*[221] decisions federal statutory protection may include trademark registration of nonfunctional features, since preventing such copying is thought not to hinder competition.

The Supreme Court, however, has unequivocally indicated that whether features be denominated functional or nonfunc-

[217] See Smith, *"In Vino (Mogen David Brand) Veritas"?*, 54 TRADEMARK REP. 581 (1964).

[218] Andrew, *supra* note 194, at 38. But see Derenberg, *supra* note 208, at 1203, where the author concludes that the mere posing of the question whether Day-Brite might have prevailed if it had taken the position that its lighting fixture's distinctive ribbing was selected solely for the purpose of indicating origin, and consequently qualified as a "mark" under section 23, or a "trademark" under section 2(f) would "seem to suggest a negative answer, or, at least, a more conservative approach than that reflected in the Court of Customs and Patent Appeals' most recent opinion [*In re* Minnesota Mining & Mfg. Co., 335 F.2d 836 (Patents 1964)]."

[219] Electric Storage Battery Co. v. Mine Safety Appliances Co., 143 U.S.P.Q. 163, 166 (Patent Office Trademark Trial & Appeal Board 1964).

[220] *In re* Deister Concentrator Co., 48 C.C.P.A. (Patents) 952, 289 F.2d 496 (1961).

[221] Application of Mogen David Wine Corp., 328 F.2d 925 (C.C.P.A. (Patents) 1964).

Unfair Competition Protection 51

tional, any prohibition of copying hinders competition in such goods and thereby contravenes federal patent policy. Section 1 of the Trademark Act, then, would appear to prevent registration of product configurations because it requires that an application for registration contain a statement "that no . . . person, firm, corporation or association . . . has the right to use such mark in commerce." [222] Since *Sears* and *Compco* hold that unpatentable articles and subjects of expired design patents are in the public domain and may be copied by anyone, it would appear that an applicant could not rightfully make the required statement respecting its right to the exclusive use of its product's configuration.[223]

If, as the *Compco* opinion indicates,[224] the *Sears* and *Compco* proscription is a constitutional prohibition and not merely a rule of federal preemption, it would then apply not only to states but to the federal government as well. Since the Constitution permits protection under the patent laws for only "a limited time" any attempt to give unlimited protection would seem to be unconstitutional. Such a severe result, however, appears to be an unwarranted extension of the *Sears-Compco* patent thesis into peripheral areas. In fact, it seems to mandate judicial accommodations of *Sears* and *Compco* with trademark registration of product configurations, necessarily, of course, on a basis more tenable than the differing philosophies of the patent and trademark laws. Also, reading *Sears* and *Compco* as a definitive constitutional prohibition of federal design protection other than through the patent mechanism necessarily renders unconstitutional any other attempt

---

[222] 60 Stat. 427 (1946), as amended, 15 U.S.C. § 1051 (1958), as amended, 15 U.S.C. § 1051 (Supp. V, 964).

[223] Electric Storage Battery Co. v. Mine Safety Appliances Co., 143 U.S.P.Q. 163. 168 (Patent Office Trademark Trial & Appeal Board 1964) (dissenting opinion).

[224] "To forbid copying would interfere with the federal policy, found in Art. I, Sec. 8, cl. 8, of the Constitution and in the implementing federal statutes of allowing free access to copy whatever the federal patent and copyright laws leave in the public domain." 376 U.S. at 237.

by Congress to proscribe commercial exploitation of designs in the public domain, possibly including the proposed "Unfair Commercial Activities" bill,[225] since injunctive relief available under the bill would be coextensive with that available under the patent laws. It is indeed difficult to conclude on the basis of *Sears* and *Compco* alone that the constitutional grant of power enabling Congress to protect designs for "limited times" should be construed to operate as a limitation on legislation concededly constitutional under the commerce clause.

COPYRIGHT PREEMPTION

STATUTORY AND COMMON LAW COPYRIGHT

Although *Sears* and *Compco* involved articles susceptible only of federal patent protection, continued state protection of uncopyrighted works in the public domain appears incompatible with comprehensive language in the opinions:

> [W]hen an article is unprotected by a patent or a copyright, state law may not forbid others to copy that article. To forbid copying would interfere with the federal policy . . . of allowing free access to copy whatever the federal patent and copyright laws leave in the public domain.[226]

The copyright clause of the Constitution secures to authors the exclusive right to their "writings."[227] This term is not limited to actual scripts, but includes all tangible expressions of intellectual creation;[228] works of art such as sculpture and paintings are therefore assumed to be within the ambit of constitutional protection.[229] But the clause is not self-operating, only permissive; it grants Congress the power to

---

[225] H.R. 4651, S. 1038, 88th Cong., 1st Sess. (1963).
[226] Compco Corp. v. Day-Brite Lighting, Inc., 376 U.S. 234, 237 (1964).
[227] U.S. CONST. art. I, § 8, cl. 8. See generally Note, *Study of the Term "Writings" in the Copyright Clause of the Constitution*, 31 N.Y.U.L. REV. 1263 (1956).
[228] NIMMER, COPYRIGHT § 8.2 (1963). [229] *Ibid.*

protect "writings." Certain classifications of subject matter eligible for statutory protection, including "works of art," musical compositions, and books, are specifically enumerated in the Copyright Act.[230] This enumeration, however, constitutes a more limited class of creations than the "writings" capable of copyright through the constitutional authorization of the copyright clause; [231] so there are a variety of literary and artistic works which are ineligible for statutory protection because Congress has chosen not to grant such protection. These include three dimensional articles which do not qualify as "works of art," titles and names of characters, covers, and the contributions of performers and conductors. Since a "writing" in the constitutional sense does not require visual expression, a performance embodied on a phonograph record, though not visually perceptible, is a "writing" within the copyright clause of the Constitution, separate and apart from the composition itself, notwithstanding that Congress has chosen not to include phonograph records in the act.[232]

In the American dichotomy between common law and federal statutory copyright, the act of publication constitutes the dividing line between the two systems of protection.[233] The Copyright Act provides that nothing in the law "shall be construed to annul or limit the right of the author or proprietor of an unpublished work, at common law or in equity, to prevent the copying, publication, or use of such unpublished work without his consent, and to obtain damages therefor." [234] Statutory copyright protection, vesting an originator with the exclusive right to reproduce and vend his work, is granted for a term of years by the federal government only if there has

[230] 17 U.S.C. § 5 (1958).
[231] Capitol Records, Inc. v. Mercury Records Corp., 221 F.2d 657 (2d Cir. 1955); see Mazer v. Stein, 347 U.S. 201 (1954).
[232] Capitol Records, Inc. v. Mercury Records Corp., supra note 231; see NIMMER, supra note 228, § 8.2.
[233] See generally Nimmer, *Copyright Publication*, 56 COLUM. L. REV. 185 (1956).
[234] 17 U.S.C. § 2 (1958).

been strict compliance with the statutory requirements.[235] On the other hand, any original and developed literary or artistic expression is capable of protection from the moment of its creation until its publication under the doctrine of common law copyright. Moreover, since the specifically enumerated categories of the federal act are not applicable to common law copyright, it seems necessarily to follow that works incapable of statutory protection may nevertheless qualify for common law protection.[236] According to this view, for example, though phonograph records are outside the scope of statutory copyright protection, they are clearly artistic expressions capable of common law copyright.

"WRITINGS" SUBJECT TO STATUTORY PROTECTION

The effect of *Sears* and *Compco* can most conveniently be discussed within the general breakdown of those "writings" subject to statutory protection and those not subject to statutory protection. The further distinction between published and unpublished "writings" is of very little significance with respect to those "writings" specifically enumerated in the federal act, but may be relevant in certain isolated cases.

A published "writing" for which copyright protection exists is, of course, protected from being copied. It is equally clear that, like the subject of an expired patent, a published "writing" for which a copyright had been obtained but which has expired is in the public domain and may be copied at will:[237] upon the expiration of a copyright the right to make the thing covered by the copyright becomes public property since it is upon this condition that a copyright is granted.[238] In many cases, published "writings" which fall within the ambit of statutory protection have never become subject to such protection. This could have occurred for either of two

[235] See Bobbs-Merrill Co. v. Straus, 210 U.S. 339, 346–47 (1908).
[236] NIMMER, *supra* note 228, § 11.2.
[237] G. Ricordi & Co. v. Haendler, 194 F.2d 914 (2d Cir. 1952).
[238] *Cf.* Singer Mfg. Co. v. June Mfg. Co., 163 U.S. 169 (1896).

Unfair Competition Protection 55

reasons: the writing failed to meet statutory standards or the creator simply failed to obtain protection for which the work was qualified. Under prior law protection was generally denied in both these situations,[239] since state protection would conflict with the "scheme which Congress has for more than a century devised to cover the subject-matter." [240] Still, there were instances where protection was afforded.[241] After *Sears* and *Compco*, however, the validity of state activity in this area is doubtful, since to protect anything subject to statutory protection would conflict with federal law.[242]

In the case of a published "writing" which fails to meet statutory standards, state protection under any common law copyright or unfair competition rationale would be unwarranted. It has recently been suggested, however, that a distinction should be drawn between "writings" which are uncopyrightable and those which are uncopyrighted.[243] In support of this suggestion the author points to language in the *Sears* opinion where Justice Black says: "States . . . [should not] allow perpetual protection to articles *too lacking in novelty to merit any patent at all under federal constitutional standards. This would be too great an encroachment on the federal patent system to be tolerated,*" [244] and that "an *unpatentable* article, like an article on which the patent has expired, is in the public domain and may be made and sold by whoever chooses to

---

[239] *E.g.*, National Comics Publications, Inc. v. Fawcett Publications, Inc., 191 F.2d 594 (2d Cir. 1951); Fashion Originators Guild of America v. FTC, 114 F.2d 80 (2d Cir. 1940), *aff'd on other grounds*, 312 U.S. 457 (1941).

[240] Cheney Bros. v. Doris Silk Corp., 35 F.2d 279, 280 (2d Cir. 1929), *cert. denied*, 281 U.S. 728 (1930).

[241] *E.g.*, Fisher v. Star Co., 231 N.Y. 414, 132 N.E. 133, *cert. denied*, 257 U.S. 654 (1921); see Ettore v. Philco Television Broadcasting Corp., 229 F.2d 481 (3d Cir.), *cert. denied*, 351 U.S. 926 (1956).

[242] See Fisher v. Star Co., 231 N.Y. 414, 435, 132 N.E. 133, 140 (Crane, J., dissenting), *cert. denied*, 257 U.S. 654 (1921).

[243] Bender, in *Symposium—Product Simulation: A Right or a Wrong?*, 64 COLUM. L. REV. 1228, 1236-38 (1964).

[244] Sears, Roebuck & Co. v. Stiffel Co., 376 U.S. 225, 232 (1964). (Emphasis added.)

do so."[245] The author points out that any conflict with the federal scheme would be slight, since a court could limit relief to that afforded by the copyright statute. Nevertheless, as the author himself suggests, this approach would totally undermine the obligatory character of the formalities to be observed in obtaining federal protection, for even if the originator failed to obtain copyright protection because of his failure to comply with statutory technicalities, he could still obtain state relief. Moreover, the author seems to use Justice Black's language out of context. Not only was Justice Black referring to the cases at bar when he spoke of unpatentable inventions, but the opinions explicitly proscribe protection for *unprotected* works, a term which includes both articles which are uncopyrightable as well as uncopyrighted. Indeed, even state protection shorter in duration than that available through the copyright grant might conceivably violate the antimonopoly implications that the Court found in the copyright clause. The restraint on copying news in *International News Serv. v. Associated Press*, for example, was limited "until its commercial value as news to the complainant and all of its members has passed away."[246] Though this type of protection might conceivably extend for only one day, it totally destroys any value inherent in the news.

States have in the past protected unpublished "writings" subject to statutory protection,[247] and it seems likely that they will be able to continue to do so.[248] *Sears* and *Compco* do not adopt the theory that the federal constitutional grant of patent

---

[245] *Id.* at 231. (Emphasis added.)   [246] 248 U.S. 215, 245 (1918).
[247] *E.g.*, Smith v. Paul, 174 Cal. App. 2d 744, 345 P.2d 546 (1959).
[248] See Edgar H. Wood Associates, Inc. v. Skene, 347 Mass. 351, 197 N.E.2d 886 (1964). Section 12 of the Copyright Act, however, provides for the registration of unpublished lectures, dramatic and musical compositions, motion pictures, and photographs. Since § 12 is merely permissive an author may still avail himself of the protection of state law. See Kaplan, *Publication in Copyright Law: The Question of Phonograph Records*, 103 U. PA. L. REV. 469, 478–79 (1955). But if the author does register, state protection is lost, and the act becomes the sole measure of his rights. Shilkret v. Musicraft Records, Inc., 131 F.2d 929 (2d Cir. 1942), *cert. denied*, 319 U.S. 742 (1943); Marx v.

Unfair Competition Protection 57

and copyright powers to Congress precludes any state activity in the area covered by the grant.[249] Adoption of this theory would substantially limit the scope of the Copyright Act's provision which specifically allows common law copyright for unpublished works.[250] Generally, the mere vesting of a power in Congress does not exclude state regulation in a particular area. True, the history or intrinsic purpose of specific constitutional grants have sometimes compelled the conclusion that state regulation is precluded even though Congress has not acted.[251] It has been suggested, however, that the present case does not warrant such treatment, since Congress can always step in and assert its control should it be dissatisfied with state regulations.[252]

WRITINGS NOT SUBJECT TO STATUTORY PROTECTION

A second major category of "writings" which have received state unfair competition or common law copyright protection are those not subject to federal protection. Here the determination of what constitutes publication is of crucial significance. After *Sears* and *Compco*, the writing must pass into the public domain once its copyright expires, or upon publication if it did not meet the statutory formalities required for a work within the Copyright Act, without any rights remaining in its creator. Thus, upon first publication the owner's common law protection is lost through a forfeiture imposed by law.[253]

United States, 96 F.2d 204 (9th Cir. 1938). *But see* DeWolf, An Outline of Copyright Law 34–35 (1925) (suggesting that an author might still elect to resort to state protection).

[249] See Note, *The Supreme Court, 1963 Term*, 78 Harv. L. Rev. 143, 312 (1964). *But see* Aro Mfg. Co. v. Convertible Top Replacement Co., 377 U.S. 476, 522 (1964) (Black, J., dissenting).

[250] 17 U.S.C. § 2 (1958).

[251] *Cf., e.g.,* H. P. Hood & Sons, Inc. v. Du Mond, 336 U.S. 525 (1949).

[252] Kaplan, *Performer's Right and Copyright: The Capitol Records Case*, 69 Harv. L. Rev. 409, 420–21 (1956).

[253] Bobbs-Merrill Co. v. Straus, 210 U.S. 339 (1908). The loss of common law protection is referred to by many as a dedication or abandonment. However,

Since common law copyright has been referred to as the right of first publication,[254] the question arises whether publication is also an abandonment of all common law rights in those works which are susceptible of copyright under the copyright clause of the Constitution, but for which Congress has not provided protection in the Copyright Act.

Many courts, prior to *Sears* and *Compco*, felt it unlikely that the constitutional provision or the Copyright Act itself precludes the states from protecting entrepreneurs after publication.[255] They reasoned that since the rights involved were not protected by the federal statute, the controversy must be exclusively between the parties and did not involve any public rights.[256] Under this rationale, copying was sometimes proscribed subsequent to technical publication.[257] Thus, despite a recognized right to copy, injunctions were traditionally granted to prevent palming off with its consequent deception of consumers.[258] Fraud upon the public, however, was not at issue in the leading case, *International News Serv. v. Associated Press*,[259] where INS obtained news from the early editions of AP's Eastern seaboard member papers and sold it to Western papers served by AP. Representing a momentous departure from the traditional passing off theory of unfair competition, the Court, notwithstanding publication by AP, granted relief on the basis of misappropriation and restrained INS from copying news "until its commercial value as news

since these words connote an intentional surrender when actually the surrender is imposed as a matter of law regardless of intent, the word forfeiture is more appropriate. National Comics Publications, Inc. v. Fawcett Publications, Inc., 191 F.2d 594, 598 (2d Cir. 1951) (L. Hand, J.).

[254] Nimmer, *supra* note 233.
[255] *E.g.*, Dior v. Milton, 9 Misc. 2d 425, 155 N.Y.S.2d 443 (Sup. Ct.), *aff'd mem.*, 2 App. Div. 2d 878, 156 N.Y.S.2d 996 (1st Dep't 1956).
[256] See Mutual Broadcasting Sys., Inc. v. Muzak Corp., 177 Misc. 489, 30 N.Y.S.2d 419 (Sup. Ct. 1941).
[257] *E.g.*, McCord Co. v. Plotnick, 108 Cal. App. 2d 392, 239 P.2d 32 (Dist. Ct. App. 1951).
[258] *E.g.*, Hesse v. Grossman, 152 Cal. App. 2d 536, 313 P.2d 625 (Dist. Ct. App. 1957).
[259] 248 U.S. 215 (1918).

to the complainant and all of its members has passed away."[260]

The misappropriation doctrine differs from previous discussions of unfair competition in that the defendant, instead of selling his goods as those of complainant, sells complainant's creation as his own. The rival, therefore, attempts a "free ride" on the product itself rather than on the reputation of its creator.[261] Thus, when it was considered that misappropriated dress designs[262] or opera performances[263] involved the expenditure of time, money, skill, and laborious effort and were of tremendous commercial value to their creators, those courts following the *INS* doctrine recognized that a property right could be acquired in such dress designs or opera performances although they were technically published and in the public domain. In appropriating and selling creations as its own, the pirate, it was thought, was endeavoring to "reap where it has not sown . . . appropriating to itself the harvest of those who have sown."[264] Thus, some courts rejected arguments of federal preemption and, until *Sears* and *Compco*, were granting increasingly broad protection to property rights of commercial value, including published works, from any form of commercial immorality.[265]

It was Judge Learned Hand's position, however, that publication is a surrender of all common law rights.[266] No action for unfair competition may thereafter be maintained because

[260] *Id.* at 245.
[261] See generally *Developments in the Law—Competitive Torts*, 77 HARV. L. REV. 888, 932–47 (1964).
[262] Dior v. Milton, 9 Misc. 2d 425, 155 N.Y.S.2d 443 (Sup. Ct.), *aff'd mem.*, 2 App. Div. 2d 878, 156 N.Y.S.2d 996 (1st Dep't 1956).
[263] Metropolitan Opera Ass'n, Inc. v. Wagner-Nichols Recorder Corp., 199 Misc. 786, 101 N.Y.S.2d 483 (Sup. Ct. 1950), *aff'd mem.*, 279 App. Div. 632, 107 N.Y.S.2d 795 (1st Dep't 1951).
[264] International News Serv. v. Associated Press, 248 U.S. 215, 239–40 (1918).
[265] See Dior v. Milton, 9 Misc. 2d 425, 155 N.Y.S.2d 443 (Sup. Ct.), *aff'd mem.*, 2 App. Div. 2d 878, 156 N.Y.S.2d 996 (1st Dep't 1956).
[266] *E.g.*, Capitol Records, Inc. v. Mercury Records Corp., 221 F.2d 657, 664 (2d Cir. 1955) (dissenting opinion); Cheney Bros. v. Doris Silk Corp., 35 F.2d 279 (2d Cir. 1929), *cert. denied*, 281 U.S. 728 (1930).

it would be anomalous to turn the grant of a statutory copyright into a detriment to the author: for if the creation was not covered by the act, its creator could obtain perpetual protection under state law. The constitutional grant to Congress of the power to secure to authors the exclusive right to their "writings" only for limited times, was thought by Judge Hand to be inconsistent with the assumption that an author, notwithstanding publication and full enjoyment of his common law property, might maintain a perpetual monopoly.[267] Since states can no longer grant greater protection than that available under the federal statute under the "guise" of unfair competition or misappropriation, an inflexible application of Judge Hand's view now seems mandated by *Sears* and *Compco*, thereby limiting state protection to the prepublication period.

Writers since *Sears* and *Compco* have found it impossible, however, to accept the proposition that *INS* has been overruled sub silentio.[268] But the Court's statement in *Compco* is difficult to circumvent:

Today we have held in *Sears* . . . that when an article is unprotected by a patent or copyright, state law may not forbid others to copy that article. To forbid copying would interfere with the federal policy . . . of allowing free access to copy whatever the federal patent and copyright laws leave in the public domain.[269]

---

[267] "It may be unfortunate—it may . . . be unjust . . . ," stated Judge Hand, "but until the copyright law is changed . . . [the designs] fall into the public demesne without reserve." Fashion Originators Guild of America, Inc. v. FTC, 114 F.2d 80, 84 (2d Cir. 1940), *aff'd on other grounds*, 312 U.S. 457 (1941).

[268] See, *e.g.*, Bender, *supra* note 243, at 1238. *Contra*, Treece, *Patent Policy and Preemption: The Stiffel and Compco Cases*, 32 U. CHI. L. REV. 80, 95 (1964) ("Compco and Stiffel can be regarded as marking the [misappropriation] doctrine's final demise"). The Second Circuit, however, after stating that Sears and Compco merely proscribe what is in effect state patent protection, applied the misappropriation doctrine to prevent defendant's continued use of plaintiff's trademark after defendant ceased to distribute plaintiff's product. Flexitized, Inc. v. National Flexitized Corp., 335 F.2d 744 (2d Cir. 1964), *cert. denied*, 380 U.S. 913 (1965).

[269] 376 U.S. at 237.

Apparently the Court adheres to the view that all published works are in the public domain and the public's right to copy published works is plenary except to the extent a patent or copyright may remove it. When the temporary incursion on the public right ends, the public right remains—no new right is born.[270] Whether an article is within or without the federal statute would appear to be of no moment; state activity seems precluded in either instance.

Yet, as several recent cases have indicated,[271] states may still afford significant protection, since *Sears* and *Compco* do not abridge the right of states to apply unfair competition principles to protect copyrightable matter prior to its initial publication. In fact, the Court recognizes that the Copyright Act expressly saves state protection of unpublished "writings."[272] One post-*Sears* and *Compco* case serves to exemplify the possible means of continued state court protection of copyrightable works and also to illustrate the alterations in pleading and proof now necessitated. Claiming exclusive rights by virtue of contract to the first run of its affiliated network's television programs, appellee television station asserted that under Idaho law the activities of community antenna operators constituted unfair competition in that the community antennas received identical programs broadcast by distant stations and distributed them for profit simultaneously with plaintiff's airings. Noting that the district court's holding for appellee was based on the premise that common law theories may be asserted to redeem what are in essence

[270] *In re* Deister Concentrator Co., 48 C.C.P.A. (Patents) 952, 962 n.4, 289 F.2d 496, 501 n.4 (1961).
[271] Cable Vision, Inc. v. KUTV, Inc., 335 F.2d 348 (9th Cir. 1964), cert. denied, 379 U.S. 989 (1965); Edgar H. Wood Associates, Inc. v. Skene, 347 Mass. 351, 197 N.E.2d 886 (1964); Capitol Records, Inc. v. Greatest Records, Inc., 43 Misc. 2d 878, 252 N.Y.S.2d 553 (Sup. Ct. 1964); New York World's Fair 1964–1965 Corp. v. Colourpicture Publishers, Inc., 141 U.S.P.Q. 939 (N.Y. Sup. Ct. 1964), aff'd mem., 21 App. Div. 2d 896, 251 N.Y.S.2d 885 (2d Dep't 1964); Columbia Broadcasting Sys., Inc. v. Documentaries Unlimited, Inc., 42 Misc. 2d 723, 248 N.Y.S.2d 809 (Sup. Ct. 1964).
[272] Sears, Roebuck & Co. v. Stiffel Co., 376 U.S. 225, 231 n.7 (1964).

copyright interests, the court read *Sears* and *Compco* as permitting only actions for statutory copyright infringement or common law actions consistent with the primary right of public access to all in the public domain.[273] The only relief state courts could still offer was reflected in the court's remand of the case to the district court so that the television station might prosecute a claim, not for unfair competition, but for common law copyright violations of any programs which the plaintiff could establish had not been published.

DEFINITION OF PUBLICATION

Assuming that prepublication protection is allowable, the question then arises as to who should define "publication." Publication has a dual effect: It not only terminates common law copyright but prevents the author from obtaining statutory protection, since a copyright may not be obtained for any work within the public domain.[274] Recent cases indicate that determining what constitutes publication for the purpose of *divesting* a creator of a common law copyright is properly left to state courts, while determining what constitutes publication in order to ascertain whether a creator has met the condition precedent for a statutory copyright—i.e., for purposes of *investing* protection in an author—is left to the federal courts.[275] As the prior law developed, however, considerably more open dissemination is required before courts are willing to find a publication sufficient to divest a creator of his common law copyright, than is required before courts will find a publication sufficient to invest a statutory copyright in the author.[276] "In each case the courts appear to so treat the

[273] Cable Vision, Inc. v. KUTV, Inc., 335 F.2d 348 (9th Cir. 1964), cert. denied, 379 U.S. 989 (1965).
[274] 17 U.S.C. § 8 (1958).
[275] Compare Blanc v. Lantz, 83 U.S.P.Q. 137 (Cal. Super. Ct. 1949), with Atlantic Monthly Co. v. Post Publishing Co., 27 F.2d 556 (D. Mass. 1928); see Kalodner & Vance, *The Relation Between Federal and State Protection of Literary and Artistic Property*, 72 HARV. L. REV. 1079, 1091–96 (1959).
[276] Edgar H. Wood Associates, Inc. v. Skene, 347 Mass. 351, 197 N.E.2d 886 (1964). Compare Pierce & Bushnell Mfg. Co. v. Werckmeister, 72 Fed. 54 (1st

Unfair Competition Protection 63

concept of 'publication' as to prevent piracy."[277] Thus, while depositing two copies of a work with the Library of Congress in compliance with the requirements of the Copyright Act has been held a sufficient publication to enable a plaintiff to sue for statutory infringement,[278] federal cases have recognized there may be a substantial distribution of material into the public domain without forfeiture of common law copyright protection.[279] In the light of *Sears* and *Compco's* insistence upon the supremacy of federal policy, state "prepublication" protection may now be subject to critical scrutiny by the federal courts.

There are three possible alternative allocations of responsibility for defining publication.[280] Since Section 2 of the Copyright Act may be read as permitting state protection only to the point at which the federal statute becomes operative, a strong inference arises that a single definition for both investive and divestive publication was intended. Still, section 2 may be read as referring to the entire body of state law, including the definition of publication, as part of the definition of the scope of common law rights, thereby sanc-

---

Cir. 1896) (holding that exhibition of a painting in a public art gallery was sufficient publication to entitle plaintiff to recover under the Copyright Act), *with* Werckmeister v. American Lithograph Co., 134 Fed. 321 (2d Cir. 1904) (holding that exhibition of a painting in a public gallery did not constitute publication divesting plaintiff of his common law protection, distinguishing the former case on the ground that it was brought under the Copyright Act). *Compare* Cardinal Film Corp. v. Beck, 248 Fed. 368 (S.D.N.Y. 1918) *and* Stern v. Jerome H. Remick & Co., 175 Fed. 282 (S.D.N.Y. 1915) (both holding that deposit of two copies of a work with the Library of Congress in compliance with the requirements of the Copyright Act was sufficient publication to enable plaintiff to maintain suit under the act), *with* Osgood v. A. S. Aloe Instrument Co., 69 Fed. 291 (C.C.E.D. Mo. 1895) (holding that deposit of two books with the Library of Congress in advance of obtaining copyright was not publication constituting dedication at common law so that plaintiff could subsequently maintain action under the federal statute when he obtained a copyright certificate).

[277] American Visuals Corp. v. Holland, 239 F.2d 740, 744, (2d Cir. 1956).
[278] Cardinal Film Corp. v. Beck, 248 Fed. 368 (S.D.N.Y. 1918).
[279] *E.g.*, Continental Casualty Co. v. Beardsley, 253 F.2d 702, 707 (2d Cir.), *cert. denied*, 358 U.S. 816 (1958)
[280] See generally Kalodner & Vance, *supra* note 275, at 1091-96.

tioning a federal definition of investive publication and a state definition of divestive publication. The third possibility would be separate definitions for investive and divestive publication, but both determined by federal law.

Discernibly, the *Sears* and *Compco* thesis is the embodiment of the doctrine espoused by Judge Learned Hand for almost half a century. It was Judge Hand's view that, through the medium of construing the word "publication," states could grant an author a perpetual monopoly on a federally nonprotected work, although he exploited the work with virtually the same freedom he would have enjoyed had it been copyrighted.[281] Because state protection clashes with what Judge Hand considered to be the federal objective of leaving nonprotectable creations in the public domain, he believed states were not free to follow their own notions in determining the proper extent of a creator's protection. To allow states such freedom, it was thought, would defeat the overriding purpose of the copyright clause—that of granting only for limited times the "untrammelled exploitation of an author's writings." [282]

In addition, Judge Hand believed that publication is a matter of constitutional significance and, as *Sears* and *Compco* palpably recognize, a policy of uniformity inheres in the copyright clause.[283] The granting of perpetual monopolies by some states under the guise of limited publication or a finding of no publication, combined with the refusal of other states to grant protection under the same circumstances, offends this constitutional policy. Similarly, if state courts retain the power to define divestive publications, they have, in effect, power to determine the scope of the constitutional grant of copyright power to Congress. The compatibility of *Sears*

[281] Capitol Records, Inc. v. Mercury Records Corp., 221 F.2d 657, 664 (2d Cir. 1955) (dissenting opinion). For an example, see Ettore v. Philco Television Broadcasting Corp., 229 F.2d 481 (3d Cir.), *cert. denied*, 351 U.S. 926 (1956).
[282] Capitol Records, Inc. v. Mercury Records Corp., *supra* note 281, at 667.
[283] See generally Kaplan, *supra* note 252, at 415–29.

Unfair Competition Protection 65

and *Compco* with Judge Hand's theory is significant, for it may conceivably herald the Court's eventual embracement of the pragmatic application of his conclusions: Publication would be a federal question [284] and the same acts that unconditionally dedicate the common law copyright in works copyrightable under the federal act would dedicate works not so copyrightable.[285]

It has been suggested, however, that adopting a single federal standard for investive and divestive publication would be unwise because of the length to which federal courts have extended investive publication in order to grant statutory protection at points early in the exploitation process, or even where no economic exploitation has taken place.[286] It has also been argued that a common law copyright should not be destroyed by a use which does not make the work fully public,[287] since the common law right of first publication is based on a desire to give the creator the initial economic benefits of his work.[288] Thus, section 2 may be read as referring to the existing law concerned only with the point of divestiture. And it does seem possible to maintain that, although the effect of federal preemption is dependent upon publication, thereby seeming to mandate a uniform federal definition of publication, this factor alone does not make illegitimate the considerations which support the maintenance of separate standards for investive and divestive publication.

[284] G. Ricordi & Co. v. Haendler, 194 F.2d 914 (2d Cir. 1952); see Treece, *supra* note 268, at 89.

[285] See RCA Mfg. Co. v. Whiteman, 114 F.2d 86 (2d Cir.), *cert. denied*, 311 U.S. 712 (1940).

[286] In Atlantic Monthly Co. v. Post Publishing Co., 27 F.2d 556 (D. Mass. 1928), the sale of a galley proof for a magazine article, consummated solely for the purpose of qualifying for copyright, was deemed sufficient investive publication. It has been suggested that a standard which allows the acquisition of copyright benefits through such colorable sales is acceptable, but that the same standard should not be employed to determine divestive publication. Kalodner & Vance, *supra* note 275, at 1093.

[287] Kalodner & Vance, *supra* note 275, at 1093.

[288] Dior v. Milton, 9 Misc. 2d 425, 438, 155 N.Y.S.2d 443, 458 (Sup. Ct.), *aff'd mem.*, 2 App. Div. 2d 878, 156 N.Y.S.2d 996 (1st Dep't 1956).

Overriding considerations, however, do appear to militate against continued state construction of publication, since states may define the term in a manner which would overrule both the statute and the Court's policy of allowing freedom to copy whatever the statutes leave in the public domain. True, some literary and artistic properties do not produce significant economic return until reproductions have been distributed to the general public for a substantial period of time. And if publication in these situations is defined as the moment of distribution to the general public, any protection of federally nonprotected works is terminated before any significant economic benefit has accrued to their creators.[289] It might even be questioned whether free competition is worth the cost when a categorical implementation of *Sears* and *Compco* causes a diversion of profit to copiers, unburdened with the expenses of creation, from originators, prevented from seeking federal protection only because Congress has made no provision for their creations.[290] Notwithstanding these inequities, however, *Sears* and *Compco* plainly indicate that the scope of relief lies with Congress and not with the states.[291]

[289] To remedy this situation, it has been suggested that a standard other than publication in its copyright sense be employed to dictate when forfeiture takes effect. The proposed standard, defined as "the active commercial exploitation of the property," contemplates continued state protection of articles which, although technically published, have not been commercially exploited to a degree repugnant to the federal policy inherent in the Copyright Act. Elman, *The Limits of State Jurisdiction in Affording Common Law Protection to Clothing Designs*, 11 VAND. L. REV. 501 (1958).

[290] Phonograph records, for example, are incapable of copyright registration under the present act. Kaplan, *supra* note 252, at 413–15. Thus, so far as the Copyright Act is concerned, an entrepreneur may duplicate records placed on sale by reputable phonograph record manufacturers and sell them in competition with the genuine articles without permission of either the artists or publishers. See H.R. REP. No. 1758, 87th Cong., 2d Sess. 1–2 (1962). See generally SUBCOMM. OF PATENTS, TRADEMARKS, & COPYRIGHT, SENATE COMM. ON THE JUDICIARY, 86TH CONG., 2D SESS., COPYRIGHT LAW REVISION, STUDY NO. 26, THE UNAUTHORIZED DUPLICATION OF SOUND RECORDINGS (Comm. Print 1960).

[291] Protection for phonograph records would be afforded by the proposed Copyright Act § 1(7), S. 3008, H.R. 11947, H.R. 12354, 88th Cong., 2d Sess. (1964).

Unfair Competition Protection 67

These considerations, however, appear to have served as the stimuli for an expansion, or at least an unquestioning application, of traditional publication principles, enabling continued state exercise of the misappropriation theory, albeit limited, to plagiarism of works found to be unpublished. The result is achieved by widely defining publication. Thus, the post-*Sears* and *Compco* cases display an intention to follow the same path as the leading pre-*Sears* case, *King v. Mister Maestro Inc.*,[292] where the public delivery of the speech, "I Have a Dream," by Dr. Martin Luther King before 200,000 people and carried over radio and television, was held not to be a general publication of the work placing it in the public domain.

A general publication occurs when a work is sold or otherwise made available to the public without restriction as to use or class of users.[293] But there can be a limited publication under traditional principles which is a communication of the work, restricted both as to persons and purpose, under circumstances showing no dedication to the public.[294] Only a general publication results in the loss of a common law copyright.[295] Recourse to this latter rule, pragmatically applied and aggrandized, has been had by courts that seem to feel that application of *Sears* and *Compco* in this area is an unwarranted incursion upon common law rights. Thus, consonant with the accepted view that ordinarily the public performance of a work such as the delivery of a speech,[296] performance of a play,[297] or radio broadcast of a script[298] is not a publication (though it has been said this rule no longer fits the "emergent

[292] 224 F. Supp. 101 (S.D.N.Y. 1963).
[293] Nimmer, *Copyright Publication*, 56 COLUM. L. REV. 185 (1956).
[294] White v. Kimmell, 193 F.2d 744 (9th Cir.), *cert. denied*, 343 U.S. 957 (1952).
[295] William A. Meier Glass Co. v. Anchor Hocking Glass Corp., 95 F. Supp. 264 (W.D. Pa. 1951).
[296] Nutt v. National Institute, Inc., 31 F.2d 236 (2d Cir. 1929).
[297] Ferris v. Frohman, 223 U.S. 424 (1912).
[298] Uproar Co. v. National Broadcasting Co., 8 F. Supp. 358 (D. Mass. 1934), *modified*, 81 F.2d 373 (1st Cir. 1936).

and developing facts of intellectual production" of today),[299] a New York court, applying the misappropriation theory, protected the common law copyright in an "off the air" recording of a news commentator's announcement later embodied in a record entitled "JFK, the Man, the President."[300] Similarly, and in accord with *Capitol Records, Inc. v. Mercury Records, Corp.*[301] which held, over a vigorous Learned Hand dissent, that the act of placing records on public sale does not constitute a dedication of the right to copy and sell the records,[302] another court enjoined the counterfeiting of "Beatle" phonograph records, purchased in retail stores, and resold under different labels after inferior reproduction.[303]

In addition, courts seeking to avoid the impact of *Sears* and *Compco* have employed nontraditional theories. Though several cases have stated that a public filing constitutes a publication,[304] a recent case has held that the filing of architectural plans with a building department was a limited publication.[305] The court felt that the publication permitted copying only for the purposes reasonably related to the objectives of the filing requirement, such as compliance with zoning laws, but that it did not permit copying which would impair the architect's common law copyright in the plans.

In another recent case the New York World's Fair Corp. sought to restrain defendant from selling postcards and allied items containing photographs of buildings, exhibits, and

[299] Kaplan, *Publication in Copyright Law: The Question of Phonograph Records*, 103 U. PA. L. REV. 469, 487 (1955). See also Selvin, *Should Performance Dedicate?*, 42 CALIF. L. REV. 40, 50–51 (1954).

[300] Columbia Broadcasting Sys., Inc. v. Documentaries Unlimited, Inc., 42 Misc. 2d 723, 248 N.Y.S.2d 809 (Sup. Ct. 1964).

[301] 221 F.2d 657 (2d Cir. 1955).

[302] *Contra*, RCA Mfg. Co. v. Whiteman, 114 F.2d 86, 88 (2d Cir. 1940) (L. Hand, J.), distinguished in Capitol Records, Inc. v. Mercury Records Corp., *supra* note 301, as not representing the law of New York.

[303] Capitol Records, Inc. v. Greatest Records, Inc., 43 Misc. 2d 878, 252 N.Y.S.2d 553 (Sup. Ct. 1964).

[304] *E.g.*, DeSilva Constr. Corp. v. Herrald, 213 F. Supp. 184 (M.D. Fla. 1962).

[305] Edgar H. Wood Associates, Inc. v. Skene, 347 Mass. 351, 197 N.E.2d 886 (1964).

Unfair Competition Protection 69

scenes of the World's Fair.³⁰⁶ Defendant contended that the leading New York case applying the *International News* doctrine ³⁰⁷ was no longer good law, since *Sears* and *Compco* had overruled the various state unfair competition cases which accord a "monopolistic" right to be free of competition by affording protection against copying to the originator of an item having commercial value. The court, however, did not take such a pervasive view of those decisions: "This court does not read either of those cases as striking down, or intending to strike down, all state laws of unfair competition in all cases and for all purposes." ³⁰⁸ Not only did the court agree that plaintiff had property rights in its giant show and in the commercial use of photographs of the various exhibits, pavilions, and scenes, but it was also willing to hold that defendant's misappropriation of those rights was unfair competition regardless of any considerations of publication or dedication:

[W]e have here a business venture purposed to gather in the harvest the seeds of which were planted and nurtured by others at great expense and with consummate skill. The conclusion here reached is not an onslaught on the currents of competition; it does not impose shackles on the arteries of enterprise. It simply quarantines business conduct which is abhorrent to good conscience and the most elementary principles of law and equity.³⁰⁹

The relief granted plaintiff could not stand, however, unless the court could overcome the *Sears-Compco* proscription against preventing the copying of anything in the public domain. Without mentioning cases which have held that the public exhibition of a work of art, though not offered for sale,

---

³⁰⁶ New York World's Fair 1964–1965 Corp. v. Colourpicture Publishers, Inc., 141 U.S.P.Q. 939 (N.Y. Sup. Ct. 1964), *aff'd mem.*, 21 App. Div. 2d 896, 251 N.Y.S.2d 885 (2d Dep't 1964).
³⁰⁷ Metropolitan Opera Ass'n v. Wagner-Nichols Recorder Corp., 199 Misc. 786, 101 N.Y.S.2d 483 (Sup. Ct. 1950), *aff'd*, 279 App. Div. 632, 107 N.Y.S.2d 795 (1st Dep't 1951).
³⁰⁸ 141 U.S.P.Q. at 942.
³⁰⁹ 141 U.S.P.Q. at 941–42 (quoting the Metropolitan Opera case).

constitutes a publication,[310] the court held that the buildings would not pass into the public domain "while . . . [they are] part of a show second to none, which is enclosed and which is viewable only upon the payment of admission and subject to conditions imposed by plaintiff."[311]

Thus, though divestive publication need not necessarily be defined by the same standards applied to investive publication, a federal definition of divestive publication seems essential if the free competition objective which the Court finds inherent in the Patent and Copyright Acts is to be immunized from the debilitating effect of divergent state standards.

ANCILLARY PROTECTION

Some of the results *Sears* and *Compco* seem to require had been termed "harsh" even by Judge Hand,[312] the strongest advocate ever of federal preemption. In the "Beatle" record case[313] and the "JFK" news announcement case,[314] for example, the competitor not only copies the product but seems to steal the very product itself. If it were possible to identify some theory, consistent with the *Sears* and *Compco* rationale, under which protection could be afforded in these and other similarly offensive situations it would seem desirable that such a theory be adopted.

As discussed above, it seems inconsistent with *Sears* and *Compco* to strain the publication concept. Another unlikely

[310] *E.g.,* William A. Meier Glass Co. v. Anchor Hocking Glass Corp., 95 F. Supp. 264 (W.D. Pa. 1951). *But see* American Tobacco Co. v. Werckmeister, 207 U.S. 284 (1907), where the Court held that a painting is not published when the public is admitted to view the painting on the implied understanding that no photographing or copying shall take place, provided measures are taken to enforce this requirement.

[311] 141 U.S.P.Q. at 942.

[312] Capitol Records, Inc. v. Mercury Records Corp., 221 F.2d 657, 667 (2d Cir. 1955) (dissenting opinion).

[313] Capitol Records, Inc. v. Greatest Records, Inc., 43 Misc. 2d 878, 252 N.Y.S.2d 553 (Sup. Ct. 1964).

[314] Columbia Broadcasting Sys., Inc. v. Documentaries Unlimited, Inc., 42 Misc. 2d 723, 248 N.Y.S.2d 809 (Sup. Ct. 1964).

possibility was raised in *Cable Vision, Inc. v. KUTV, Inc.*,[315] where affiliated network television programs were rebroadcast for the profit of others. The argument was made that relief was warranted irrespective of publication under the theory of interference with contractual relations. The court quite properly denied relief on this basis. It would undermine *Sears* and *Compco* if complainants were able to preclude copying by asserting the existence of contractual relations with a third party. Were it otherwise, parties could "bootstrap" into existence rights in subject matter in the public domain through the mere expedient of an exclusive contract.

A third possible alternative theory of relief was presented in a similar situation, where the exclusive licensee of a motion picture sought damages for the use of a substantial segment of the picture on a television program.[316] The court noted that *Sears* and *Compco*, which dealt with articles of trade copied so as to imitate or resemble original products, are to be distinguished from the kind of situation where the complaint is essentially of an *appropriation* of the very item involved. If defendants had copied the movie concerned and produced their own movie based upon the same plot and themes, the court reasoned, plaintiffs, because of *Sears* and *Compco*, would not be entitled to state protection. If this distinction between the copying of an idea or a physical article and the use of the identical product were applied to the "Beatle" and "JFK" cases, it is apparent that no necessity would have existed for those courts to have considered the issue of publication. In the "Beatle" case, for example, defendants would have been found guilty of having *appropriated* for their own profit the audible manifestation of the performers' talents and skills.

Although this theory is more tenable than those discussed

[315] 335 F.2d 348 (9th Cir. 1964), *cert. denied*, 379 U.S. 989 (1965).
[316] Flamingo Telefilm Sales, Inc. v. United Artists Corp., 141 U.S.P.Q. 461 (N.Y. Sup. Ct., 1964), *rev'd on other grounds*, 22 App. Div. 2d 778, 254 N.Y.S.2d 36 (1st Dep't 1964).

above, no apparent difference exists in the moral position of one who "copies" and one who "appropriates" another's talents. The mere difference in terminology should not yield a difference in treatment. Also, this theory appears to miss the mark since in granting relief a court would still be concerned with the commercial exploitation of a property right. It is just such protection, based upon proprietary interests, which *Sears* and *Compco* disallow.

It appears, therefore, that any protection afforded must be for a noncommercial interest. The most likely possibility is the right to privacy. Relief under the right to privacy rationale depends ultimately upon the nature of that right. One theory, expounded principally by Dean Prosser,[317] is that there is no right to privacy as such, only a group of individual torts which courts treat under the generic term "privacy." One interest which this theory includes is the individual's "proprietary interest" in his person and talents. Any such approach, with its commercial overtones, would necessarily doom the use of the right to privacy, as a basis of ancillary relief.

But as Professor Bloustein has recently demonstrated,[318] the right to privacy as originally conceived by Warren and Brandeis,[319] and as it is reflected in other areas of the law, is more than a mere conglomeration of traditional torts. Privacy is an aspect of human dignity, based on the principle of "inviolate personality."[320] Concededly, an invasion of privacy may sometimes involve the misappropriation of something of pecuniary value; but this is not the essence of the wrong. The wrong is reflected in the many, many ways the human personality is violated: the exposure to ridicule,

---

[317] Prosser, *Privacy*, 48 Calif. L. Rev. 383 (1960).
[318] Bloustein, *Privacy as an Aspect of Human Dignity: An Answer to Dean Prosser*, 39 N.Y.U.L. Rev. 962 (1964).
[319] Warren & Brandeis, *The Right to Privacy*, 4 Harv. L. Rev. 193 (1890).
[320] *Id.* at 205.

the invasion of intimate, highly personal occasions, the commercial exploitation of a person's name, body, or property.[321]

It can readily be seen that relief in the "Beatle" and "JFK" cases, and in other situations, may be possible if Professor Bloustein is correct. It would seem out of the question to attempt to protect, in the case of a vocal performance, the words and music of an uncopyrighted song, or even the techniques and inflections of the performer. These things seem to be in the public domain, and no violation of personality is apparent. When the copier goes further and lifts the performer's voice, however, there may indeed be the type of violation a flexible concept of privacy might encompass. Here, just as in the leading *Pavesich* case [322] where plaintiff's picture was used for advertising purposes without authorization, the individual is made a "slave" to the will of another. If one may prohibit unauthorized use of his picture, no reason exists to deny him the same relief when his voice is appropriated and utilized for another's purposes.

There are, of course, numerous weighty objections to this theory of relief. And even if all the objections are answered, there are numerous unanswered questions. Thus, it may be objected that relief is not warranted under a right to privacy rationale because the performer has exercised his control of publication, and has willingly placed his performance in the public domain. One possible answer lies in a distinction between the performer's voice and the other aspects of the performance. It is arguable that a man's voice is an extension of his personality, and that it cannot be treated as part of the performance, as being in the public domain. More generally, the performer may be validly complaining not of his being heard, but of commercial exploitation as a form of human denigration. The "spiritual characteristic" which is

---

[321] See generally Bloustein, *supra* note 318.
[322] Pavesich v. New England Life Ins. Co., 122 Ga. 190, 50 S.E. 68 (1905).

then at issue is not a form of trauma, mental illness, or distress, but rather an individual's freedom to decide how his personality will be used.[323]

Assuming this to be true, however, it may well be asked where the line is to be drawn. Certainly, there is no difference between the human voice in song and in speech. Can the voice be distinguished from the sounds made by a musical instrument? It might be suggested that the distinction must be drawn along lines which separate artistic activities from those activities which are not only artistic but also represent the very embodiment of an individual's expression. But a composer's sheet of music embodies his expression, and is just as much an extension of his personality as a singer's voice. Even a master potter's vase may fulfill this test. Would such a wide exception to the *Sears-Compco* thesis be acceptable?

An answer to this objection, if there is one, may be found in the type of remedy which is afforded for a breach of the right to privacy. If courts are able to restrict the availability and nature of relief to the preservation of human dignity and individuality, the widest scope may be given to the "substantive" right without too great an infringement of the *Sears-Compco* goal.

Relief would, of course, be available only to the creator.[324] A record company or any other commercial medium would have no standing to assert the artist's claim. The extent of damages to be accorded presents problems. Damages probably could not be measured by the commercial value of the performance or creation.[325] To permit such a measure would

---

[323] See Bloustein, *supra* note 318, at 1000–07. See also Waring v. WOAS Broadcasting Station, Inc., 327 Pa. 433, 456, 194 Atl. 631, 642 (1937) (concurring opinion), where Judge Maxey discussed the right of privacy as a theory of relief in record cases.

[324] See Flamingo Telefilm Sales, Inc. v. United Artists Corp., 22 App Div. 2d 778, 254 N.Y.S.2d 36 (1st Dep't 1964), *reversing* 141 U.S.P.Q. 461 (Sup. Ct. 1964).

[325] See Birmingham Broadcasting Co. v. Bell, 259 Ala. 656, 68 So. 2d 314 (1953).

Unfair Competition Protection 75

achieve the same result *Sears* and *Compco* proscribed. But even in traditional right to privacy cases damages are often measured by the amount the performer could obtain for the use of his voice or other creative talent. Here, however, such a measure may be objected to on the ground that a poor performer should be able to obtain damages equal to the measure obtainable by the best performer, since the offense to privacy is the same in both cases. Though difficult, this problem should not be insurmountable. And even if relief were restricted to grants of injunctions, the remedy would be highly significant.

It therefore seems that ancillary relief will be limited. Any relief based on the commercial value of a creation would in all likelihood conflict with the *Sears-Compco* thesis. Relief based on the right to privacy is a significant possibility, but that path presents numerous problems, some of which may be insurmountable. The "harsh" or perhaps even offensive results in some cases may, however, spur scholarly and judicial ingenuity to advance solutions and, possibly, new theories of relief.

CONCLUSION

It is apparent that *Sears* and *Compco* absolutely prohibit injunctions against copying commercial products "regardless of the copier's motives." Labeling, then, as the only practicable form of relief available, assumes tremendous importance, necessitating re-evaluation of its traditional concepts. While traditional methods of court-imposed labeling may now be in need of curtailment to avoid possible anticompetitive effects, it is arguable that the secondary meaning requirement may be dispensed with, in specific instances, without violating the *Sears-Compco* thesis. An issue also arises as to whether states may continue to proscribe the copying of bottle and package configurations in order to prevent customer source confusion. Prohibiting the simulation of bottles or packages that are essential selling features of their enclosed products appears to conflict with the *Sears* and *Compco* free competition rationale. On the other hand, no reason exists why states may not prohibit simulation of bottles which serve only as a means of primary source identification.

Nor is the *Sears-Compco* proscription confined to articles subject to patent protection. States can no longer protect copyrightable articles in the public domain whether they be within or without the Copyright Act. States, of course, may continue to give common law copyright protection prior to publication. It now seems, however, that the definition of divestive publication will be a federal question, for if it is otherwise states will determine the scope of the federal act. Articles not subject to statutory protection may receive protection where it is found that an appropriation of the very item involved, not a copying, has occurred. Similarly, it has been argued here that artists might receive state protection against unauthorized reproduction of their performances and creations based on the theory of invasion of the right of privacy.

Although prior to *Sears* and *Compco* it had been argued that a codification in the area of unfair competition would induce an interpretation of words instead of a consideration of the nature of the problems,[326] and would be too inflexible to furnish a satisfactory solution for the innumerable and varied situations which arise,[327] the need for such a statute for those who feel the results of *Sears* and *Compco* are undesirable is now manifest.[328] The decisions are certain to

[326] Callmann, *He Who Reaps Where He Has Not Sown: Unjust Enrichment in the Law of Unfair Competition*, 55 HARV. L. REV. 595 (1942).

[327] Sell, *The Doctrine of Misappropriation in Unfair Competition*, 11 VAND. L. REV. 483 (1958); Note, *Protection of Styles and Designs in the Garment Industry*, 26 U. CINC. L. REV. 86 (1957).

[328] See *Hearings on H.R. 4651 Before the Subcommittee on Commerce, and Finance of the House Committee on Interstate and Foreign Commerce*, 88th Cong., 2d Sess. 44, 47–49 (1964).

Unfair Competition Protection 77

have a pervasive effect upon the relief, which courts have traditionally provided against various forms of commercial piracy, causing many "harsh" results.[329]

It has been said that one of the most deplorable effects of *Sears* and *Compco* is their apparent endorsement of a low standard of commercial morality.[330] The proposed "Unfair Commercial Activities" bill[331] would counter this result, and direct the law toward increasingly higher standards of commercial morality by creating a uniform nationwide unfair competition law.[332] The view of unfair competition embodied in this bill rests on the broad principle that property rights of commercial value will be protected from any form of commercial immorality, and that courts of equity should penetrate and restrain every guise resorted to by the wrongdoer.[333] The basic purpose of the bill is to fill the hiatus between existing federal statutes and the general area of unfair competition.[334]

[329] See Capitol Records, Inc. v. Mercury Records Corp., 221 F.2d 657, 667 (2d Cir. 1955) (L. Hand, J., dissenting).

[330] Statement of Sidney A. Diamond, *Hearings on H.R. 4651 Before the Subcommittee on Commerce and Finance of the House Committee on Interstate and Foreign Commerce,* 88th Cong., 2d Sess. 18, 26 (1964).

[331] H.R. 4651, S. 1038, 88th Cong., 1st Sess. (1963). The bill is reprinted in 54 Trademark Rep. 781-84 (1964).

[332] See generally *Hearings on H.R. 4651 Before the Subcommittee on Commerce and Finance of the House Committee on Interstate and Foreign Commerce,* 88th Cong., 2d Sess. (1964); Diamond, *The Proposed Federal Unfair Commercial Activities Act,* 23 OHIO ST. L.J. 110 (1962); Kunin, *The Lindsay Bill Before and After the Stiffel Case,* 54 TRADEMARK REP. 731 (1964); Note, *Misrepresentation and the Lindsay Bill: A Stab at Uniformity in the Law of Unfair Competition,* 70 YALE L.J. 406 (1961).

[333] This legislation does not seek to explore new territory in the area of unfair competition; instead it simply outlines broad boundaries which are recognizable under common law precedents and grants power to the federal courts to act within those boundaries. *Hearings on H.R. 4651 Before the Subcommittee on Commerce and Finance of the House Committee on Interstate and Foreign Commerce,* 88th Cong., 2d Sess. 86 (1964).

[334] The proposed Design Protection Act, S. 776, 88th Cong., 1st Sess. (1963), would narrow this haitus by providing short term federal statutory protection for many designs not susceptible to the more substantial protection of design patents. The bill is limited to designs of useful articles, the term "design" referring to those features intended to give an ornamental appearance. Mechani-

To the paramount objection that this legislation would create a potentially dangerous anticompetitive weapon,[335] its draftsmen have replied that they fully appreciate the importance of preserving our competitive system of free enterprise.[336] They think it equally important, however, that competition be conducted on a fair basis. The two positions seem irreconcilable.[337] And even though many courts have felt that competition and morality can, in fact, be reconciled, the difficulty of achieving such a resolution lends substantial support to leaving the task to Congress.

---

cal design, or features dictated solely by function or purpose, are not included. See generally S. Rep. No. 686, 88th Cong., 1st Sess. (1963) ; Latman, *The New Design Protection Proposals Before Congress*, 8 BULL. COPYRIGHT SOC'Y 356 (1961).

[335] Report of U.S. Dep't of Justice, *Hearings on H.R. 4651 Before the Subcommittee on Commerce and Finance of the House Committee on Interstate and Foreign Commerce*, 88th Cong., 2d Sess. 6, 7 (1964).

[336] Letter of the Ass'n of the Bar of the City of New York, *Hearings on H.R. 4651 Before the Subcommittee on Commerce and Finance of the House Committee on Interstate and Foreign Commerce*, 88th Cong., 2d Sess. 84, 85 (1964).

[337] *But see* Sell, *supra* note 327, at 497.

NATIONAL SECOND PRIZE, 1965

Design Protection

By MATTHEW NIMETZ
HARVARD UNIVERSITY LAW SCHOOL

IN A CIVILIZED STATE men have sufficient leisure and affluence to concern themselves with more than the bare necessities of survival. They can afford to make ordinary things—tools, utensils, shelters—more pleasing aesthetically as well as more efficient technically. And societies are measured, as much as we can ever measure societies, for their artistic accomplishments as well as for their technical achievements. It is therefore no exaggeration to assert that the promotion of the arts, particularly such applied arts as architecture and design, is a traditional and important social endeavor.

To promote economic progress we strive generally toward a norm of competition. To promote advancement in the realm of abstract ideas we likewise encourage freedom of investigation and freedom in the use of the ideas of others; we speak of the open market-place of ideas. To promote the inventing of new and useful devices we have a different policy. We grant limited monopolies in the form of patents which are meant to encourage inventors and investors and to induce early publication of new ideas. And to promote the creation, improvement, and proliferation of designs, we have sought to adopt the monopoly approach, limiting free competition through copying, by adopting a system of various types of monopolies—patent, copyright, trademark, and the common law of unfair competition. This paper attempts to describe the various methods by which design protection has been sought, to examine some of the problems raised by their interaction, and to evaluate the economic effects of such protection.

AN OUTLINE OF DESIGN PROTECTION: VARIATIONS AND FUGUE

THE DESIGN PATENT

The design patent seeks to protect appearances. Although included in the overall patent system, design protection is difficult to conceptualize as an aspect of conventional patent law.[1] It seems to fit more easily somewhere between patents and copyrights, and this peculiar status is largely responsible for many of its difficulties.[2] The basic structure of the design

---

[1] The design patent statute was enacted in 1842. Act of August 29, 1842, 5 Stat. 543. In a message to Congress in 1841, Patent Commissioner Ellworth noted that "competition among manufacturers for the latest patterns prompts to the highest effort to secure improvements, and calls out the inventive genius of our citizens. Such patterns are immediately pirated. . . . If protection is given to designers, better patterns will, it is believed, be obtained. . . ." Report to 27th Cong., 2d Sess., Feb. 8, 1841, reprinted in Hudson, *A Brief History of the Development of Design Patent Protection in the United States*, 30 J. PAT. OFF. SOC'Y 380–81 (1948). Commissioner Ellworth, like most supporters of design protection, spoke explicitly of the public interest in the creation of superior designs, but made clear also the ethical overtones of his plan to protect creators. The statute was amended several times—in 1861, 12 Stat. 246; in 1870, 16 Stat. 198; in 1902, 32 Stat. 193; and in 1952, 66 Stat. 805—but the central theme of case development was never tied to the particular language of the particular statute. The design patent statute is presently codified in 35 U.S.C. § 171 (1964) as follows: "Whoever invents any new, original and ornamental design for an article of manufacture may obtain a patent therefor, subject to the conditions and requirements of this title. The provisions of this title relating to patents for inventions shall apply to patents for designs, except as otherwise provided."

[2] No thought appears to have been given in 1841 to utilizing copyright rather than patent law to protect designs. Evidently, no consideration was given to the *type* of protection required, but only to the subject matter believed deserving of governmental protection. Perhaps because this subject matter was manufactured goods, and not purely artistic endeavors, the patent approach was deemed more suitable. See Hudson, *supra* note 1, at 382–83. Other reasons have also been given for the use of the patent form: The Commissioner of Patents initiated the legislation; there was in 1841 no central copyright registration system; and a French statute of 1802, based on a patent approach, provided the best known model for design protection. See *ibid.*; Pogue, *Borderland—Where Copyright and Design Patent Meet*, 52 MICH. L. REV. 33, 62 (1953).

patent system is straightforward. A design merits a patent if it meets four criteria: it must be new, original, ornamental, and involve an inventive effort.[3] Of these, the inventive requirement has proved most troublesome and will be analyzed later. Here it is important only to note that the integration of design protection into the patent scheme has had the effect of making applicable to designs all the principles, standards, and jargon used to test mechanical patents.

The protection afforded by the statute to designs that qualify is substantial. Unlike the copyright, which prohibits only copying, the design patent prohibits any manufacturing of the patented configuration. The test for infringement was established in *Gorham v. White*.[4] In order "to give encouragement to the decorative arts," the Court stated, appearances must be tested by their effect upon the ordinary observer, for he will be the purchaser through whose actions the design will be transformed into profits: "if in the eye of an ordinary observer, giving such attention as a purchaser usually gives, two designs are substantially the same, if the resemblance is such as to deceive such an observer, inducing him to purchase one supposing it to be the other, the first one patented is infringed by the others."[5] This test, based on consumer confusion, with overtones of trademark and unfair competition law, granted far-reaching protection. In many areas of commerce the type of design available is limited, and consumers often appear to want certain styles that may be popular at the moment. Under the *Gorham* test even if a second design was originated independently and was capable of being distinguished from the patented one, infringement could still be found. Several factors have modified the harsh effects of the test. First, courts do not apply an "ordinary man" standard but rather, as *Gorham* specifically authorized, a test based on the investigation of a prudent purchaser who would compare

[3] 35 U.S.C. § 171 (1964); see Michaelson, *The Nature of the Protection of Artistic and Industrial Design*, 37 J. PAT. OFF. SOC'Y 543, 553 (1955).
[4] 81 U.S. (14 Wall.) 511 (1871). [5] *Id.* at 528.

the two items with care.[6] Second, patent law has applied the rule defining infringement as a test for anticipation in prior art.[7] In widening the protective effect of a patent, the Court indirectly made it more difficult to obtain a valid patent. Third, the effectiveness of a patent against an innocent infringer may have moved courts to strengthen their standard of invention to ensure that this monopoly power was awarded only to worthy creators.

For a number of reasons the design patent law has not been successful in protecting creators and investors. Indeed, while the number of ordinary patents applied for and granted in the last decade has increased steadily and substantially, the design patent statistics have remained static, even in periods of great economic activity.[8] One reason for the statute's low level of utilization is the length of time [9] involved in obtaining a patent. In many industries, such as the garment trade, immediate protection is important. Yet a patent is effective only from the date of its issue, in contrast to a copyright, which is effective from the date of publication.[10] Moreover, the cost of obtaining a patent and defending it is often beyond the means of designers and small manufacturers, especially those who produce large numbers of designs regu-

[6] See, *e.g.,* Monroe v. Anderson, 58 Fed. 398 (3d Cir. 1893); W. D. SHOEMAKER, PATENTS FOR DESIGNS 78–81 (1929).

[7] See Franklin Lamp Mfg. Co. v. Albe Lamp & Shade Co., 26 F. Supp. 960, 962 (E.D. Pa. 1939); Shoemaker, *op. cit. supra* note 6, at 99. *But see* 1 DELLER, WALKER ON PATENTS 247–48 (2d ed. 1964).

[8] It is interesting to compare statistics of patent applications and grants during the last two decades. The following are taken from 1963 U.S. PAT. OFF. ANN. REP. 10.

	Inventions		Designs	
	Applications	Granted	Applications	Granted
1944	50,027	29,305	3,711	2,270
1948	73,188	21,336	7,323	3,102
1954	74,987	38,499	5,501	2,573
1958	76,565	43,407	4,838	2,573
1963	84,620	53,958	4,841	2,411

[9] See Michaelson, *supra* note 3, at 560–61, who reports an average lag of 5–8 months.

[10] *Compare* 17 U.S.C. §§ 10, 13 (1964), *with* 35 U.S.C. §§ 151, 271 (1964).

larly.[11] Most important, the hostility of the courts to patents in general and to design patents in particular makes a design patent a most uncertain form of protection.

COPYRIGHT

The practical deficiencies of the design patent have led to a search for other techniques by which creative effort might be protected. Although the copyright approach is limited constitutionally to the protection of "writings," statutory developments [12] as well as administrative policies [13] and judicial opinions have gradually widened its coverage. The courts have extended the scope of permissible copyright protection by liberalizing two standards, namely, the constitutional definition of "writings" and the statutory meaning of "art." [14] Most recently, the Supreme Court faced the question of the contours of permissible copyright protection in deciding whether statuettes designed for commercial use as lamp bases were copyrightable. In *Mazer v. Stein* the Court decided solely the question whether the Copyright Act limited protection to fine arts, and held that it did not.[15] Mr. Justice Douglas, in a separate opinion, argued strongly that a rehearing should have been granted on the question whether such works could constitutionally be copyrighted as writings.[16]

[11] See *Hearings Before the Subcomm. on Patents, Trademarks & Copyright of the U.S. Senate Comm. on the Judiciary on the American Patent System*, 84th Cong. 1st Sess. 104–05 (1955); F. L. VAUGHAN, THE UNITED STATES PATENT SYSTEM 263–66 (1956).
[12] The first copyright act protected only books, maps, and charts, 1 Stat. 124 (1790), but subsequent acts added prints, 2 Stat. 171 (1802), musical compositions, 4 Stat. 436 (1831), public performances of dramatic works, 11 Stat. 138 (1856), photographs, 13 Stat. 540 (1865), statues, Rev. Stat. § 4948–71 (1870), and—in the present codification—"works of art," 17 U.S.C. § 5(g) (1964).
[13] See Derenberg, *Copyright No-Man's Land: Fringe Rights in Literary and Artistic Property*, 35 J. PAT. OFF. SOC'Y 627, 646 (1953).
[14] See Burrow-Giles Lithograph Co. v. Sarony, 111 U.S. 53 (1884); Bleistein v. Donaldson Lithographing Co., 188 U.S. 239 (1903).
[15] 347 U.S. 201 (1954). *Compare* Stein v. Expert Lamp Co., 188 F.2d 611 (7th Cir. 1951), *with* Stein v. Rosenthal, 205 F.2d 633 (9th Cir. 1953).
[16] 347 U.S. at 221.

In spite of Mr. Justice Douglas's opinion, and in spite of the fact that the Court explicitly eschewed the constitutional issue, most commentators appear to have little doubt that three-dimensional works of applied art, even when used only for commercial purposes, can be copyrighted as writings.[17] One recent opinion cites *Mazer v. Stein* for the proposition that "it is now settled beyond question that practically anything novel can be copyrighted." [18] Such assertions seem premature. The writings standard certainly stands for something: it was not the intention of the drafters that everything visible should be protectable. The constitutional concern was for "authors" who, even in the broadest sense, have distinct social and cultural functions and special economic needs which make the copyright a useful device to encourage their efforts. Other creators, say of industrial design, besides not being authors in the ordinary sense of the word, do not require copyright protection as a means to ensure their continued productive effort.

The writings requirement need not serve solely to determine what is protectable and what is not; it can serve as well to distinguish what is copyrightable from what is patentable. The statuettes at issue in *Mazer v. Stein* might well have been submitted for design patents; but most likely they would have failed for lack of invention. It can be argued that such nonpatentable designs should be copyable by all, and that the purpose of the patent scheme is as much to free up uninventive designs as it is to protect inventive ones.[19] The Court, however, rejected this argument. Disregarding the question whether the statuettes were patentable, Mr. Justice Reed stated that "Neither the Copyright Statute nor any other says that

---

[17] See, *e.g.*, Note, *The Meaning of "Writings" in the Copyright Clause of the Constitution*, 31 N.Y.U.L. REV. 1263 (1956); NIMMER, COPYRIGHT § 19.3, at 87–91 (1964).

[18] Dan Kasoff Inc. v. Novelty Jewelry Co., 209 F.2d 745, 746 (2d Cir. 1962).

[19] See discussion *infra* of Sears, Roebuck & Co. v. Stiffel Co., 376 U.S. 225 (1964), and Compco Corp. v. Day-Brite Lighting, Inc., 376 U.S. 234 (1964).

Design Protection 85

because a thing is patentable it may not be copyrighted."[20] Because this short answer is framed solely in statutory terms, and because the Court explicitly excluded any constitutional discussion of the case, it is possible that although no statute requires a distinction between patentable and copyrightable materials the Court may yet find that the Constitution imposes such exclusive categories.

The overlap permitted in *Mazer v. Stein* can, however, be defended on both practical and conceptual grounds. Designs intended for commercial use do stand somewhere between the paradigm subjects for patents and copyrights. From a practical viewpoint, there is nothing objectionable in allowing a designer a choice between the two types of protection.[21] Moreover, copyright and patent protect different interests: The former recognizes an interest in preventing copying, the latter grants a monopoly over the invention. If a particular design is both an invention and a writing and meets the statutory requirements, there is no great harm in allowing the designer to choose the type of protection he thinks most appropriate. A problem arises, though, if an item is given protection under both statutes. Most courts facing this problem have refused double protection,[22] but the Supreme Court in *Mazer* refused to rule on this point.[23]

[20] 347 U.S. at 217.
[21] See Jones Bros. v. Underkoffler, 16 F. Supp. 729, 731 (M.D. Pa. 1936); De Jonge & Co. v. Breuker & Kessler Co., 181 Fed. 150 (E.D. Pa. 1910).
[22] See, *e.g.,* Taylor Instrument Co. v. Fawley-Brost Co., 139 F.2d 98 (7th Cir. 1943); Korzybski v. Underwood & Underwood, Inc., 36 F.2d 727 (2d Cir. 1929).
[23] The regulations of the Copyright Office state that the potential patentability of a work of art does not affect its claim under the Copyright Act, but that a copyright will not be issued on a patented object. 37 C.F.R. § 202.10(b) (1960). If this rule is based on the theory that the application for a patent is a form of publication (see Korzybski v. Underwood & Underwood, Inc., *supra* note 22), then, perhaps, although a prior patent precludes a copyright, a prior copyright will not preclude a patent. More likely the rule is based on the unarticulated but fundamentally sound view that the creator might have an election between the two forms of protection (see cases cited in note 21 *supra*), but that the federal protective scheme never intended double protection; if one desires the long-term protection against plagiarizers one must be willing to give

Assuming the writings standard to be as broad as most interpreters have recently read it, the more immediate problem in analyzing design protection through copyright is to define the scope of statutory protection of works of art. The cases hold, as noted earlier, that commercial purpose is not a disqualification; the statute has been held to include an "applied design." [24] Nevertheless, cultural relativism does not demand that everything be accepted as a work of art. The copyright regulations speak of granting protection only to a work that must "embody some creative authorship in its delineation or form." [25] This standard is a loose one, following the traditionally liberal application of the copyright law. Section 202.10(c) asserts, however, that "if the sole intrinsic function of an article is its utility the fact that the article is unique and attractively shaped will not qualify it as a work of art." [26] Most contemporary goods have both utilitarian and aesthetic functions, and apparently such designs are copyrightable under the regulation.

Statuettes, for instance, even when used to make lamps, are very difficult to distinguish from sculpture. *Mazer v. Stein*, therefore, does not necessarily open the copyright approach to all applied designs. It is likely that future litigation will limit the availability of the copyright in this area; it would be strange for a Supreme Court so intent on restricting patents to strain constitutional and statutory language in order to

up one's "idea" to the public; if one wants a total monopoly over any use of the design, one must be satisfied with the terms and conditions of the design patent statute. This restrictive approach to double protection is most consistent with overall governmental policy toward monopolies, although it does not square easily with the ruling in *Mazer v. Stein* that there is an overlap between patentable and copyrightable subjects and with the argument that because the statutes protect different interests both should be available concurrently. See Note, 42 COLUM. L. REV. 290, 294–95 (1942), suggesting that both forms of protection may be obtainable, citing Wilson v. Haber Bros., 275 Fed. 246 (2d Cir. 1921), a suit for infringement of a design patent *and* a copyright on a "kewpie doll." The question of double protection was not, however, argued in that case, and the court did not rule on the point.

[24] Loomskill, Inc. v. Puritan Dress Co., 134 U.S.P.Q. 20 (S.D.N.Y. 1962).
[25] 37 C.F.R. § 202.10(b) (1960).   [26] 37 C.F.R. § 202.10(c) (1960).

Design Protection 87

grant wide copyright protection. Although a copyright does not grant the complete monopoly of a patent, there are serious objections to allowing its extensive use in the design field. The copyright term can be as long as fifty-six years, which is very broad protection for a design; whereas the design patent protects truly inventive designs for a maximum of only fourteen years.[27] Since copyright law has no standard of invention and no registration system, trivial designs receive the same protection as more worthy creations. The copyright rules of notice,[28] deposit,[29] and publication [30] were devised for written material and hence they raise difficult problems when applied to the variety of materials now submitted for copyright protection. Also it is unclear precisely what kind of protection a copyright affords to a design of an article of manufacture. It clearly protects a bookend against copies of that bookend, but does it protect against pictures of the bookend, or against the use of the design on a radically different material such as a fabric? [31] A copyright protects the expression of an idea, but not the idea itself. How then is this rubric applicable to a design, where the expression is itself the idea?

In spite of such conceptual problems, the copyright ap-

[27] *Compare* 17 U.S.C. §§ 24–25 (1964), *with* 35 U.S.C. § 173 (1964).

[28] *Cf.* H. M. Kolbe Co. v. Armgus Textile Co., 315 F.2d 70 (2d Cir. 1963); Peter Pan Fabrics, Inc. v. Martin Weiner Corp., 274 F.2d 487 (2d Cir. 1960).

[29] See statement of Register Kaminstein, in *Hearings Before the Subcomm. on Patents, Trademarks and Copyrights of the Senate Comm. on the Judiciary on S. 1884*, 87th Cong., 1st Sess. 152 (1961).

[30] *Ibid.; cf.* Richard J. Cole, Inc. v. Manhattan Modes Co., 2 App. Div. 2d 593, 159 N.Y.S.2d 259 (1956).

[31] See King Features Syndicate v. Fleischer, 299 Fed. 533, 535 (2d Cir. 1924), where the court found that a doll infringed a copyrighted cartoon. The court stated: "Copying is not confined to a literary repetition, but includes various modes in which the matter of any publication may be adapted, imitated, or transferred. . . . We do not think it avoids the infringement of the copyright to take the substance or ideas, and produce it through a different medium. . . ." See also Jones Bros. Co. v. Underkoffler, 16 F. Supp. 729 (M.D. Pa. 1936) (copyrighted design of a memorial infringed by the manufacture of the memorial stone). On the other hand, see Fulmer v. United States, 103 F. Supp. 1021 (Ct. Cl. 1952) (copyrighted design of camouflaged parachute is not infringed by the manufacture of the parachute).

proach is attractive because of the ease and rapidity with which it operates, and because it applies only to actual copiers and not to those who may develop the same product independently. Thus, most attempts to devise new forms of design protection have been based on copyright theory, with modifications to suit the special requirements of the applied arts.

TRADEMARKS

The federal trademark law [32] protects symbols and configurations that serve to identify a particular manufacturer's product. It is possible for a design to serve this function; indeed, in one sense all trademarks other than names are designs. In the nineteenth century, when trademark law was totally within the common law, the design patent statute, then loosely applied, was used to give statutory trademark protection.[33] The Patent Office discontinued this practice when passage of the Trademark Act gave specific protection; the Commissioner of Patents noted that it was "only by a forced construction" of the design patent statute that trademark protection had previously been granted.[34] His decision is an example of the gradual accommodation among various interrelated forms of federal protection through administrative and judicial rule making. Here a strained construction of the design patent statute was reversed because it tended to overlap the trademark law's primary area of coverage. So in the copyright-design patent field it might be argued that copyright coverage should be withdrawn to avoid any interference with the workings of the patent system.

Trademark and design patent protection are fundamentally different in purpose. The patent seeks to encourage the arts by granting monopolies on new products with unique appearances. The trademark aims to prevent consumer confusion by

[32] 60 Stat. 427 (1946), 15 U.S.C. §§ 1051–1127 (1964).
[33] See SYMONS, THE LAW OF PATENTS FOR DESIGNS 35 (1914).
[34] William King, 1870 C.D. 109 (Comm'r of Patents); see William Whyte, 1871 C.D. 304 (Comm'r of Patents).

Design Protection 89

designating exclusive use of a mark that serves to identify the origin of a good.[35] But although these goals are easily distinguishable in theory, in practice they tend to overlap. A unique configuration of a good—a particular bottle, for example—may become so closely associated with a particular producer that it would qualify as a trademark, with the right to perpetual protection. Some early cases under the 1946 trademark statute ruled that a configuration of patentable character would not qualify as a trademark.[36] One opinion noted that the act "clearly was not intended to repeal the law as to design patents and it is not believed that an alternative form of protection, without limitation as to time, could have been intended."[37] Although this approach was one way to reconcile the two federal statutes, it did not take full account of the trademark law's purpose of preventing deception of the public. Nor did it take account of the specific statutory provision allowing registration of configurations on the Supplemental Register,[38] or of language that might permit such registration on the Principal Register.[39] *Ex parte Haig & Haig Ltd.*[40] presented a set of facts favoring a more thorough analysis of these factors and a more precise evaluation of the interests involved. Here the applicant's "Pinch Bottle" was held registrable as a distinctive means of identifying the producer's liquor. And in *In re Mogen David Wine Corp.*[41] a

---

[35] See SHOEMAKER, *op. cit. supra* note 6, at 26–27.

[36] *E.g.*, Lucien Lelong Inc. v. Lenel, Inc., 181 F.2d 3 (5th Cir. 1950); *Ex parte* Mars Signal-Light Co., 85 U.S.P.Q. 173 (Ass't Comm'r of Patents 1950); *Ex parte* Minnesota Mining & Mfg. Co., 92 U.S.P.Q. 74 (Patent Office Examiner-in-Chief 1952); see Note, *Registrability of Package & Configuration of Goods on the Supplemental Register*, 23 GEO. WASH. L. REV. 82 (1954).

[37] *Ex parte* Mars Signal Light Co., 85 U.S.P.Q. 173, 176 (Ass't Comm'r of Patents 1950).

[38] 60 Stat. 435 (1946), as amended, 15 U.S.C. § 1091 (1964).

[39] 60 Stat. 428 (1946), as amended, 76 Stat. 769 (1962), 15 U.S.C. § 1052 (1964): "No trade-mark by which the goods of the applicant may be distinguished from the goods of others shall be refused registration on the principal register on account of its nature. . . ."

[40] 118 U.S.P.Q. 229 (Comm'r of Patents 1958).

[41] 328 F.2d 925 (C.C.P.A. 1964), 78 HARV. L. REV. 1269 (1965), *reversing* 134 U.S.P.Q. 576 (Pat. Off. Trademark Trial & App. Bd. 1962).

distinctive decanter in which wine was sold was held registrable even though it had already been patented as a design.

Mogen David points up the difficulty of reconciling the patent and trademark statutes. If the design patent has the purpose of freeing up designs for any type of use after the period of statutory protection, then the subsequent or contemporaneous grant of trademark protection surely conflicts with this purpose. Moreover, the statutory monopoly granted by the patent is intended to give the producer time to recover his development costs; it is not intended to supply a period in which to develop consumer association of the design with the producer so that it will qualify as a trademark.[42] On the other hand, trademark protection does not grant a patent type of monopoly; presumably use of the pinch bottle or the Mogen David decanter in contexts other than the sale of liquor would be permitted.

Although it is still arguable that some design protection is being afforded by the trademark, the danger of serious conflict between the policies of the statutes is not great. For one thing, patent policy is concerned with promoting competition in the manufacture of desirable goods by the freeing up of designs (as well as other inventions). Yet the trademark law protects only distinctive and identifiable forms of packaging for the purpose of eliminating deception of consumers. To allow copying here would not promote the usual cost-reducing goals of competition; rather, it would tend to confuse the consumer as to source.[43] Thus, under these circumstances, the federal patent interest in promoting beneficial copying is exceedingly

[42] The Canadian Royal Commission on Patents, Copyright, Trade Marks and Industrial Designs dealt with this very problem, REPORT ON INDUSTRIAL DESIGNS 33 (1958). A designer, they said, "should not be permitted under the cover of his design monopoly to build up distinctiveness of his design . . . so that it . . . can be registered as a distinguishing guise and thereby prolong his monopoly beyond the period of the design protection."

[43] See Note, *Unfair Competition Protection after Sears and Compco*, 40 N.Y.U.L. REV. 101, 131-35 (1965). This essay, which was submitted in the 1965 National Nathan Burkan Memorial Competition, is published *supra* as the First National Award essay.

Design Protection

small,[44] while the federal trademark interest in prohibiting such copying is substantial.

Second, the courts have drawn a strict line to prevent the trademarking of configurations that may have a functional purpose.[45] These cases usually deal with shapes that serve a mechanical function; for example, irregular grooves in plywood to eliminate stresses,[46] treads on metal plate flooring to prevent slipping,[47] or a distinctively shaped deck for an oreshaking apparatus,[48] each of which may also serve to identify the manufacturer. One commentator has noted that just as the trademark cannot grant a monopoly on such mechanically functional features, neither should it be able to forbit the copying of aesthetically functional features.[49] If the Haig & Haig bottle were purchased primarily for use as a vase, the policies of the patent scheme would indeed be violated by the allowance of a trademark. The policies of both statutes are satisfied, however, if a trademark is allowed only to those configurations that serve no purpose except to identify for consumers the source of the particular product.

A third method of limiting possible undesirable effects of this class of trademark is to require a strict test as to whether the configuration does in fact serve as a true trademark. In fact, this factual question has always been the greatest stumbling-block to registration of containers.[50] In *Mogen David*, for example, after winning the legal point, the applicant lost on remand;[51] the Board found that the evidence did not sustain the contention that consumers identified the product by

---

[44] See Rich, *Trademark Problems As I See Them—Judiciary*, 52 TRADEMARK REP. 1183, 1188–89 (1962); *cf.* Sears, Roebuck & Co. v. Stiffel Co., 376 U.S. 225, 232 (1964).
[45] See Wehringer, *Two for One: Trademarks and Design Patents*, 50 TRADEMARK REP. 1158, 1163 (1960).
[46] United States Plywood Corp. v. Watson, 171 F. Supp. 193 (D.D.C. 1958).
[47] Wood Steel Co. v. Watson, 150 F. Supp. 861 (D.D.C. 1957).
[48] *In re* The Deister Concentrator Co., 289 F.2d 496 (C.C.P.A. 1961).
[49] See 78 HARV. L. REV. 1269 (1965).
[50] See Wehringer, *supra* note 45, at 1162.
[51] 145 U.S.P.Q. 58 (Pat. Off. Trademark Trial & App. Bd. 1965).

the shape of the bottle and not by name. If the factual requirements are held to the same high level as in *Mogen David*, there should be relatively little fear that the trademark law will be used to circumvent the patent act.

UNFAIR COMPETITION

Reconciliation of the various forms of federal design protection outlined above requires both analysis of statutory policies and interpretation of the patent clause of the Constitution. These factors must be supplemented by considerations of the interrelation of federal and state law when a study of design protection through unfair competition law is undertaken. Unfair competition law, particularly pre-*Erie* federal law, granted important protection to designs, at least when the copying of a nonfunctional design confused the buyer as to source.[52] At least so far as this tort of passing off was concerned, the interest protected was essentially the same as that afforded by the trademark. Some courts also recognized a property interest in intangibles, which they protected against misappropriation.[53] Although the contours of unfair competition protection were never fully clear, the language of the leading case, *International News Serv. v. Associated Press*,[54] was framed in the widest possible terms, granting relief against one who "reaps where he has not sown." Attempts to apply the misappropriation doctrine to design protection were occasionally successful,[55] although Judge Learned Hand

---

[52] See generally *Developments in the Law—Competitive Torts*, 77 HARV. L. REV. 888, 908–23 (1964).

[53] *Id.* at 932–46.   [54] 248 U.S. 215 (1918).

[55] In Oneida, Ltd. v. National Silver Co., 25 N.Y.S.2d 271 (Sup. Ct. 1940), a state court granted relief against the copying of the plaintiff's patterns for silver plate. The designs had been patented, but the court recognized no problem of preemption. Indeed, it noted that "the general principles governing infringement actions and those for unfair competition are the same; but the rules to be applied in the latter are much broader." *Id.* at 281. In a later case, Mastercrafters Clock & Radio Co. v. Vacheron & Constantin–Le Coultre Watches, Inc., 221 F.2d 464 (2d Cir.), *cert. denied*, 350 U.S. 832 (1955), protection was granted on unfair competition grounds to the manufacturer of the Atmos clock, the distinctive appearance of which resulted from the full disclosure of its complex mechanism which operates without electricity or

Design Protection

rejected the applicability of *INS* in a suit against the copier of a dress design: "We are meant to suppose that the court meant to create a sort of common-law patent or copyright for reasons of justice," Judge Hand wrote. "Either would flagrantly conflict with the scheme which Congress has for more than a century devised to cover the subject matter." [56]

The major attempt to reconcile the federal scheme with the common law of unfair competition occurred in 1964.[57] In *Stiffel* the defendant had manufactured and sold pole lamps that were almost exact copies of the plaintiff's; in *Compco* it was the plaintiff's grill for a lighting fixture that was copied. In both cases, although design patents were declared void, the lower court granted relief on unfair competition grounds even though there was no showing, at least in *Stiffel*, that consumers had in fact been deceived. More important than the precise holdings of the Supreme Court was its wide language.[58]

How far the *Stiffel* and *Compco* cases, in which the Court forbade the application of unfair competition law on grounds of federal preemption, will affect the law of unfair competition has already been widely discussed.[59] The broad strictures

---
winding. Finally, in Dior v. Milton, 9 Misc. 2d 425, 155 N.Y.S.2d 443 (Sup. Ct.), *aff'd mem.*, 2 App. Div. 2d 878, 156 N.Y.S.2d 996 (1956), a state court specifically applied *INS* (a nondesign case) to grant relief to Dior against those who made and sold sketches of his original garments.

[56] Cheney Bros. v. Doris Silk Corp., 35 F.2d 279, 280 (2d Cir. 1929), *cert. denied*, 281 U.S. 728 (1930).

[57] Sears, Roebuck & Co. v. Stiffel Co., 376 U.S. 225 (1964); Compco Corp. v. Day-Brite Lighting, Inc., 376 U.S. 234 (1964).

[58] *E.g.*, 376 U.S. at 236-38: "Today we have held in *Sears, Roebuck & Co. v. Stiffel Co., supra*, that when an article is unprotected by a patent or a copyright, state law may not forbid others to copy that article. To forbid copying would interfere with the federal policy, found in Art. I, § 8, cl. 8, of the Constitution and in the implementing federal statutes, of allowing free access to copy whatever the federal patent and copyright laws leave in the public domain. Here Day-Brite's fixture has been held not to be entitled to a design or mechanical patent. Under the federal patent laws it is, therefore, in the public domain and can be copied in every detail by whoever pleases."

[59] For the best studies see *Symposium—Product Simulation: A Right or a Wrong*, 64 COLUM. L. REV. 1178 (1964); Treece, *Patent Policy and Preemption: The Stiffel and Compco Cases*, 32 U. CHI. L. REV. 80 (1964); Note,

expressed in the decisions would appear to preclude, either on grounds of statutory preemption or on constitutional grounds,[60] such application of the unfair competition law as conflicts with the purposes of the patent and copyright scheme. This in itself is not startling; more important to understanding the implications of *Stiffel* is an examination of the wide scope of preemption brought about by the Court's interpretation of the patent and copyright systems. Patent and copyright have traditionally been viewed as protective in purpose: To encourage creative effort the Government gives a bounty to inventors and writers. If this were the sole purpose of federal protection, then additional state grants of protection would be in harmony with the patent clause. According to Mr. Justice Black, however, the constitutional clause has another purpose: to limit monopolization and ensure a certain amount of competitive effort, including copying, by emphasizing the "inventive" requirement and the "limited times" restrictions.

Although this latter interpretation of the clause is by no means self-evident, either from its language or history,[61] it is the reading accepted by the Court and probably the interpretation best able to integrate the constitutional clause and its statutory development with other federal economic policies. Surely the patent scheme cannot be construed in an economic vacuum; it is designed to stimulate economic and social progress and must not only be justified in terms of that end, but reconciled as well with other statutes and judicially created policies designed to further the same purpose. Thus, the

---

Unfair Competition Protection after Sears and Compco, 40 N.Y.U.L. Rev. 101 (1965).

[60] The opinions are unclear on the question whether the Constitution itself forbids state protection in this field. Some language in the opinions indicates that they are constitutionally grounded. See also Aro Mfg. Co. v. Convertible Top Replacement Co., 377 U.S. 476, 522 (1964) (Black, J., dissenting).

[61] See Handler, in *Symposium, supra* note 59, at 1188–89; Kaplan, *Performer's Rights and Copyright: The Capitol Records Case*, 69 Harv. L. Rev. 409, 420–25 (1956).

Design Protection

scope of patent protection has been limited when its effects appear to violate the broader, complementary policies of the antitrust laws.[62] *Stiffel* and *Compco* may be seen as attempts to delineate this area of overlap and to determine the dominant interests.

Accepting Mr. Justice Black's reading of the patent clause and statutory policies, there is simply no place in the cosmos of design protection for the traditional torts of passing off and misappropriation insofar as they apply to designs. The tort of passing off, although meant to protect only nonfunctional recognitional features, was in practice applied more broadly.[63] Furthermore, when passing off is seen for what it was meant to accomplish, it appears to be little more than a common law counterpart of trademark law. Since the protection of recognitional features, including configurations, can be obtained within the federal system, there is no need to tolerate a state system that at most protects these same interests but more usually serves to undercut the entire federal scheme for protection and freeing up designs. Moreover, other methods of protection, such as labeling requirements, still remain open to the states.[64]

---

[62] See, *e.g.*, Mercoid Corp. v. Mid-Continent Inv. Co., 320 U.S. 661 (1944); International Business Mach. Corp. v. United States, 298 U.S. 131 (1936); United States v. United Shoe Mach. Co., 247 U.S. 32, 57–59 (1918); *Report of the Attorney General's National Comm. to Study the Antitrust Laws: Chapter V—Patent-Antitrust Problems*, reproduced in 37 J. Pat. Off. Soc'y 331 (1955). *Cf.* Walker Process Equip., Inc. v. Food Mach. & Chem. Corp., 382 U.S. 172 (1965).

[63] 78 Harv. L. Rev. 309, 311 (1964): "For example, claims for the protection afforded by passing off have often been appended to charges of patent infringement, as in *Stiffel*, and the reason for their inclusion was more to obtain a monopoly than to vindicate consumer rights. Moreover, the present tendency of courts in this area, as exemplified by the Seventh Circuit's opinions, has been to dilute the requirements of secondary meaning and nonfunctionality, thereby raising the spectre of conflict with the patent systems. Coupled with these threats to the integrity of the patent laws is the fact that when the limitations on the tort have been rigorously applied, plaintiffs have had a very poor record of success. Thus the elimination of this branch of tort law, may, in practice, prove to be a small loss." [Footnotes omitted.]

[64] The *Compco* opinion makes this explicit, 376 U.S. at 238–39.

The tort of misappropriation can be analyzed in the same way. The protection afforded by state unfair competition law against misappropriation of designs does nothing more than create a common law design patent. Since federal law already grants this protection, but in a context that weeds out uninventive creations and frees up inventive ones after a specified time, there is nothing positive and much that is detrimental in allowing the common law tort to apply to "misappropriation" of designs. Protectable intangibles in designs still exist, but they are to be defined solely by federal law. In other areas of law, such as trade secrets, common law protection will remain available. Here state protection does not usually undercut the patent-copyright-trademark scheme because consumer lists, for example, are not intangibles that the federal law is designed to protect or meant to free up. Moreover, this tort raises questions of agency, trust, contract, and criminal law, over which the states have always had dominant control.

A trade secret in a patentable process held secret for more than the federal statutory limit, however, may well be unprotectable by state law on the ground that such protection encourages inventors to avoid the patent system with its emphasis on publicity and on a monopoly limited in time. In general, the *Stiffel* and *Compco* cases indicate that problems of preemption lurk in many different applications of state unfair competition law. Their solution requires rigorous analysis of the policies behind the federal scheme as well as those supporting the apparently conflicting state law. According to *Stiffel* and *Compco*, when a conflict occurs, it is federal law that governs; more important, this federal law must be viewed not only as a limited method of protecting certain classes of material, but also as a comprehensive, constitutionally-imposed system of protection subject to qualification and of freeing up subject to condition, of aiding creators in some instances and of encouraging copying in others.

Design Protection 97

THE ECONOMICS OF DESIGN PROTECTION

Most studies of the problems of design protection emphasize the ineffectiveness of statutory and common law attempts to grant protection. Commentators speak of the "need" for better protection; they argue that creators "deserve" to be shielded from the activities of "pirates." Even courts have been dissatisfied with the law, and they have recommended new protective legislation.[65] In this area, economic sense, as well as virtue, is generally thought to reside with the designer.

And yet, there must be good reason why, in spite of the rhetoric on the side of stronger design protection, no new legislation has in fact been enacted although for years it has been introduced, why the design patent has been reduced to a bare shadow, why unfair competition law in this field has been largely dissipated, why the antitrust laws have been applied to prevent designers from combining to prevent copying,[66] and why the copyright law, in spite of recent extensions, has not provided substantial relief. The most helpful way of analyzing the proper role of design protection is through an economic analysis. This approach starts with a presumption opposite to that of most studies of design law. Whereas they presume that protection is desirable and view its legal background as unfortunate, we shall presume that the absence of protection is the natural condition, that manufacturers and creators should be free to use the ideas of others freely, that any interference with this laissez-faire environment, any imposition of restrictions on free use, any grant of monopoly, is acceptable only to the extent that it may be justified economically. Such an analysis of design protection must be derived from studies already undertaken of the economic functioning of the whole patent system.

[65] See White v. Leanore Frocks, Inc., 120 F.2d 113 (2d Cir. 1941) ; Cheney Bros. v. Doris Silk Corp., 35 F.2d 279 (2d Cir. 1929). See also White v. Lombardy Dresses, Inc., 40 F. Supp. 548 (S.D.N.Y. 1941).
[66] Fashion Originators' Guild of America, Inc. v. FTC, 312 U.S. 457 (1941).

THE PATENT SYSTEM

The fundamental question of patent economics is, simply, whether technical advancement and other advantages induced by the patent system outweigh its restraining effects on the economy. "The issue," writes one economist, "is not one of principle but of practical social engineering: *how much* protection against competitive appropriation or imitation and of what kind is required and worth paying for the optimum rate of innovation in a capitalistic economy?" [67] Patents have been justified in a number of ways:

1. The patent is said to provide an incentive to inventors which stimulates and accelerates technical progress.[68] This was the most important rationale for the monopoly grant in the nineteenth century when the patent was seen as a method of encouraging the single inventor, or creative hobbyist, to spend more of his time on inventive endeavors.[69] Although the self-employed inventor is still a factor in the modern economy, he is rapidly becoming a negligible one. If the patent reward did serve once to encourage individual creative efforts, it is another question whether today the patent system "stimulates business corporations to hire more of these talents than they otherwise would for this task." [70] For the large business, especially in fields such as electronics, chemicals, and the like, there is a constant need to innovate on various levels. Innovating with the purpose of reducing costs or distinguishing one's goods from those of competitors will nearly always be worthwhile. And, with particular relevance

---

[67] Kahn, *The Role of Patents*, in MILLER, COMPETITION, CARTELS AND THEIR REGULATION 311 (1962).

[68] See, *e.g.*, DEPARTMENTAL COMMITTEE OF THE BOARD OF TRADE, SECOND INTERIM REPORT ON PATENTS & DESIGNS ACT, Cmd. No. 6789, at 3 (1946).

[69] SUBCOMM. ON PATENTS, TRADEMARKS, AND COPYRIGHTS, SENATE COMM. ON THE JUDICIARY, 85TH CONG., 2D SESS., COPYRIGHT LAW REVISION STUDIES, Machlup, *Study No. 15, An Economic Review of the Patent System*, (Comm. Print 1958).

[70] *Id.* at 36. See Abramson, *The Economic Bases of Patent Reform*, 13 LAW & CONTEMP. PROB. 339, 341 (1948).

Design Protection 99

to design innovation, manufacturers are likely to continue to change "models and styles where a head start of a month or a year makes the difference between competitive success and failure. . . ." [71] Because of the high standard of invention applied to patent applications, inventors can never be certain that their creations will qualify, especially if attacked in the courts; this uncertainty lowers the incentive value of the patent. In the present economic structure, then, we might conclude—although there would doubtless be argument even on this—that the patent reward is not a major contributory factor in run-of-the-mill innovation, although it may occasionally help to encourage significant inventive efforts in new fields.[72]

2. Patents, it is often said, induce an inventor to disclose his invention, so that by making it available to others and thereby advancing their knowledge, further innovation is stimulated. It is certainly true that publicity is better than secrecy, but the argument that the patent system is an important method of spreading knowledge that would otherwise be unavailable can be largely discounted.[73] First, firms tend to patent only those processes or inventions that they cannot keep secret or that they fear might be discovered independently. Processes and techniques that can be kept within the firm without fear of disclosure or independent discovery, such as the formula for Coca-Cola, will usually not be patented. Thus, the patent system protects inventions that would

[71] Kahn, *supra* note 67, at 319. Compare Atlantic Works v. Brady, 107 U.S. 192, 199 (1882).

[72] Kahn, *supra* note 67, at 319, gives some statistics to show that patent applications have declined per capita in this country. Another thorough study shows that between 1941 and 1954 there was a 120% increase in the number of research scientists and engineers, but a drop in the number of patents granted; over a longer period, from 1900 to 1954 the number of all scientists and engineers increased by 1,600%; patents increased less than 83%. See SUBCOMM. ON PATENTS, TRADEMARKS, AND COPYRIGHTS, SENATE COMM. ON THE JUDICIARY, 85TH CONG., 2D SESS., COPYRIGHT LAW REVISION STUDIES, Melman, STUDY NO. 11, THE IMPACT OF THE PATENT SYSTEM ON RESEARCH, (Comm. Print 1958).

[73] See Kahn, *supra* note 67, at 317.

soon become available to the public anyway, and does not really induce the publicity of those that can be kept secret.[74] Second, even when an invention is patented, only seldom does the patent give sufficient information to be of value even to those well versed in the field.[75]

3. Some commentators have argued that whereas in the nineteenth century patents were needed as rewards for inventors, today they are needed to persuade investors to put their capital into the development of new products and new methods.[76] The cost of introducing a new product to the market is usually much greater than the cost of inventing it.[77] A patent may be needed to assure investors that this development cost can be recovered. It can also be important in aiding a small business built around a single new product to obtain financial backing and to develop its product without fear of immediate competition by established concerns.

These rationales are difficult to evaluate conclusively; only a detailed study of business practices and inventor psychology can resolve the question of the actual effect of the patent system on the economy. Yet there are certain other objections to patents, aside from the ones mentioned above, which should be articulated more fully. The argument for the patent, especially paragraph 3 above, is based on the premise that an artificial stimulus is needed to ensure the necessary amount of innovation in the economy, *i.e.*, that the market structure is incapable of allocating capital and talent adequately. Under traditional economic analysis, individuals invest their capital, time, and talent according to decisions based on marginal utility. They ask the question where the next dollar (or hour) would most profitably be spent.[78] In our society there must be

---

[74] See Melman, *supra* note 72, at 46–48; *cf.* Picard v. United Aircraft Corp., 128 F.2d 632, 640 (2d Cir. 1942) (Frank, J., concurring).

[75] See EDWARDS, MAINTAINING COMPETITION: REQUISITES OF A GOVERNMENTAL POLICY 222 (1949); Melman, *supra* note 72, at 34–35.

[76] See, *e.g.*, Picard v. United Aircraft Corp., *supra* note 74, at 642 (Frank, J., concurring); Edwards, *op. cit. supra* note 75, at 217–18.

[77] Machlup, *supra* note 69, at 36–37.   [78] See *id.* at 48.

an allocation of talent and capital among many spheres; "the decision to increase inventive activities is fully rational only when it appears likely that productivity can be raised faster and maintained more securely by more new technical knowledge than by more education and more capital equipment." [79] The introduction of the patent, a governmental bounty, adds an extraneous consideration into this decision-making process that may lead to misallocation in the economy. The misallocation argument has also been used in another way. Not only is a patent said to favor inventing at the expense of other economic activities, but also within the inventing field, it emphasizes activities leading to patentable results at the expense of basic research.[80]

Many other objections have been voiced against the patent system, and these will be mentioned briefly. It is indisputable that patents impose a cost on society because they prevent the fullest utilization of available knowledge.[81] They prevent effective competition in certain goods by allowing monopoly profits to the patentee and at the same time cutting of productive lines of research by others. Although the argument in defense of this monopoly element has been that it forces competitors to explore alternatives,[82] such "inventing around" is usually wasteful and can at best mitigate the social loss caused by monopoly use.[83] Firms holding patents are tempted to patent and suppress competing techniques or products. Moreover, patents can be used to create and reinforce market power, especially of large corporations. The uncertain validity of most patents and the expense of litigation accentuate this effect. As Thurman Arnold has observed: "A very weak

[79] *Ibid.*
[80] *Id.* at 50; Kahn, *supra* note 67, at 313; see Nelson, *The Simple Economics of Basic Scientific Research*, 67 J. POL. ECON. 297, 304 (1959).
[81] See Machlup, *supra* note 69, at 61.
[82] Frost, *The Patent System and the Modern Economy*, Study No. 2 of the Subcomm. on Patents, Trademarks, and Copyright, Senate Comm. on the Judiciary, 84th Cong., 2d Sess. 19 (1957).
[83] See Kahn, *supra* note 67, at 312.

patent in strong hands is pretty powerful. A very strong patent in weak hands is not worth anything." [84] Finally, the patent system itself, in terms of administration, is an economic burden on society.

The foregoing brief exposition of the arguments for and against a patent system is necessarily inconclusive. There are very clear disadvantages to a system in which monopoly grants over knowledge are awarded by the Government. Such a system is justifiable only if these disadvantages—inhibition of the free use of knowledge and the free competition of goods as well as misallocation of social resources—are outweighed by more rapid innovation motivated by the patent incentive. Although a full quantitative investigation remains to be done, studies of inventing methods and investment patterns suggest that, whereas the patent can sometimes be an incentive, its importance as a positive force in the economy is doubtful.[85]

THE ECONOMICS OF THE DESIGN PATENT

The preceding survey of patent theory was phrased in general terms; still, it is obvious that nearly all economic analysis in the patent field has been made in the context of technological innovation. It is clear, from even a cursory examination of the arguments for and against the patent system, that design protection does not easily fit into this model. One rea-

[84] *Hearings Before the Subcomm. on Patents, Trademarks, and Copyright, Senate Comm. on the Judiciary on the American Patent System*, 84th Cong., 1st Sess. 221 (1955); see Edwards, *supra* note 75, at 221–22.

[85] Most economists are unsympathetic to the patent and have advocated limiting its scope. Several favor an economic test, allowing patents only for those inventions that require systematic research and thus need patent protection in order to permit recovery of development costs. See Kahn, *supra* note 67, at 331; Edwards, *supra* note 75, at 237–38; Machlup, *supra* note 69, at 14. Other suggestions include shorter and perhaps more flexible periods; compulsory licensing; more rigorous administrative examination; insistence on fuller disclosure; and more intensive use of the antitrust laws to narrow the effects of the patent monopoly. For more extensive treatment of these approaches, see Abramson, *The Economic Bases of Patent Reform*, 13 LAW & CONTEMP. PROB. 339, 346–51 (1948); Hamilton & Till, *What is a Patent?*, 13 LAW & CONTEMP. PROB. 245, 253–56 (1948); Machlup, *supra* note 69, at 14; VAUGHAN, THE UNITED STATES PATENT SYSTEM 227–37 (1956).

son for the neglect of the design patent by economists is that they consider it much less important than mechanical patents. This judgment strikes two ways. One might argue that a rapid rate of technological innovation is of critical national importance; it is therefore worth risking some monopoly abuse in order to accelerate the rate of innovation. Designs do not present the same urgency; consequently, we need not offer a government bounty in order to hurry up advancement in the applied arts; we can let popular desires, as reflected in the market, set the rate of change.

On the other hand, the relative unimportance of designs can also be used to justify design protection. Because technical formulae and other scientific information are so important, it is dangerous to tie up this kind of knowledge in long-term monopolies. Permitting an exclusive franchise on a design, however, although it may not benefit society greatly, can do very little harm. Because there are so many possible designs and no one design is particularly important, society can afford to be lenient in granting exclusive rights.[86] This argument for supporting design protection cannot in itself be a reason for maintaining the expense of a complete design protection system; it can at most bolster the defense of a system established for more positive reasons.

As was noted earlier, an important rationale for the patent system is that it induces publicity of new technical knowledge that would otherwise be kept secret. In spite of the uncertain merit of this argument in terms of actual practice, it is important to see that the argument itself does not apply to design patents. There are no secret processes involving technical know-how in respect to designs as such. What is patented is the outward appearance, and that, of course, is made public as soon as the product is first exhibited. Technical knowledge should be publicized so that other inventors and scientists in

[86] See testimony of the Hon. Thurman Arnold, in *Hearings, supra* note 84, at 54.

the field can build upon it; the patent system is always justified as a means to progress in the sciences. This justification, too, lacks persuasiveness in the design field, where there is no real concept of progress but only of variety. Here the notion of accelerating a rate of progress is nearly meaningless. There are, of course, major innovations in aesthetics, but these are usually related to some deep-seated social change, for example the acceptance of "modern art," or to a major technological breakthrough, for example the invention of plastics or the engineering revolutions in steel framing and preformed concrete that have made possible contemporary architecture. Such major changes define progress in the applied arts; grants of exclusive rights to particular new configurations have had little or nothing to do with major design changes.

The chief argument for patents is that they induce more invention and more investment of capital in innovating-type activities. This basic rationale is not easily sustained when it is applied to designs. A survey of the types of items that have been patented or presented to the Patent Office for patents, indicates that the possibility of obtaining an exclusive right to produce them could not have been the primary motivating force leading to their development. In one case a manufacturer had patented a bottle of a particular shape which, at least from the drawings reproduced in the opinion, was virtually indistinguishable from most other bottles. The court declared the patent void, noting that the constitutional grant "was never intended to grant a monopoly just for the purpose of stimulating the natural instincts of mankind to make goods and merchandise attractive . . . ."[87] The court was clearly right, and the economic argument underlying its statement can be developed further. All products, if they are visible, must have an appearance; that is, they must be designed. Every maker of lamps, of dishes, of houses must give his prod-

[87] Charles Boldt Co. v. Turner Bros. Co., 199 Fed. 139, 143 (7th Cir. 1912).

Design Protection

uct some design, whether or not a patent is available. Thus, at least with products that are not sold primarily for decorative purposes, the availability of a design patent will not call into existence a greater number of designs. The desire to attract customers will generally induce manufacturers, who have to give their goods some appearance, to choose appealing designs. Yet courts have continued to give patents for goods that are not significant creations and that would have been "invented" whether or not a patent was available. A better approach is that of an early Seventh Circuit decision [88] in a dispute over a design patent for a lamp. In declaring the patent void, the court stated: "Lamps are indispensable. . . . New features are constantly being added. Success in trade demands it. The beneficent provisions of the federal statutes were never meant to support [such protection]. . . ." [89] Perhaps the *reductio ad absurdum* was reached when an attempt was made to patent the shape of a noodle.[90]

The argument that a patent is not necessary as a stimulus to the creation of designs is reinforced by the modern emphasis on design. As one commentator observed, today "most products have aspects of nonfunctional design, and these aspects are a major factor in their sales promotion." [91] Because of the importance of attractiveness as a matter of sales technique, the need for a patent as an additional inducement is minimal.

The little empirical data that is available affords further support for this position. It has often been stated that the designing art would suffer without protection. Yet there is no indication that this has ever occurred. The Canadian Royal

---

[88] Bolte & Weyer Co. v. Knight Light Co., 180 Fed. 412 (7th Cir. 1910).
[89] *Id.* at 415.
[90] C. F. Mueller Co. v. A. Zeregas Sons, 12 F.2d 517 (2d Cir. 1926).
[91] Dalsimer, *New Concepts of Design Protection,* in Eighth Annual Public Conference of the Patent, Trademark & Copyright Institute, 8 IDEA: THE PATENT, TRADEMARK, & COPYRIGHT JOURNAL OF RESEARCH & EDUC. 168 (1964); see Hudson, *A Brief History of the Development of Design Patent Protection in the United States,* 30 J. PAT. OFF. SOC'Y 380, 397 (1948).

Commission on Patents, Copyright, Trademarks and Industrial Design cited the weakness of United States design protection, but noted that:

> We have not heard it suggested that progress in design there is unsatisfactory. Design protection in Canada is virtually non-existent. Yet can it be said that design progress is wanting? Two members of this Commission examined the situation with respect to industrial designs in some other countries and were impressed with the high level of design excellence in at least one country which affords no protection.[92]

A study of the American dress industry is also instructive.[93] In this industry built on design, protection has been especially ineffective. Competition is keen and the turnover of firms is among the highest.[94] Yet, from the public's point of view, the results are satisfactory. Competition keeps prices down, and contrary to the claims of protectionists, there has been no cessation of designing; neither has there been any noticeable lack of investment in the industry.

Even if design patents are not essential to a high level of designing, it is said that the level would be even higher if effective protection were available. Assuming *arguendo* that this can be demonstrated, a number of important questions remain. Is there really a public interest in the proliferation of designs? Who is to say what the proper level of design innovation should be, what rate of design "progress" is best? In technology, we can perhaps speak of a greater need for technological growth in terms of military necessity or of maintaining a proper base for an expanding, full-employment economy. These considerations cannot be applied to design creation. The allocation argument, outlined in the preceding section, becomes particularly relevant here. Goods must be

---

[92] Canadian Royal Commission on Patents, Copyright, Trade Marks and Industrial Designs, REPORT ON INDUSTRIAL DESIGNS 10 (1958).

[93] See Meiklejohn, *Dresses—The Impact of Fashion on a Business*, in HAMILTON, PRICE AND PRICE POLICIES (1938); Weikart, *Design Piracy*, 19 IND. L.J. 235 (1944).

[94] See Meiklejohn, *supra* note 93, at 324.

useful, sturdy, attractive, effectively merchandised, and as inexpensive as possible. The proper mixture of these and other qualities is always uncertain; it is a function of investment decisions made by entrepreneurs, who have first made an evaluation of market needs. Thus, at a particular moment in a particular industry a manufacturer, let us say of garments, finds that a given amount of money would be most profitably spent on fancy designing; at another time he thinks it wise to cut the price of his dresses; another time to invest in better cloth. There is no "right" decision in these matters, at least so far as our economic premises are concerned. Yet the grant of special design protection carries with it the implication that investment in designing is particularly beneficial; it thus has the effect of disturbing the entrepreneur's "rational" decision-making process by giving him a special inducement to invest in the design rather than in some other aspect of his product.

It is not even clear, however, that effective design protection would induce more designing. Indeed, some advocates of strong protection argue that its great advantage is in *reducing* the rate of design change. Given a hypothetical firm that invests a great deal to produce an attractive design, under present conditions the design is immediately copied. The copiers, because they need not recover the initial investment needed to design the product, can undersell the initial producer. This "unfair" competition compels the producer to create another new design, which is again copied, and so on. One producer testifying before a Senate committee argued this point vigorously. He noted that a copied article is "cheapened, vulgarized, and promoted to the point of banality. It becomes stale and tiresome through the process of endless and degraded repetition long before its natural lifespan has ended and long before maximum efficiency in production has been achieved. . . . This accelerated obsolescence is very wasteful." [95] The Canadian Royal Commission found it

[95] Testimony of William F. Blitzer, in *Hearings, supra* note 29, at 106.

"impossible to say with any assurance whether design protection promotes activity or stability. . . ."[96] In the face of such doubts as to practical consequences and of such conflicting rationales for the patent, it is difficult to avoid the conclusion that the market mechanism is the best guide to determining the proper amount of designing in our economy.

It is occasionally said that it is unfair to put designers and producers at the mercy of copiers.[97] It is important to see that this is no longer an argument that the public need for designs requires the patent. It is an ethical argument, supporting the claim of producers who create their own designs against producers who imitate the designs of others. It is no exaggeration to say that in the design area, the moral arguments are really more basically important than the economic arguments in shaping opinion. Design "pirates" do not elicit the sympathies of courts or legislators, whereas manufacturers tell a compelling tale. One fabric executive explained that his company produced two-hundred designs a year. The cost of each, including designing, copper rollers, sample runs, was $5,000 a pattern, or $1,000,000 a year.[98] Only a handful of these patterns are successful, and all of the initial investment must be recovered from the sales of these few. Of course the copiers, operating with no designers and needing no sample runs, are able to manufacture the successful models on a large scale almost immediately.[99] Indeed, the speed of the copiers in some fields is quite amazing. In one case a new form of wood molding was copied by means of a rubber mold taken from the original; the copy was on the market two days after the original was first exhibited.[100] Cer-

---

[96] REPORT ON INDUSTRIAL DESIGN, *op. cit. supra* note 92, at 11 (1958).
[97] See, *e.g.*, Nat Lewis Purses, Inc. v. Carole Bags, Inc., 83 F.2d 475 (2d Cir. 1936); *Developments in the Law—Competitive Torts*, 77 HARV. L. REV. 888, 936 (1964).
[98] Testimony of Irwin W. Malvin, in *Hearings, supra* note 29, at 87–88; see Jackson, *Industrial Designs in the United Kingdom*, 45 J. PAT. OFF. SOC'Y 488, 492–93 (1963).
[99] See *Hearings, supra* note 29, at 44–54, 67–81.   [100] *Id.* at 72.

Design Protection 109

tainly these factors, which come to light in studying the business conditions of individual manufacturers in various industries, are relevant to the case for design patents. Where design is a relatively minor aspect of the total product, there is little reason to be concerned with copying. Where design is the primary quality of the product, as in most garments, the concern is great. Nevertheless, it is a fact that some businesses fail and others—perhaps less creative and more willing to copy—prosper; indeed, it is the norm of the competitive system.

There is in truth little reason to sympathize with the entrepreneur who fails, for he is presumed to have entered his field with knowledge of the market and industrial structure. As an example, let us consider an individual preparing to enter the garment industry. He has a choice: to be a creative manufacturer, hiring designers and hoping to make vast profits on a successful new model, or to be a copier. If everyone already in the industry were a creator, there would probably be artistic chaos: thousands of styles and models, too many to allow intelligent consumer choosing, and each costing far too much for the average purchaser. Our entrepreneur, faced with such an industrial environment, would probably become a copier, in which capacity he would serve the public interest by producing cheaper versions of the most successful models. On the other hand, if everyone in the industry were a copier, the selection available to the public would be exceedingly dull, old styles being redone season after season. If our entrepreneur believed that consumers were interested in new designs, then he would enter the industry in a creative capacity. Obviously, a healthy society requires some sort of balance between creators and copiers, for both serve useful functions. The new investor will analyze the market and the industry to decide in which way he is likely to be more successful. Probably he will do a little of both—copy some successful standard models and create some new ones.

And this is not far from what in fact happens. According to an estimate of the executive director of the National Dress Manufacturers Association, "in one way or another ninety percent of the industry engages in style piracy. In fact, only about forty firms live by their own original designs or by those they've legitimately purchased from French designers."[101] Most industries appear to have managed well despite the lack of effective design protection. The individual investor who fails because he has spent too much on new designs when the market does not demand such creative effort has suffered a fate no different from that of other entrepreneurs who have tried to sell products that consumers are unwilling to buy.

We may conclude that in general the market will arrive at the most productive combination of designing and nondesigning elements in every industry. But there remains one troublesome exception. It can happen that, when the design is the only or the major aspect of a product for which the reproduction process is very rapid, new designs will not be created even though society is willing to pay for them. For most situations the market can be relied upon to provide sufficient rewards so that supply moves to meet demand. In certain situations this mechanism is inadequate: the market cannot call forth the higher price needed to reward the maker of the desired good.[102] For example, if there were no copyright law, new books could be copied immediately, and the copies would be less expensive than the originally published version. No publisher would then be willing to pay royalties to an author; each would wait for the other to make the initial investment of buying the manuscript, advertising the work, and risking fi-

---

[101] Note, 33 CINN. L. REV. 382, 400 n.101 (1964).

[102] This argument is occasionally used to justify retail price maintenance. It is argued that retailers must provide certain services, *e.g.*, a radio and television shop should have models for exhibition and trial. But if they perform this service, people will try out equipment there but buy the goods at lower prices from discount houses which do not perform the services. *Cf.* Dr. Miles Medical Co. v. John D. Park & Sons Co., 220 U.S. 373 (1911).

Design Protection 111

nancial loss if the public is unreceptive. The number of new works published, it is argued, would drop to near zero.[103]

This argument can be answered, although not conclusively. It is doubtful that publication of new works would cease completely; some other method of maintaining the flow of new works would probably be devised. Perhaps publishers would create a common fund to subsidize writers; or, if culture is truly a national resource, perhaps the Government would pay a bounty to authors and let the reading public benefit from the lowered price of books. But even if citing the exception to the general market rule can be persuasive when referring to book publishing and map making, it is much less so in the design field. In some industries one can recover an initial investment just by being first on the market with a design. But it is rare that one sells a design and nothing more. A maker of noodles is selling more than just the shape, and copying of the shape should not affect the noodle maker in the same way that copying of a book would affect the original publisher. Of course the force of this distinction varies with the product. But as the design aspect of a particular good approaches the point at which it is the major element of the good, as for example in manufactured *objects d'art*, it becomes relatively easier to obtain copyright protection, thus mitigating the harmful effects of direct plagiarism. It would seem, then, that design protection is really unnecessary except to prevent direct copying of articles that are sold exclusively or primarily for their design content and that can be copied easily and rapidly.

One last factor should be mentioned even when considering such limited design protection. Goods, even though of similar or identical design, may not be fungible. Chagall and Picasso, Dior and Eames can still sell their originals even though cheap reproductions are available. The designs of expensive furniture can be copied using cheaper wood and inferior

[103] *Cf.* International News Serv. v. Associated Press, 248 U.S. 215 (1918).

workmanship; the design of expensive silverware can be used for inexpensive plate;[104] the plans used to build a high-priced home can be adapted for use in low-priced developments. And all the products will be profitable. Some consumers prefer originals just because they are originals. When we add the factors of superior craftsmanship and material, prior availability, and distinctive methods of merchandising, the plight of the original producer appears less tragic. In such situations, the decision as to the legal consequences of commercial copying has important social consequences. In the garment industry, for example, it has been said that the freedom of low-price manufacturers to imitate "the most popular innovations in the higher price ranges has . . . given to the majority of American women clothes which have blurred all class distinctions."[105] To the extent that copying is of this type, high-price designers can be assured that they will always have customers for their exclusive originals, and at the same time people who can afford only mass-produced goods of generally inferior quality will benefit by the rapid spread of styles.[106]

THE DESIGN PATENT: SOME CONCEPTUAL PROBLEMS

The foregoing economic analysis suggests that the case for design protection is a weak one. Although some help against direct copying may be defensible in industries in which design plays a predominant role and in which exact copies can be rapidly produced, the type of relief afforded by the patent would appear to be unnecessary and even detrimental. The drawbacks of the design patent statute are not confined to its economic effects; the legal problems it raises also seem to

[104] *Cf.* Graff, Washbourne & Dunn v. Webster, 195 Fed. 522, 524 (2d Cir. 1912).
[105] Meiklejohn, *supra* note 93, at 337.
[106] *Cf.* Forestek Plating & Mfg. Co. v. Knapp-Monarch Co., 106 F.2d 554 (6th Cir. 1939).

Design Protection 113

demand that the patent protection be withdrawn from this field.

Superseding all other problems is the central anomaly presented by the integration of design protection into the patent system. In few areas of the law do judges and administrators have such trouble applying legal standards. As early as 1927 it was noted that "in no branch of the Patent Office service is there more opportunity for arbitrary judgment on the part of administrative officials, and in no branch is there a more hazy and indefinite line of decisions from which to endeavor to extract principles and rules which should lead to the establishing of definite standards of what is, and what is not, patentable in the way of a design." [107] Recent commentators have expressed the same view.[108] The inability of the Office and the courts to establish predictable standards is particularly noticeable in this area. A number of the problems involved are discussed below. They should be viewed not as minor questions of statutory construction that can be solved by a skillfully drafted amendment or a brilliant Supreme Court decision, but rather as manifestations of the basic inappropriateness of the design patent statute.

OF ORNAMENTATION AND FUNCTION

The design patent statute requires that a design be "ornamental" if it is to qualify for coverage. To some courts this has meant that a judgment as to the quality of the design must be made. A very early opinion asserted of one design that "it is difficult, if not impossible, to conceive of any article of manufacture, the value of which would be the least enhanced in the estimation of the public, by the permanent attachment to it of the design in question. There is too little of the beautiful or even the grotesque in it. . . ." [109] Judge

[107] Allen, *Design Patentability*, 9 J. PAT. OFF. SOC'Y 298, 299 (1927).
[108] See *e.g.*, A. C. Gilbert Co. v. Shemitz, 45 F.2d 98 (2d Cir. 1930) (A. Hand, J.) ("The subject for design patents is difficult, for there are no standards."); testimony of Judge Rich, *Hearings, supra* note 29, at 33–34.
[109] *Ex parte* William Whyte, 1871 C.D. 304 (Comm'r of Patents).

Hand was more sophisticated in voiding a design patent on a tricycle: [110]

> We recognize that in aesthetics there are no standards, and that the design need not please such sensibilities as we may personally chance to possess. Nevertheless, we must find that the disclosure has at least a rudimentary aesthetic appeal, for so we interpret the word, "ornamental." . . . The plaintiff's tricycle has neither proportion, ornament, nor style, which could in our judgment make the remotest appeal to the eye.

Even Judge Hand's formulation does not clarify the issue. Although it establishes the proposition that judges should not consult their own tastes, it still defines "ornamental" in terms of actual effect upon the viewer. Most other cases are no more helpful. Courts have variously asserted that a design " 'must be one which appeals to the aesthetic sense'; 'to the artistic sense'; 'to the sense of beauty and the beautiful'; or as one poetically inclined phrased it for us, 'the design must be a thing of beauty which is a joy forever. . . .' " [111] One authoritative treatise states flatly: "The possession by a design of ornamentality is determined by whether or not it appeals to the aesthetic emotions. A design is ornamental if it appeals to the aesthetic emotions." [112] The 1964 edition of *Walker on Patents* states: "The term 'ornamental' as applied to designs relates to something beautiful, something giving a pleasing appearance, something which appeals to the aesthetic emotions or has artistic merit." [113] Of course these gropings toward a standard do not really elucidate the statutory term "ornamental." Indeed, they confuse the issue by introducing questions of aesthetics without resolving them.

In fact no one takes seriously these occasional lapses into

---

[110] H. C. White Co. v. Morton E. Converse & Sons Co., 20 F.2d 311, 312 (2d Cir. 1927).
[111] Franklin Lamp Mfg. Co. v. Albe Lamp & Shade Co., 26 F. Supp. 960 (E.D. Pa. 1939).
[112] SHOEMAKER, PATENTS FOR DESIGNS 113 (1929).
[113] 2 Deller, WALKER ON PATENTS 752 (2d ed. 1964).

the jargon of aesthetics. Judges are not interested in enforcing standards of beauty. What does concern the courts is the possibility that shapes defined solely by mechanical necessity might be given design patents. This concern relates to the economic argument against design patents: Because the design is to a great extent a manifestation of the object's mechanical function, there is no need to grant a special inducement for its creation. In *R. E. Dietz Co. v. Burr & Starkweather Co.*[114] the question was the patentability of the shape of a lantern. The court held the shape unpatentable on the ground that it had no "appeal to the eye" or "to the aesthetic sense." The real reason behind the decision was more substantial: "McArthur's lantern . . . represents nothing more than a convenient shape for an article purchased and used for what it will do—not for its looks." [115]

Such cases can be interpreted as using the ornamental criterion to withhold patents from shapes that, however pleasing, are so related to the functional aspects of the product that no patent reward is necessary to induce their creation. Although the courts never rely explicitly on such an economic test, they very often attempt to resolve the question of patentability by considering the purpose of the design: If it was prompted by "the purpose of improving [the object's] appearance merely, without changing its function or increasing its practical efficiency" then a design patent might be available; if it was developed to improve the functioning of the device, then no design patent is available.[116] This test assumes, illogically, that the disjunctive holds true; that producers have only one purpose in mind when they make a new or improve an old product. Moreover, the difficulty of applying such a purposive test makes it unattractive to the courts, although a reading of the cases suggests that, even when not

---

[114] 243 Fed. 592 (2d Cir. 1917). [115] *Id.* at 594.
[116] Oglesby, 3 O.G. PAT. OFF. 211 (Feb. 24, 1873), reprinted in SIMONDS, THE LAW OF DESIGN PATENTS 121 (1874); see SIMONDS at 189.

explicitly articulated, this consideration often underlies court decisions.

It would be rational economically, although a strain on statutory language and legislative intent, to interpret the ornamental requirement not as merely a loose threshold criterion, but rather as a standard requiring a showing that the particular configuration was so unrelated to the functional and other nondesign qualities of the product that only the inducement of a patent could have elicited it. A shape is not ornamental, most courts agree, if it is determined by mechanical necessity; why then should it be classified as ornamental if it is determined by the necessities of salesmanship and advertising?[117] The adoption of such a test of aesthetic functionality would probably eliminate most design patents.

Although no court has taken such an extreme view, many have seized upon the ornamentation criterion to attempt a distinction between what is protected by design and mechanical patents. Until relatively recently the standard of patentability for design patents was considerably more lenient than for other patents. Manufacturers were consequently tempted to use design patents as substitutes for mechanical ones. In an effort to resist this misuse of the statute, courts used the ornamental standard to distinguish between items for which design patents may be available and those requiring mechanical patents. In an early case testing the validity of a design patent on the appearance of the treads of a rubber tire, the court stated: "this patent is a plain effort to secure, under the guise of a design, a monopoly of the mechanical excellences thought to inhere in the peculiar arrangement of ridges and hollows resulting from the revealed combination of stripes, crosses, and squares."[118] This distinction is not a

---

[117] Compare the notion of aesthetic functionality in unfair competition law. *Developments in the Law—Competitive Torts*, 77 HARV. L. REV. 888, 919–21 (1964).
[118] North British Rubber Co. v. Racine Rubber Tire Co., 271 Fed. 936, 939 (2d Cir. 1921). Compare Application of Bigelow, 194 F.2d 545 (C.C.P.A.

Design Protection 117

difficult one when the item can be said to have absolutely no decorative function. A classic example is the attempt to patent the design of horseshoe calks—steel pieces protruding downward to prevent slipping. In two separate cases, design patents were voided or refused. One court talked of the need to produce "pleasant emotions," of appeals "to the eye, to the esthetic emotions, to the beautiful." [119] The other spoke of the need to produce something "which is artistically worth the while." [120] And yet the real question was not one of aesthetics at all, but a question of attempting to evade the stricter standards of the mechanical patent law. Indeed, in one case the plaintiff had only applied for a design patent after his application for a mechanical one had been rejected; in the other the applicant had applied for both types of patents.

Most cases present more difficulty, for the configurations of most goods are guided both by mechanical necessity *and* by artistic considerations. The rule generally accepted is that "a design patent on an article cannot be denied simply because that article has a mechanical or functional utility." [121] A design patent can issue on such an article, but only on its design, while the rules for mechanical patent control the utilitarian elements of the article. Although this formulation is theoretically unobjectionable, it raises practical difficulties. In *Ex parte Crane* [122] the applicant sought a patent on a paper box "with compartments conveniently arranged for holding each of the articles comprising a set of ladies' furs." A general patent had already been refused, but the Commissioner here allowed the design patent under the 1842 act, stating that Crane sought only the "more limited" protection

---
1952) (aircraft tire tread design). See generally SHOEMAKER, *op. cit. supra* note 112, at 33.
[119] Rowe v. Blodgett & Clapp Co., 103 Fed. 873, 874 (D. Conn. 1900).
[120] William Calk Co. v. Neverslip Mfg. Co., 136 Fed. 210, 215 (M.D. Pa. 1905), *aff'd*, 145 Fed. 928 (1906).
[121] SHOEMAKER, *op. cit. supra* note 112, at 128.
[122] 1869 C.D. 7 (Comm'r of Patents).

of a design patent. Yet the effect of the grant was the same as it would have been under a regular patent: the box was nothing more than its shape, and if only Jason Crane can manufacture such a shape then Jason Crane possesses an absolute monopoly.

More clearly wrong still is *In re Koehring*,[123] an appeal from the Commissioner's refusal to grant a design patent for a concrete-mixer truck. The design placed "the different elements of the whole machine, including the hood, gas tank, mixer, etc. into a more symmetrical and compact whole."[124] The purpose of the design patent statute was the "elimination of much of the unsightly repulsiveness that characterizes many machines," said the court when it ordered the grant of a patent. The implications of this decision for other concrete-mixing companies was not considered. The compact shape of the Koehring mixer may have reflected important structural advantages that made the machine easier, safer, or more economical to operate. In giving Koehring a patent on the shape, the court in effect gave him a monopoly over structural changes that probably were not sufficiently inventive to qualify for a mechanical patent. Other courts have realized the danger of such patents, and find excuses for refusing to grant them. A streetcar was held not to possess "any distinctiveness";[125] a pair of pliers was held graceful but not sufficiently inventive;[126] a machine was refused a design patent because it had movable parts;[127] other decisions say, more simply, that the particular item is functional and not ornamental.[128]

---

[123] 37 F.2d 421 (C.C.P.A. 1930).   [124] *Id.* at 422.
[125] Hammond v. Stockton Combined Harvester & Agricultural Works, 70 Fed. 716 (9th Cir. 1895).
[126] Application of Johnson, 175 F.2d 791 (C.C.P.A. 1949).
[127] *Ex parte* Adams, 1898 C.D. 115 (Comm'r of Patents). *But see* Chandler Adjustable Chair & Desk Co. v. Heywood Bros. & Wakefield Co., 91 Fed. 163 (D. Mass. 1898).
[128] See, *e.g.*, Spaulding v. Guardian Light Co., 267 F.2d 111 (7th Cir. 1959) (fluorescent lighting equipment); Hueter v. Compco Corp., 179 F.2d 416 (7th Cir. 1950) (bar on automobile dashboard); Circle S Prods. Co. v. Powell Prods., Inc., 174 F.2d 562 (7th Cir. 1949) (photographic lamp holder); *In re*

Design Protection 119

In all these cases some designing may have been necessary to produce the final product, and courts waver between rejecting the design patent outright or granting it with the offhand remark that it covers only the design and not the functional elements of the work. A better standard would be to refuse a design patent whenever the grant may work to circumvent the rigorous standard of invention applied to mechanical patents. Such a strict rule is the best way to reconcile the two patent statutes. It fulfills the aim of the patent scheme to encourage wide use of useful (and incidentally attractive) innovations that are not patentable; at the same time it does not undercut the aims of the design patent statute for it is unlikely that the patent has any effect in encouraging these kinds of industrial designs. In *In re Lobl* [129] the applicant sought a design patent on the shape of a nose inhaler. The court in a well-reasoned opinion asserted that the peculiar function of a nose inhaler allowed only a limited number of possible designs, and refused the patent on the formal ground that the design required only ordinary skill. Even if the design took inventive skill to create, the patent should have been refused because of its inhibiting effect upon competitors.

The approach suggested here would reject the traditional question: Is the item ornamental or is it functional? Since the answer is usually "both," it would be better to analyze the practical effects upon the public and possible competitors if the configuration were given design protection. If such protection would interfere with functional imitation, the patent should be refused as nonornamental. One objection to the strict application of this test was seen as early as 1869: it leads to "the absurdity that if a design is useless, it may be patented, whereas if it is useful, it is entitled to no protec-

---

Stimpson, 24 F.2d 1012 (D.C. Cir. 1928) (riveting machine). *But see In re Horne,* 83 F.2d 692 (C.C.P.A. 1936) (design for playground climbing bars held patentable); *In re* Muldoon, 56 F.2d 894 (C.C.P.A. 1932) (design for electric light socket held patentable.
[129] 75 F.2d 219 (C.C.P.A. 1935).

tion." [130] One answer to this critique is that a "useful" design might still be patentable if it involves no interference with free copying of unpatented functional elements. Second, such a test would probably not lower the rate of design innovation because when design changes are so closely tied to changes in function they will continue to be produced whether or not a design patent is available. Far from being absurd, such a test would make good economic sense; the only absurdity is that the established design patent scheme requires such a strained approach if one is to define rationally the contours of design protection.

The distinction between ornamental and functional qualities, which the courts have long sought to establish, takes on an almost humorous aspect when its premise is contrasted with the theories underlying modern design. The elaboration of the ornamental standard is based on the notion that design and function are easily separable. Of course, this is not the case, at least not without a more detailed articulation of the reasons for the rule. Even if it were an easy distinction to make, it does not reckon with modern design, which is heavily influenced by Louis Sullivan's dictum "Form follows function." Contemporary design avoids decoration: "The stark simplicity of much modern design, both industrial and architectural, is a violent reaction against the ginger-bread of the nineteenth century." [131] Yet the law in this area is built upon a gingerbread conception of design; [132] it sees design as something added to a product, an ornamentation, an embellishment, not as an integral part of the product itself. The contemporary designer does not take a finished good and decorate it; he helps to create it as much as does the production engineer.[133] The designer does not seek to add something special to the product; rather he seeks, if he is in the vanguard

[130] *Ex parte* William N. Bartholomew, 1869 C.D. 103 (Comm'r of Patents).
[131] VAN DOREN, INDUSTRIAL DESIGN 127 (1954).
[132] See Bowen, *Design Patents and Modern Industrial Design*, 37 J. PAT. OFF. SOC'Y 744 (1955).
[133] GLOAG, INDUSTRIAL ART EXPLAINED 204 (2d ed. 1946).

Design Protection 121

of artistic innovators, to strip away and reveal basic forms.[134] The design patent, in particular its requirement of ornamentation, is not only difficult to apply through the establishment of legally respectable standards; it is also grounded conceptually in an aesthetic outlook inconsistent with the art it seeks to encourage.

THE SEARCH FOR INVENTION

Although four criteria are said to establish the right to a design patent—originality, novelty, ornamentation, and invention—it is the last of these that raises the greatest problems, for it is the standard of invention that represents the starkest example of the transferral of a difficult mechanical and process patent standard to the wholly alien world of design. The invention standard is troublesome in all areas of patent law;[135] yet in the case of mechanical patents courts can look at prior art more objectively, seeing what can be done with prior know-how and what changes the innovation causes. True,

---

[134] See TEAGUE, DESIGN THIS DAY 167–70 (1949): "The current severity of exterior is vastly preferable to elaboration by application of classical order and ornaments in which the earlier builders of steel buildings indulged, but it is not true simplicity. . . . If the modern designer could leave his steel exposed, the material out of which he could construct his rhythmic relationships of area and line would be enormously enlarged, and it would all be essential and significant material; his design would gain thereby in unity, and hence in simplicity."

[135] See, *e.g.*, Picard v. United Aircraft Corp., 128 F.2d 632 (2d Cir. 1942) (Frank, J., concurring); Frost, *supra* note 82, at 59.

Since this paper was written, the Supreme Court, in Graham v. John Deere Co., 383 U.S. 1 (1966), dealt at some length with § 103 of the 1952 Patent Act, 35 U.S.C. § 103 (1964), which declares: "A patent may not be obtained . . . if the differences between the subject matter sought to be patented and the prior art are such that the subject matter as a whole would have been obvious at the time the invention was made to a person having ordinary skill in the art to which said subject matter pertains. Patentability shall not be negatived by the manner in which the invention was made."

The Court stated that "the revision was not intended by Congress to change the general level of patentable invention." It concludes that "the section was intended merely as a codification of judicial precedents . . . with congressional directions that inquiries into the obviousness of the subject matter sought to be patented are a prerequisite to patentability." 383 U.S. at 17. The effect of any shift in inquiry from "inventiveness" to "nonobviousness" in the design patent area will be interesting to observe, especially as it may affect the analysis in this paper of the invention standard.

the particular improvement required to distinguish a workmanlike innovation from a true invention remains elusive, but within certain limits the nature of the innovation itself can be determined with some claim to objectivity. Design innovation, on the other hand, is especially subjective, in part because it can exist only in the minds of onlookers and in part because our society has no accepted concept of artistic progress. Invention, in truth, is not a word that has any reference value whatsoever in dealing with design. Perhaps this means that, if strictly applied, no design patents should be issued because none meets this inapplicable standard. The courts, however, have struggled to make sense of the requirement in a way that allows the finding that some designs are inventions while others are not.[136]

Hundreds of judicial opinions deal with the question of invention, and nearly all follow a regular pattern. The court states that the design must meet the test of invention, observing that this requires something more than ordinary skill but that precise articulation of the standard is impossible. The product is then described: it may be a kewpie doll, a garment, a lighting fixture. The decision concludes with an assertion either that a patent is proper because the creation required inventive genius or that no patent can issue because the article required no more than the effort of a skilled craftsman. In spite of the superficial similarity of all these opinions, a survey of them does reveal some substantial changes in the application of the standard. The extremely permissive practices of the Patent Office in the middle of the nineteenth century are well known.[137] In fact, there was at that time no real test of invention; challenges to the validity of patents in early cases were more likely to be based on the novelty requirement.[138]

[136] See Dienner, *Protection of Industrial Designs*, 45 J. PAT. OFF. SOC'Y 673, 676 (1963); Note, 66 HARV. L. REV. 877, 885 (1953).
[137] See SHOEMAKER, *op. cit. supra* note 112, at 20.
[138] *E.g.*, Booth v. Garelly, 1 Blatch. 247 (S.D.N.Y. 1847), reprinted in SIMONDS, THE LAW OF DESIGN PATENTS 11 (1874); Worcester v. Crane, 2

Design Protection

Even in the celebrated case of *Gorham v. White* [139] there was no attack on the validity of the patent itself, although by recent standards it is doubtful that the requisite invention would be found. In *Dobson v. Dornan* [140] the Court in sustaining a design patent for a carpet spoke of testing for "novelty" [141] but never mentioned invention. This early neglect of invention should not seem surprising. The design patent statute was not really seen as an integral part of the patent system, and the jargon of invention does not mix easily with the rhetoric of aesthetics. It has been argued that this neglect of the invention standard was not unjustified, and that the design patent act was never intended to impose the standard because the statutory language referred to any one who "invented or produced" a design.[142] This argument was never accepted, and in 1893 the Supreme Court established the invention requirements for a design patent in the same sense as it applied to mechanical patents.[143] The design patent was henceforth to be applied on the basis of all the rules laid down for ordinary patents; there must be "the exercise of the inventive faculty. . . . Mere mechanical skill is insufficient. There must be something akin to genius." [144]

Once the invention criterion had been recognized, debate shifted to whether the same degree of invention was needed to sustain a design patent as was required for mechanical patents.[145] The controversy was largely an academic one, since even if it had been agreed that the standard was the same, its application in a totally different context made comparison impossible. The opinions show that the application of the invention standard in fact made little difference if a court

Fisher's Pat. Cases 583 (S.D.N.Y. 1865), reprinted in SIMONDS 16; see Michaelson, *The Nature of the Protection of Artistic and Industrial Design*, 37 J. PAT. OFF. SOC'Y 543, 546 (1955).

[139] 81 U.S. (14 Wall.) 511 (1871).   [140] 118 U.S. 10 (1886).
[141] *Id.* at 15.   [142] See Michaelson, *supra* note 138, at 557.
[143] Smith v. Whitman Saddle Co., 148 U.S. 674 (1893); see Northrup v. Adams, 18 Fed. Cas. No. 10,328 (E.D. Mich. 1877).
[144] 148 U.S. at 679.
[145] See SIMONDS, *op. cit. supra* note 138, at 193–94; SYMONS, THE LAW OF PATENTS FOR DESIGNS 41 (1914).

thought a patent proper. In *Smith v. Stewart*[146] the plaintiff had patented masonic designs arranged "in an orderly and tasteful manner" for a rug. The court thought it "absurd" to say that the standard of invention for designs was the same as for mechanical inventions: "The invention in a majority of patented designs is very small, and of low order. All the statute, as commonly interpreted, requires is the production of a new and pleasing design. . . ."[147] The leading case for the permissive application of the standard was a Second Circuit opinion[148] dealing with a design patent on the Queen Ann pattern for spoons and forks. If any sort of economic argument had been recognized, the patent would not have been sustained. Although the appearance of the handles was distinctive, the pattern consisted merely of rearrangements of older features. Such combinations of elements from prior art are often permitted in a design patent, although the public interest in encouraging mere variation is surely insubstantial. Moreover, in this case the defendant manufactured only plated ware whereas the plaintiff used only sterling silver, three times as expensive. It is doubtful that the markets for these goods overlapped appreciably, and there is a strong social interest in allowing goods for low-price markets to make use of the advances introduced by more expensive goods. The court dealt with none of these considerations but concentrated upon "invention," which it seemed to equate with "novelty," a standard it associated with copyright law:[149]

> A design patent must of course disclose invention. It must show a novel design, but a very different set of faculties are brought into play from those required in producing a new machine or a chemical or electrical combination. . . . The policy which protects a design is akin to that which protects the works of an artist, a sculptor or a photographer by copyright. It requires but little invention, in the

---

[146] 55 Fed. 481 (E.D. Pa. 1893).   [147] *Id.* at 483.
[148] Dominick & Haff v. R. Wallace & Sons Mfg. Co., 209 Fed. 223 (2d Cir. 1913).
[149] *Id.* at 223–24. See also Untermeyer v. Freund, 37 Fed. 342 (S.D.N.Y. 1889).

Design Protection 125

sense above referred to, to paint a pleasing picture, and yet the picture is protected, because it exhibits the personal characteristics of the artist, and because it is his. So with a design. . . . A design patent necessarily must relate to subject matter comparatively trivial and the courts have looked with greater leniency upon design patents than patents for other inventions. The object of the law is to encourage those who have the industry and genius to originate objects which give pleasure through the sense of sight.

The Second Circuit, known for its liberality in these matters, became the spokesman for the stricter approach in 1916. In *Steffens v. Stevens* [150] a district judge felt compelled, on the basis of Second Circuit precedents, to grant design patents to obviously commonplace cigar bands. This result was too extreme for the Court of Appeals, which might have sensed that such protection was not necessary to encourage cigar manufacturers to design their bands. A "new" test was therefore announced: "To sustain a design patent the design must involve something more than mere mechanical skill. There must be invention." [151] The newness of the test was not in its words, which of course represented nothing more than the old *Whitman Saddle* formulation,[152] but in a new emphasis on the voiding of patents. That same year Judge Hand, sitting with the court of appeals, reaffirmed *Steffens*, equated the design test with that for mechanical patents, and articulated the invention standard as follows: "Was the new combination within the range of the ordinary routine designer?" [153]

The Second Circuit went on to reject more design patents, applying the same incantation, but obviously imputing to it greater vitality.[154] In *Nat Lewis Purses, Inc. v. Carole Bags, Inc.*[155] it supported its application of the invention standard by asking whether "the law should create such a monopoly,

---

[150] 232 Fed. 862 (2d Cir. 1916) [151] *Id.* at 865.
[152] Smith v. Whitman Saddle Co., 148 U.S. 674 (1893).
[153] Strause Gas Iron Co. v. William M. Crane Co., 235 Fed. 126, 131 (2d Cir. 1916).
[154] *E.g.*, Knapp v. Will & Baumer Co., 273 Fed. 380 (2d Cir. 1921); Berlinger v. Bush Jewelry Co., 48 F.2d 812 (2d Cir. 1931).
[155] 83 F.2d 475 (2d Cir. 1936).

unless the monopolists' contribution is something out of the common." This kind of analysis suggests that the strengthening of the invention standard was tied to more fundamental economic considerations, but the language of the opinions still spoke in terms of the degree of creativeness of the designer. The garment industry found it particularly difficult to meet the test.[156] In a 1941 handbag case the court found "uniqueness of appearance and an aesthetic appeal not found in any prior patent or publication," but still did not find the requisite inventiveness.[157] The more stringent application of the invention criterion was not a Second Circuit manifestation alone. Supreme Court opinions in the mechanical patent field, which had rarely sustained a patent and often rebuked the Patent Office and lower courts for their leniency, had an important effect in design patent litigation.[158] The force of the latest opinions [159] as well as statistical data [160] indicate that although some courts are occasionally lenient in applying the invention standard,[161] very few design patents are likely to be sustained in litigation.

Like the search for the meaning of the ornamental criterion,

[156] See, *e.g.*, Neufeld-Furst & Co. v. Jay-Day Frocks, Inc., 112 F.2d 715 (2d Cir. 1940).
[157] Gold Seal Importers, Inc. v. Morris White Fashions, Inc., 124 F.2d 141, 142 (2d Cir. 1941).
[158] See Cuno Eng'r Corp. v. Automatic Devices Corp., 314 U.S. 84, 89 (1941); Picard v. United Aircraft Corp., 128 F.2d 632 (2d Cir. 1942). *But see* Frost, *supra* note 82, at 59. Compare Harris, *Some Aspects of the Underlying Legislative Intent of the Patent Act of 1952*, 23 GEO. WASH. L. REV. 658, 677–79 (1955).
[159] See Kono Mfg. Co. v. Vogue Optical Mfg. Co., 94 F. Supp. 251 (S.D.N.Y. 1950); Roseweb Frocks Inc. v. Moe Feinberg-Mor Wiesen, Inc., 40 F. Supp. 979 (S.D.N.Y. 1941); Michaelson, *supra* note 138, at 552.
[160] See *supra* note 8. In Amerock Corp. v. Aubrey Hardware Mfg., Inc., 275 F.2d 346, 349 (7th Cir. 1960), the court reviews in a footnote all the Seventh Circuit design patent cases in recent years; between 1937 and 1960, of the 21 cases in which design patent validity was litigated, none was found valid. A more general survey also showing an extremely high percentage of patents declared invalid can be found in Walter, *A Ten Year Survey of Design Litigation*, 35 J. PAT. OFF. SOC'Y 389 (1953).
[161] *E.g.*, Glen Raven Knitting Mills, Inc. v. Sanson Hosiery Mills, Inc., 189 F.2d 845 (4th Cir. 1951); Application of Park, 181 F.2d 155 (C.C.P.A. 1950).

Design Protection

the question whether a creation required sufficient inventive effort is an unsatisfying one. We found in our analysis of ornamentation that courts were not really interested in standards of beauty and that they used ornamentation as a method of weeding out designs that were too closely related to functional elements, both because they feared giving mechanical protection and because designs closely tied to utilitarian needs probably require less of an inducement. In respect to inventiveness, we find that in spite of the language used by the courts, they are not really interested in the romantic and imprecise notion of what sort of genius is needed to create various designs.[162] The invention standard is said to be one of the four criteria for a valid patent, but actually courts do not and cannot approach items such as kewpie dolls,[163] hosiery,[164] fruit bowls,[165] and dart boards [166] in terms of the genius of the creator. Instead, they use the invention standard to choose between those designs deserving a monopoly and those that should be freely copyable.

A standard thus relating to the appropriateness of the reward, even when unarticulated in the opinions and even if based on a feeling rather than on analysis, can be objectified more easily than the abstraction "invention." To be sure, most courts have only been feeling their way toward what seemed to be a proper solution in individual cases. When the design is attractive, and the defendant is a plagiarist, and no precedent based on economic or social theories of monopoly exploitation is available, it is not surprising that courts, particularly the nineteenth century courts, would interpret "inventiveness" in such a way as to sustain the patent. In those days, too, most patentees appear to have been individuals

---

[162] Cf. Charles Boldt Co. v. Turner Bros. Co., 199 Fed. 139 (7th Cir. 1912).
[163] See Pfeffer v. Western Doll Mfg. Co., 283 Fed. 966 (7th Cir. 1922).
[164] See Glen Raven Knitting Mills, Inc. v. Sanson Hosiery Mills, Inc., 189 F.2d 845 (4th Cir. 1951).
[165] See Imperial Glass Co. v. A. H. Heisey & Co., 294 Fed. 267 (6th Cir. 1923).
[166] See Capex Co. v. Swartz, 166 F.2d 5 (7th Cir. 1948).

who had come up with a simple but attractive and profitable improvement. The possibility of obtaining a design patent did no doubt motivate many of these designers to do their work. As modern industry moved away from the homecrafts of Jason Crane to the large-scale production of inexpensive goods for a wide market, as economic analysis became more penetrating, as antitrust laws were passed and gained vitality, as mechanical patents became suspect as fetters on competition, the attitude of the courts began to change. As an economic matter, the patent was less important to sustain a high level of designing; as an equitable question, it was less clear that a creator needed this protection; as a social policy, the interest of the public seemed to correspond more with that of the copier.

These complex policies and social changes were never fully stated and only occasionally hinted at; they manifested themselves, however, in findings of lack of inventiveness, findings that ostensibly related to the nature of the creative process, not to the social and economic system in which that creative process occurred. If the analysis presented here is correct, and invention is just a judicial shorthand for the basic policies underlying the entire patent policy, two results can be expected. First, the standard will remain strict, preventing effective use of the statute by designers. Second, the standard will remain a fundamentally unpredictable and clumsy device because it is, if not a legal fiction, at least a fantasy.

REPRISE

This analysis of design protection, and in particular our examination of the operation of the design patent statute, leads to several conclusions.

1. The economic case for design protection is a weak one at best. There is no need in the present economy to provide extramarket inducements to encourage the manufacture of more

Design Protection 129

attractive goods; the market mechanism, the producers' desire to differentiate goods, the public's preference for variety, and the integration of designing into the production process are sufficient to ensure the maintenance of a high level of design activity. There is no need to provide a special inducement in order to encourage disclosure because designs by their nature are fully public once displayed. There is no need to concern ourselves with speeding "progress" in the field of applied design because first, it is relatively unimportant even if we could define it, and second, we have at best only a vague notion of what such progress is; moreover, if there is such a thing as important innovation in design, it comes from major conceptual and structural breakthroughs and not from the proliferation of shapes and forms. The empirical data we have, and they are admittedly slight, indicate that design creativity remains vital without protection and that, in certain areas at least, the grant of protection might lead to stabilization rather than experimentation. Decisions as to whether there should be a proliferation of designs or a slowing down of the rate of change should be left to the market. Economic considerations, then, militate generally against design protection in any form.

2. The design patent is, from an economic viewpoint, particularly harmful. The cost of administering the system is substantial; the standard of infringement is wide; and the nature of the monopoly is inappropriate. If some design protection is necessary, it is to allow producers to recoup their investment in the design element of a product without being undersold by copiers who do not bear the development costs. But the patent grants a total monopoly, which treats as infringers both the producer who independently creates a similar design (and thus did bear the development cost) and the copier against whom we may wish to grant some protection.

3. The patent is inappropriate for another reason: If designs are to be given some protection the problems and inter-

ests involved should be faced and resolved. The historical accident that led to the incorporation of design protection into the patent system has resulted in an anomaly which seriously hampers efforts to establish intelligent contours to the protected area. At the beginning these grants, with their extensive monopoly power, were given out freely. This liberality was soon recognized as unwise. Using the clumsy tools provided by the "ornamental" and "invention" tests, courts, although not always the Patent Office,[167] were able to limit the application of the act, but only by making use of arbitrary and unpredictable standards that do not explicitly operate in terms of the real interests at issue. If some protection were thought necessary and the patent the only available approach, then continuation of the patent system would not be objectionable. The cost of litigation and the time lag before a patent issues would deter many; the hostility of the courts to these monopoly grants and the unpredictability of the invention standard would deter many more. However, other possible forms of protection are available to replace the patent approach.

4. If we take no protection as the norm, there would seem little reason to grant protection except in the following circumstances: In some situations the market structure may not function so as to induce as much designing as consumers in fact desire. This phenomenon will occur in an industry in which (a) products are purchased solely or primarily because of their attractiveness, e.g., statuettes; (b) the cost of designing and developing new products requires an investment that makes up an important part of the good's total cost; and (c) copying is effective in reproducing the quality of the originals and is rapid enough to prevent the designer from recovering his development costs merely by being first on the market. In such a market, a manufacturer may with good

[167] The looser standard applied by the Patent Office has often been the subject of comment. See, e.g., VAUGHAN, THE UNITED STATES PATENT SYSTEM 299 (1956).

Design Protection 131

reason fear that his new designs will be copied immediately by competitors who do no designing themselves and who will undersell him because they have no development costs to recover. In such an industry, permitting free copying will probably deter desired design innovation. If an industry exists that operates in this way, there is a public interest in granting the manufacturer who designs limited protection against copying, but not a patent monopoly against those who may have developed the same design independently. The need for protection against copying suggests a copyright approach to protection.[168]

5. Concerning the class of goods thus delineated there is a serious question whether any social interest is served by protecting trivial changes of form. If a straight copyright approach were established, or a special design act passed, this type of protection—preventing copying but not establishing a total monopoly—would be more rational, but the coverage would be much wider than that of the patent: There is no invention standard in copyright law; any configuration, however uninspired, is copyrightable. One possible approach would be to carry the invention standard over into the design copyright area; this, however, would introduce new complexities while retaining many of the drawbacks of the design patent. Another method would be to follow the British statute,[169] which includes no criterion based on creative effort, but requires that the design be "new or original." British courts interpret this to mean that something substantially innovative has been designed.[170] This approach, like the patent, requires

[168] A number of important commentators have argued for a copyright approach to designs. See Vacheron & Constantin-Le Coultre Watches, Inc. v. Benrus Watch Co., 260 F.2d 637, 644 (2d Cir. 1948) (Clark, C. J., dissenting); Derenberg, *Copyright No-Man's Land: Fringe Rights in Literary and Artistic Property*, 37 J. Pat. Off. Soc'y 690, 705 (1953); L. Hand, in *Hearings, supra* note 84, at 114; Frost, *supra* note 82, at 56.

[169] Registered Design Act of 1949; Copyright Act of 1956; 12, 13, and 14 Geo. 6 c.88; 4 & 5 Eliz. 2 c.74; see Jackson, *Industrial Designs in the United Kingdom*, 45 J. Pat. Off. Soc'y 488 (1963).

[170] See discussion of the British Act by Hamilton, in Royal Comm'n on

a registration system, with its inevitable time lag and expense. Perhaps the simplicity of the copyright approach is worth its unnecessarily wide coverage. Perhaps it would be best to allow any designer whose design is covered by the criteria of paragraph 4 to copyright his work on publication simply by applying a proper notice, but also to strengthen the novelty test itself, thus allowing a copier to challenge the copyright for lack of novelty.

6. Whether such protection, limted as it may be, is permissible under a broad reading of *Stiffel* and *Compco* may be open to challenge. If the Supreme Court is reading the patent clause to embody a purpose of encouraging copying of those goods not protected by either a patent or a copyright, then wider protection under a design statute enacted under the Commerce Clause is suspect. We have already seen that the patent approach is undesirable. The copyright standard, however, may provide an appropriate method of granting design protection to the limited class of goods defined in paragraph 4. The Constitution extends copyright protection only to "writings," but as noted earlier, this definition has been broadly interpreted. The "writings" standard may provide a convenient and effective device for extending protection to those goods, defined in economic terms in paragraph 4, that are purchased by consumers primarily for their design element. Such goods are, like an author's book, primarily an artistic effort. Also, like the works of novelists and cartographers, they may require some protection in order to induce their manufacture. The "writings" standard should not be too widely extended, however; it is well to remember that *Mazer v. Stein* was not a constitutional decision. Designs that are mere adjuncts of mechanical devices, products that are not sought primarily for the sake of their appearance, industrial designs in general—these goods are clearly not

---

Patents, Copyright, Trade Marks and Industrial Designs, REPORT ON INDUSTRIAL DESIGNS 41–45 (Canada 1958).

Design Protection 133

"writings" either in the artistic sense or in the economic sense that they need this protection in order to induce producers to turn them out. This limited approach to design protection through copyright—limited both in the type of protection afforded [171] and in the class of goods covered—would seem the most rational solution to the design protection problem.

[171] If copyright is used to give design protection the term of years of such protection should be reduced substantially; a 3–5 year term would be as much of an inducement to designers as is the current 28-year term.

NATIONAL THIRD PRIZE, 1965

The Effect of the Copyright Act and the Proposed Revision on Educators as Users of Copyrighted Materials

By MICHAEL E. MECSAS
CORNELL LAW SCHOOL

THE UNITED STATES COPYRIGHT ACT grants authors certain exclusive rights to exploit their works in order to encourage authorship which will inure to the benefit of all mankind.[1] The Act has a significant bearing on the use, recording, and re-use of materials for educational purposes. Because of the vital role of education in American society, educators desire maximum availability of all kinds of teaching materials and resources.[2] On the other hand, without economic or other incentives, authors may not prepare the very materials educators need. Both the United States Constitution and the Copyright Act recognize that there must be a proper balance between free use of creative works and incentive necessary to encourage authorship of those works.[3]

[1] See 17 U.S.C. §§ 1–5 (1964). For purposes of simplicity, the term author, as used in this essay, includes the copyright owner.

[2] HOUSE COMM. ON THE JUDICIARY, 88TH CONG., 2D SESS., COPYRIGHT LAW REVISION, PART 4, FURTHER DISCUSSIONS AND COMMENTS ON PRELIMINARY DRAFT FOR REVISED U.S. COPYRIGHT LAW 216, 218 (Comm. Print 1964). (Hereafter cited as COPYRIGHT LAW REVISION, PART 4.)

[3] U.S. CONST. art. 1, § 8, cl. 8, provides: "The Congress shall have the power . . . To Promote the Progress of Science and useful Arts, by securing for limited Times to Authors and Inventors the exclusive Right to their respective Writings and Discoveries."

The provisions of the Copyright Act discussed in this essay demonstrate that the act strives to balance the need for incentives for authors against the need for widespread availability of creative works.

Effect of the Copyright Act on Educators 135

The present Copyright Act, subject to a few minor amendments, was passed in 1909. Technological advancements and new patterns of relations between authors and users of copyrighted materials prompted Congress, in 1955, to authorize the Copyright Office to undertake a program of studies leading to a general revision of the Act.[4] H.R. 4347 [5] is the culmination of these studies as well as of long debate and the rejection of several proposals for revision.[6]

EDUCATORS USING COPYRIGHTED MATERIALS IN THE CLASSROOM

In addition to traditional teaching materials such as books, many classrooms are, or soon will be, provided with audiovisual devices such as slides, filmstrips, radios, television sets, projectors, phonograph records, and tape recorders. Copyright law may place severe limitations on the use of these materials for educational purposes. In the discussions leading to H.R. 4347 educators focused attention on three primary areas: photocopying, "public performances," and the doctrine of "fair use."

[4] See HOUSE COMM. ON THE JUDICIARY, 87TH CONG., 1ST SESS., COPYRIGHT LAW REVISION, REPORT OF THE REGISTER OF COPYRIGHTS ON THE GENERAL REVISION OF THE U.S. COPYRIGHT LAW (Comm. Print 1961). (Hereinafter cited as COPYRIGHT LAW REVISION, PART 1.)
[5] S. 1006, 89th Cong., 1st Sess. (1965).
[6] See, e.g., SUBCOMM. ON PATENTS, TRADEMARKS, AND COPYRIGHTS, SENATE COMM. ON THE JUDICIARY, 86TH CONG., 1ST & 2D SESS., COPYRIGHT LAW REVISION STUDIES (Comm. Prints 1960–61) (Hereafter cited as COPYRIGHT LAW REVISION STUDIES); COPYRIGHT LAW REVISION, PART 1; HOUSE COMM. ON THE JUDICIARY, 88TH CONG., 1ST SESS., COPYRIGHT LAW REVISION, PART 2, DISCUSSION AND COMMENTS ON REPORT OF THE REGISTER OF COPYRIGHTS ON THE GENERAL REVISION OF THE U.S. COPYRIGHT LAW" (Comm. Print 1963) (Hereinafter cited as COPYRIGHT LAW REVISION, PART 2); HOUSE COMM. ON THE JUDICIARY, 88TH CONG., 2D SESS. COPYRIGHT LAW REVISION, PART 3, PRELIMINARY DRAFT FOR REVISED U.S. COPYRIGHT LAW AND DISCUSSIONS AND COMMENTS ON THE DRAFT" (Comm. Print 1964) (Hereinafter cited as COPYRIGHT LAW REVISION, PART 3.); COPYRIGHT LAW REVISION, PART 4; HOUSE COMM. ON THE JUDICIARY, 89TH CONG., 1ST SESS., COPYRIGHT LAW REVISION, PART 5, 1964 REVISION BILL WITH DISCUSSIONS AND COMMENTS 33–139 (Comm. Print 1965) (Hereinafter cited as COPYRIGHT LAW REVISION, PART 5).

PHOTOCOPYING

The present Copyright Act provides that the author has the exclusive right "to print, reprint, publish, *copy,* and vend the copyrighted work."[7] Photocopying for educational purposes is, therefore, an infringement of the author's copyright unless it can be justified under the doctrine of fair use.[8]

Educators have pressed for statutory recognition of limited copying for instructional purposes.[9] They argue that the teacher has no time to obtain the requisite permission to copy and distribute an excerpt of a book, and, if he must obtain permission, he will not use the particular work. Consequently, the students suffer.[10] Because modern copying machines are very efficient and easy to handle, and becoming relatively inexpensive and even commonplace, it is feared that statutory recognition of a limited copying right will lead to widespread copying, amounting to confiscation of the author's product.[11] The opponents of a copying privilege for educational uses point out that copying machines are currently used by libraries and schools to copy articles from encyclopedias, works of history, source books, dictionaries, atlases, and many other books that are not read entirely but used a few pages at a time.[12] The result of this copying is that a school or even a school district need have only one copy of such books where formerly it had many.[13] This reduction in the publisher's market reduces the very incentive copyright legislation is designed to promote.

Objection to a provision on copying is not limited to books. Future technology is expected to make it possible for a school system to store all types of audiovisual materials in a centralized electronic device which will distribute these

---

[7] 17 U.S.C. § 1(a) (1964). (Emphasis added.)
[8] The doctrine of fair use and its effects on photocopying are discussed in text accompanying notes 38–48 *infra.*
[9] See, *e.g.,* COPYRIGHT LAW REVISION, PART 5, at 115.   [10] *Ibid.*
[11] See, *e.g.,* COPYRIGHT LAW REVISION, PART 4, at 273.   [12] *Ibid.*
[13] *Ibid.*

materials to the various classrooms on a demand basis.[14] Such devices would be of little value if they were to stilt the growth of creative audiovisual materials needed for effective use of these devices.

It has recently been reported that most of the nation's 30,000 school districts may soon be able to afford to purchase videotape recorders.[15] Such recorders are being hailed as a useful teaching device because they enable the teacher to "record important telecasts . . . and then play them back during school hours on classroom TV screens." [16] If the work being taped is protected under common-law or statutory copyright, this teaching exercise would appear to be an infringement under present law.

The consequence of the debates over photocopying is that H.R. 4347 is, like the present statute, silent on photocopying. Each case, therefore, will presumably be decided on the question of whether or not it is a fair use.[17]

As a practical matter, use of photocopying machines to make copies of copyrighted materials is widespread. All such copying certainly cannot be justified under the doctrine of "fair use." A recent report of a survey of the reproduction of copyrighted materials in the scientific and technical fields concluded that no significant damage occurs to copyright holders in scientific and technical fields although duplication of copyrighted materials is widespread and is growing rapidly.[18] The report cautioned, however, that new methods of copying and a decrease in the cost of copying could result in economic damage to the authors and publishers of scientific and technical books.[19]

---

[14] *Id.* at 292. [15] Time, Feb. 19, 1965, p. 92.
[16] *Ibid.* Followed to its logical conclusion, this would imply that school districts may make hundreds of copies of such a videotape for educational use. If the work being taped is copyrighted, it seems that such copying clearly would be an infringement of the author's rights.
[17] See text accompanying notes 38–48 *infra.*
[18] *Survey of Copyrighted Material Reproduction Practices in Scientific and Technical Fields,* 11 BULL. COPYRIGHT SOC'Y 69, 71 (1963).
[19] *Id.* at 73.

The major reasons an educator copies a work without obtaining prior permission are the need for immediate use of the materials and the bother involved in seeking such permission. The delay in obtaining permission seriously handicaps the efforts of the scientist and educator. It has been suggested that a school district, or an individual scholar or student, however poor, would willingly pay to copy short articles if there were some efficient way of doing this.[20] The problem, therefore, is to find a procedure by which the small copyright royalty could be paid within the time necessary to obtain the copy.[21]

This procedure might include some method to ascertain the number of copies made at the source, a central clearinghouse, and an organization to administer the program.[22] The American Textbook Publishers Institute has volunteered to cooperate with educators to help establish a licensing system to provide for immediate use of copyrighted materials with reasonable compensation for authors and publishers.[23] The Institute would extend the licensing system to photocopying, educational television, and all other uses of copyrighted materials for educational purposes.[24] Because of the broad scope of this proposal, and its antitrust ramifications, possibly some agency of the federal government, e.g., the Copyright Office, may be better equipped to administer the program. In any event, until such a procedure is perfected the doctrine of fair use will continue to serve as a stop-gap measure to deal with the need for rapid, unscheduled copying.

"PUBLIC PERFORMANCES"

The present Copyright Act provides that the author has the exclusive right "to perform or represent the copyrighted work publicly if it be a drama or, if it be . . . dramatic work."[25] *Any* public performance of a copyrighted dramatic work, including "dramatico-musical" works, is an infringement of

[20] COPYRIGHT LAW REVISION, PART 3, at 171.   [21] *Id.* at 172.
[22] *Id.* at 172–73.   [23] COPYRIGHT LAW REVISION, PART 5, at 123–24.
[24] *Ibid.*   [25] 17 U.S.C. § 1(d) (1964).

the copyright unless permission to perform is secured or the performance can be justified under the doctrine of fair use.

With respect to nondramatic literary and musical works, the author's exclusive rights are limited to performing them *"publicly for profit."* [26] The "for profit" limitation on the author's exclusive rights enables schools to perform (both in classroom and through educational broadcasting) nondramatic copyrighted historical, poetical, literary, musical, and other materials.[27]

Three reasons are given to support the distinction between dramatic and nondramatic works. First, the main source of revenue from a dramatic work is usually public performance whereas revenue from nondramatic works is often available from the sale of copies and sound recordings.[28] Generally, "the audience at a nonprofit performance of a dramatic work is less likely to pay to attend another performance than is the case with nondramatic works." [29] And finally, as a practical matter, dramatic works are not as readily or as frequently performed for charitable and educational purposes as are nondramatic works.[30]

Opponents of the "for profit" limitation have flatly denied the validity of all three arguments for the distinction. They argue that the United States should adopt the philosophy of "most civilized countries" and give composers and poets the same rights as playwrights or motion picture producers.[31]

H.R. 4347 would abolish the "for profit" limitation and, in its place, introduce several specific exemptions to the author's exclusive right to perform his work.[32] This approach, in addition to being in line with a number of foreign copyright laws,[33] lends itself to precise specification, by statute, of the performances for which the public interest is deemed

[26] 17 U.S.C. § 1(e) (1964). (Emphasis added.)
[27] See, *e.g.*, COPYRIGHT LAW REVISION, PART 5, at 115.
[28] COPYRIGHT LAW REVISION, PART 1, at 28.   [29] *Ibid.*
[30] *Ibid.*   [31] See COPYRIGHT LAW REVISION, PART 2, at 283.
[32] S. 1006, H.R. 4347, 89th Cong., 1st Sess. § 109 (1965).
[33] See Varmer, *Study No. 16: Limitations on Performing Rights*, in COPYRIGHT LAW REVISION STUDIES, *supra* note 6, at 112 (1960).

to warrant an exception. The price H.R. 4347 pays for this approach is that, unlike the "for profit" limitation, it is neither flexible nor adaptable to changing circumstances.

From the standpoint of education, the most important provisions of H.R. 4347 are the exceptions to the author's exclusive right to perform his work. The bill provides that "performance or exhibition of a work by instructors or pupils in the course of face-to-face teaching activities in a classroom or similar place normally devoted to instruction" [34] is not an infringement of copyright. This, in effect, is equivalent to the present Act's "publicly for profit" limitation for all face-to-face performances for instructional purposes.

H.R. 4347 also provides a limited exemption for performances given for educational purposes other than instruction. The bill provides that "performance of a nondramatic literary or musical work, otherwise than in a transmission to the public, without any purpose of direct or indirect commercial advantage and without payment of any fee or other compensation for the performance to any of its performers, promoters, or organizers" [35] is not an infringement of copyright if either of two conditions is met. First, such a performance is exempt if "there is no direct or indirect admission charge." [36] Second, if there is an admission charge the performance still may be exempt if the proceeds "are used exclusively for educational, religious, or charitable purposes and not for private financial gain." [37] If an organization wishes to rely on this provision, it should beware of the technical limitations. For example, if every member of an orchestra except the harpist were donating his services, the exemption presumably would not apply. Furthermore, this exemption, like the present Act, applies only to nondramatic literary or musical works.

[34] S. 1006, H.R. 4347, 89th Cong., 1st Sess. § 109(1) (1965).
[35] S. 1006, H.R. 4347, 89th Cong., 1st Sess. § 109(4) (1965).
[36] *Ibid.*   [37] *Ibid.*

FAIR USE

The Copyright Act is silent on the topic of fair use. Nevertheless the doctrine has been judicially established as a limitation on the author's exclusive rights. Fair use eludes precise definition. In broad terms it means that a reasonable portion of a copyrighted work may be reproduced without permission when the purpose is not competitive with the author's market for his work.[38] For example, under this doctrine, teachers and students are allowed to reproduce a small part of a copyrighted work for the purpose of illustrating a lesson.[39]

Since the limitations on fair use are not clearly defined, each case must be decided on an *ad hoc* basis. Educators have argued that since the limits of fair use remain controversial even among sophisticated lawyers, a classroom teacher cannot be expected to know when the doctrine is applicable.[40] On the other hand, there are apparently no cases where a teacher has been sued for overstepping fair use.[41]

Furthermore, since "fair use" is not a technical doctrine, but rather one of reasonableness with common-sense standards, it would seem that some educational organization, e.g., the National Education Association, could disseminate information concerning "fair use" to educators. If educators had some basic knowledge of "fair use," much of their uncertainty would dissipate. The Copyright Office has stated that under the doctrine of "fair use" educators are "free to publish short extracts or quotations from copyrighted works, without permission of the copyrighted owner, for the purpose of illustration or comment." [42]

---

[38] COPYRIGHT LAW REVISION, PART 1, at 24.
[39] *Ibid.* Because of the practical limitations of hand-copying, scholars have been allowed to copy by hand from copyrighted works for purposes of their own private research and study. *Id.* at 25.
[40] See, *e.g.*, COPYRIGHT LAW REVISION, PART 5, at 97.
[41] *Id.* at 102. (Opinion expressed by Mr. Schulman before the panel.)
[42] United States Copyright Office *Circular No. 20* (June 1962): "In the broadest terms, the doctrine of 'fair use' means that copyrighted material may

One authority has noted that there are no decisions dealing with the question of a person making photocopies for his own use.[43] This would indicate that such copying is either justified as a fair use or tolerated because of its lack of economic importance. This is not to say that mass copying with modern machines will be sanctioned.[44] For instance, when copying reaches the point where it diminishes the volume of sales, publishers can be expected to resist the practice and argue that it oversteps fair use.[45]

H.R. 4347 states that notwithstanding the exclusive rights of an author, "the fair use of a copyrighted work is not an infringement of copyright." [46] This is not intended to change the present law on fair use but merely to give statutory recognition to the firmly established judicial doctrine. There was some support for the position that H.R. 4347 should carry forward the provision in a prior draft [47] which specified some

be used to a limited extent, without obtaining permission, in some circumstances where the use is reasonable and not harmful to the copyright owner's rights. For example, this is the doctrine under which scholars and critics have been held free to publish short extracts or quotations from copyrighted works, without the permission of the copyright owner, for the purpose of illustration or comment."

[43] Varmer, *supra* note 33, at 50.

[44] A prior draft of the proposed revision contained a provision allowing libraries to duplicate a copyrighted work and supply a single copy upon request, providing: (1) the copy was limited to one article or other contribution to a copyrighted collection; (2) if the copy was an entire work, or more than a relatively small part of it, the library made a reasonable investigation to determine that a copy of the copyrighted work could not readily be obtained from trade sources; and (3) the library attached a warning that the work appeared to be copyrighted.

[45] Varmer, *supra* note 33, at 61.

[46] S. 1006, H.R. 4347, 89th Cong., 1st Sess. § 107 (1965).

[47] COPYRIGHT LAW REVISION, PART 1, at 6: "§ 6. Limitations on Exclusive Rights: Fair Use. All of the exclusive rights specified in section 5 shall be limited by the privilege of making fair use of a copyrighted work, for determining whether, under the circumstances in any particular case, the use of a copyrighted work constitutes fair use rather than an infringement of copyright, the following factors, among others, shall be considered: (a) the purpose and character of the use, (b) the nature of the copyrighted work, (c) the amount and substantiality of the material used in relation to the copyrighted work as a whole, and (d) the effect of the use upon the potential value of the

Effect of the Copyright Act on Educators 143

general criteria for the application of "fair use." [48] A narrow definition of the doctrine of "fair use" would seem to place limitations on the courts in the future when they will be forced to deal with such unforeseen circumstances as special technological advancements. The advantage of having no definition is that the court is free to evaluate the use in terms of contemporary standards. Moreover, in the area of public performances, the specific exemptions provided by H.R. 4347 would seem to minimize the effect of lack of preciseness of the fair use doctrine.

EDUCATORS USING COPYRIGHTED MATERIALS OVER BROADCASTING MEDIA

The present Copyright Act is silent on the subject of educational broadcasting. Both open-circuit television and radio are considered public performances so that, once again, the "for profit" limitation becomes decisive.[49] Also, in some instances, depending upon the nature and circumstances of the broadcast, closed-circuit television and radio transmissions may be public performances. Nondramatic literary and musical materials may be used in nonprofit educational broadcasts, whereas copyrighted dramatic works cannot be used without prior permission.

There has been a great deal of opposition to free use of copyrighted materials in educational radio and television.[50] The basic argument is that all modern teaching tools are useful only because they utilize "the funds, talents, and time of authors and publishers." [51] Publishers claim that the free use of copyrighted materials in nonprofit educational broadcasts

---

copyrighted work." See also Mr. Justice Story's opinion in Folsom v. Marsh, 9 Fed. Cas. 342, 348 (No. 4901) (C.C.D. Mass. 1841).
[48] See, *e.g.*, COPYRIGHT LAW REVISION, PART 5, at 97.
[49] See COPYRIGHT LAW REVISION, PART 1, at 30.
[50] See authorities cited note 6, *supra*.
[51] See COPYRIGHT LAW REVISION, PART 3, at 343.

reduces profits and, consequently, the incentive to create new material. The magnitude of this problem is increasing with the growth of educational television. A textbook used on an educational television program may reach hundreds of thousands of students.[52] A poem, instead of being published and sold, may be read to many thousands of students over television or radio.[53] Authors and publishers are as much entitled to compensation for this educational use of their copyrighted work as they are when the educational use is through the medium of print.[54]

The economic aspect is undoubtedly the most significant force behind the opposition to the "for profit" limitation. All agree that education must flourish, but some argue that it should pay its own way. Colleges pay their way; textbooks bear royalty; there is no reason why educational television should not "be fit into the capitalistic system as we understand it in this country." [55]

Proponents of the "for profit" limitation argue that "educational television is only one part of the educational process." Education does not change because it is transmitted to the student by a camera rather than by a printed page.[56] The purpose being to assist the educational process, in some cases educational broadcasting is the only effective way to reach the students.[57] The television camera, like the printed book, is only the means; the goal is education.[58]

Even if some limitations were imposed on open-circuit broadcasting, educators consider it to be illogical to place limitations on closed-circuit television. Why grant privileges

---

[52] See COPYRIGHT LAW REVISION, PART 2, at 228.
[53] *Ibid.*   [54] *Ibid.*   [55] COPYRIGHT LAW REVISION, PART 3, at 155.
[56] See COPYRIGHT LAW REVISION, PART 3, at 144; COPYRIGHT LAW REVISION, PART 5, at 94–95.
[57] Proponents of free use of copyrighted materials over educational television would have us consider invalids unable to leave their homes, adults unable to attend regularly scheduled classes at a school, and the extremely poor who are unable to afford formal classroom education.
[58] See COPYRIGHT LAW REVISION, PART 5, at 112.

Effect of the Copyright Act on Educators 145

to the teacher who addresses the students face-to-face in the classroom or auditorium, and deny them to the teacher who talks to the students over closed-circuit radio or television? [59]

It is generally assumed, by both sides, that use of copyrighted materials in educational radio or television has a detrimental effect on the sales of these materials. No evidence has been presented to verify this assumption. It can be argued that television takes the place of the teacher and not of the materials he uses. Since open-circuit television reaches many persons who would not otherwise be exposed to these materials, sales may even be increased with television exposure. When an instructor reads a long passage from a book, he is, in substance, advertising that book. Furthermore, there may be instances involving textbooks where students cannot prepare their assignments without purchasing a copy of the text. In short, there appears to be a need for statistical evidence as to the effect of educational television on the sales or sales potential of the materials used.

The exemptions from the author's exclusive rights provided in H.R. 4347 distinguish between closed-circuit and open-circuit television.[60] When a performance of a nondramatic literary or musical work over closed-circuit television is "made primarily for reception in classrooms or similar places normally devoted to instruction and is a regular part of the systematic instructional activities of a non profit educational institution," it is not an infringement of copyright.[61] Similarly an exhibition of a work over closed-circuit educational television is not an infringement of copyright.[62] These provisions essentially preserve the "for profit" limitation for closed-circuit educational television.

H.R. 4347 also has an exemption for nonprofit open-circuit broadcasting. It provides that "the further transmitting to the

---
[59] See COPYRIGHT LAW REVISION, PART 3, at 150.
[60] *Compare* S. 1006, H.R. 4347, 89th Cong., 1st Sess. § 109(2) (1965), *with* § 109(5) of the same bill.
[61] S. 1006, H.R. 4347, 89th Cong., 1st Sess. § 109(2) (1965).   [62] *Ibid.*

public" of a performance or exhibition that is valid under either the closed-circuit exemption or the face-to-face exemptions discussed above is not an infringement of copyright if "the further transmission is made without altering or adding to the content of the original transmission, without any purpose of direct or indirect commercial advantage, and without charge to the recipients of the further transmissions. . . ."[63] Under what circumstances, then, can a copyrighted nondramatic literary or musical work be used over open-circuit educational television? First, exempted closed-circuit and classroom performances or exhibitions can be transmitted to the public. Second, a performance can, without compensation to any of the "performers, promoters, or organizers," be transmitted to the public where there is no admission charge to the performance or, if there is a charge, where the proceeds are used "exclusively for educational, religious, or charitable purposes and not for private financial gain."[64] In both of these situations the broadcast itself must be "nonprofit" and the "without altering or adding" requirement must be met.[65]

How can a performance or exhibition in an educational television studio for *direct* transmission to the public employ copyrighted works? First, there can be a simulated classroom exercise, i.e., teacher and students in a face-to-face confrontation. Second, the nonprofit performance or exhibition can be directly given so long as the "performers, promoters, or organizers" are not compensated.[66] This second situation raises several interesting questions. Under these circumstances are the teachers "performers"? Are the employees of the educational television stations "promoters" or "organizers"? If so, and if they are receiving compensation, copyrighted mate-

---

[63] S. 1006, H.R. 4347, 89th Cong., 1st Sess. § 109(5) (1965).
[64] S. 1006, H.R. 4347, 89th Cong., 1st Sess. § 109(4) (1965). For a discussion of face-to-face and other performances sanctioned by the bill, see text accompanying notes 30–35 *supra*.
[65] See text accompanying note 58 *supra*.
[66] See text accompanying notes 33–35 *supra*.

Effect of the Copyright Act on Educators 147

rials cannot be used. The statute is not clear on these and related questions, but seems rather to take the approach that such questions are better left to the courts.

One further provision of H.R. 4347 is relevant to educational broadcasting. An "organization lawfully entitled to transmit a performance or exhibition of a copyrighted work to the public" may make "no more than one copy or phonorecord of the work solely for purposes of the organization's own lawful transmissions or for archival preservation." [67] In any event, the copy cannot be "used for transmission after six months from the date it was first made." [68] The reason for the latter requirement is not readily apparent. Since the same performance may be given live in seven months, there is little reason to prohibit the tape from being shown. Reading the provision as a whole, it seems to recognize educational television as an "organization lawfully entitled" to broadcast to the public. This might be used to refute the argument that employees of the educational television station are promoters or organizers. The statute, however, is not explicit on this point.

EDUCATORS AS AUTHORS OF COPYRIGHTED MATERIALS

"Publish or perish" is a well-known phrase in educational circles. From the point of view of copyright law, this means that many educators who use copyrighted works are also authors seeking copyright protection for their efforts as authors. Under the present Act they may copyright books, composite works, lectures, addresses, tests, periodicals, dramatic or dramatico-musical compositions, musical compositions, maps, works of art, models or designs for works of art, reproductions of a work of art, drawings or plastic works of a scientific or technical character, photographs, prints and pictorial illustrations, motion pictures and other visually per-

[67] S. 1006, H.R. 4347, 89th Cong., 1st Sess. § 110 (1965).   [68] *Ibid.*

ceivable works.[69] There is no judicial decision on the question of whether a videotape, as distinguished from a film, is copyrightable. Phonograph records and other sound recordings may not be copyrighted.[70] Although the written expression of an idea is copyrightable, the idea itself cannot be copyrighted.[71]

Under the present Act the author is granted the exclusive right: (1) to print, publish, and sell his work; (2) to make other versions if it is a literary, dramatic, or musical work; (3) to complete, execute, and finish it if it is a model or design for a work of art; (4) to perform nondramatic literary and musical works in public and for profit; (5) to perform dramatic works in public; and (6) to reproduce a literary, dramatic, or musical work in a transcription or recording.[72] These rights are secured for twenty-eight years with a renewal provision for an additional twenty-eight years.[73]

[69] 17 U.S.C. § 5 (1964).   [70] 37 C.F.R. § 202.8(b) (1960).

[71] 37 C.F.R. 202.1(b) (1960). For example, a scientist can copyright a report describing an experiment but, as far as copyright law is concerned, anyone is free to perform the experiment and report the findings as his own. There is a growing body of law, however, which is affording some protection to "ideas" on theories such as breach of trust, breach of contract, and unfair competition; see NIMMER, COPYRIGHT 714–60 (1963); RINGER & GITLIN, COPYRIGHTS 14 (1963).

[72] 17 U.S.C. § 1 (1964).

[73] 17 U.S.C. § 24 (1964). The present act requires that certain types of works be manufactured in the United States in order to secure a full-term copyright; see 17 U.S.C. § 16 (1964). "No other country requires domestic manufacture as a condition of copyright protection." COPYRIGHT LAW REVISION, PART 1, at 120. Many foreign works, however, may be manufactured outside the United States and still secure United States copyright protection. In 1961 the Register of Copyrights recommended that the "requirement of manufacture in the United States as a condition of copyright . . . should be eliminated." *Id.* at 124. Proponents of the manufacturing clause fear that its abolition would cause a "surge of 'runaway foreign printing production.'" See COPYRIGHT LAW REVISION, PART 2, at 201. Educators, on the other hand, have argued that the "manufacturing clause" has no place in the Copyright Act, which was designed to protect authors, not to protect the printing trades and unions. COPYRIGHT LAW REVISION, PART 4, at 332. Furthermore, many authors lose their copyright protection under this provision when a publisher, with or without the author's knowledge, has the work printed outside of the United States. *Ibid.* Unfortunately, H.R. 4347 has a manufacturing clause and its accompanying inequities. S. 1006, H.R. 4347, 89th Cong., 1st Sess. § 601 (1965).

Effect of the Copyright Act on Educators 149

Once the author has secured statutory copyright protection he still must face the possible widespread use of his work because of "fair use" and the rather limited statutory enumeration of his exclusive rights under the current Act. Often the primary users of a scholastic writing are educators. In this situation, the privileges granted to educators as users of copyrighted materials may effectively deny the educator-author copyright protection. However, many modern teaching tools, e.g., filmstrips, slides, motion pictures, etc., are prepared by professional organizations on a regular basis. When these organizations use copyrighted works to prepare audiovisual materials for sale or leasing they are required to obtain the author's permission and pay the stipulated royalty unless, because the copying is minimal, such use can be justified as "fair use." Thus, authors receive some compensation for this type of organized widespread educational use of their copyrighted works.

H.R. 4347, if passed, would broaden the scope of material which can be copyrighted; for example, videotape and sound recordings would become copyrightable.[74] The duration of the copyrighted period would be extended to the "life of the author and 50 years after his death," [75] or, where no natural person is identified as the author, "the copyright endures for a term of 75 years from the year of its first publication. . . ." [76] Under H.R. 4347, the exclusive rights vary with the types of materials.[77] In general, those rights afforded under the present Act are preserved and, in some instances, expanded. For some of the newly copyrightable items, such as sound recordings, the exclusive rights are somewhat narrower than for other works.[78] The bill gives statutory recognition to the common-law doctrine of "fair use" and, unlike the

---
[74] See S. 1006, H.R. 4347, 89th Cong., 1st Sess. §§ 101–02 (1965).
[75] S. 1006, H.R. 4347, 89th Cong., 1st Sess. § 302(a) (1965).
[76] S. 1006, H.R. 4347, 89th Cong., 1st Sess. § 302(c) (1965).
[77] See S. 1006, H.R. 4347, 89th Cong., 1st Sess. §§ 106–14 (1965).
[78] See, e.g., S. 1006, H.R. 4347, 89th Cong., 1st Sess. § 112 (1965).

present Act, provides for a number of specific exemptions from the author's exclusive rights.

From the standpoint of educators as authors, H.R. 4347 intensifies the basic problem presented by the current Act, i.e., by exempting specified educational uses of copyrighted materials, H.R. 4347, as a practical matter, deprives the educator-author of effective copyright protection.

CONCLUSION

The Copyright Act does not present a significant barrier to educators intending to use copyrighted materials for educational purposes. Because the Act is over fifty years old, however, it does not specifically address itself to many of the problems raised by modern educational techniques. The proposed general revision to the Act, H.R. 4347, attempts to clarify the rights of educators as users of copyrighted materials. Basically, it first grants the author somewhat broader copyright protection, and then provides a number of specific exemptions for educational uses,[79] in addition to expressly preserving the doctrine of "fair use."

Some problem areas remain unresolved under both the present Act and H.R. 4347. The fundamental criticism of both statutes is that they do not specifically consider the interests of the author (often an educator) who creates works solely for educational purposes. Since there are a great many more educators who use copyrighted works than there are educators who are authors, the educational associations, e.g., the National Education Association, seem to be quite vociferous in advocating the viewpoint of the former whereas they

---

[79] It might be argued that specific provisions relating to the duration period could be used to allow educators broader privileges than other users. For instance, the term of protection for the exclusive right to copy could be reduced for educational uses to 5 or 10 years after the last printing, after which time educators would be allowed to make photocopies.

Effect of the Copyright Act on Educators 151

seem to minimize the interests of the educator-author.[80] Most other authors have a wide market from which to derive economic benefit, e.g., through magazines, motion pictures, sound recordings, commercial radio and television, etc., and hence they can afford to grant broad exemptions for educational uses. On the other hand, the author writing solely for educators may suffer such severe economic detriment from the broad exemptions granted to education that his incentive to create will be reduced. If this happens, education, and consequently society as a whole, will suffer. There are, however, practical problems in drafting a provision to protect the author who writes principally for educational users. What works would qualify as being written "solely" or "principally" for education? If such authors were given rights not subject to the educational exemptions, would this, in effect, deprive education of the prime value of the present exemptions?

Neither the present Act nor H.R. 4347 allows copying of a copyrighted work without prior permission. Yet, copying for educational purposes is widespread and all indications point to an increase in this practice as photocopying becomes less and less expensive. It has been suggested that educator-users are willing to compensate the author but that they cannot afford the bother or delay in seeking permission.[81] What is needed is a procedure whereby educator-users could, probably through their school districts, enjoy licenses to copy from pools of copyrighted materials under prescribed circumstances, subject to reasonable compensation to the respective authors.[82]

H.R. 4347 contains special provisions for educational broadcasting, whereas under the present Act it is subject to the same treatment as classroom education. The opposition to free use of copyrighted materials in educational television

---

[80] See, e.g., COPYRIGHT LAW REVISION, PART 4, at 217–28; COPYRIGHT LAW REVISION, PART 5, at 108–19.
[81] COPYRIGHT LAW REVISION, PART 3, at 171.   [82] Id. at 171–72.

is strong, and it is increasing with the expansion of educational television. H.R. 4347 adopts the position that, under certain circumstances, copyrighted materials can be used in television broadcasts to the public. The limitations are not entirely clear and apparently have been left to the courts for clarification.

In the area of educational television, as with photocopying, it has been suggested that a procedure to allow for immediate use of copyrighted materials with reasonable compensation to the author would be desirable.[83] Such procedures may possibly be used as a means of providing incentives for authors who write exclusively for educational users.

[83] COPYRIGHT LAW REVISION, PART 5, at 123–24.

HONORABLE MENTION, 1965

Is CATV Infringing Proprietary Rights in Television Broadcasts?

By DANIEL E. NESTER
SETON HALL UNIVERSITY SCHOOL OF LAW

THE FUTURE IMPORTANCE of defining legally protectable proprietary interests in broadcast television programs was recognized relatively early in the development of the television industry.[1] In addition to copyright interests, it was suggested that other valuable interests might well be present in television broadcasts of a class appropriate for legal protection.[2] Subsequently, a further opinion was expressed to the effect that the rebroadcast of television programs did not violate any proprietary rights.[3] During the past few years, the rapid growth of a new segment of the television industry has focused attention on legal issues surrounding the protectable interests of television networks and broadcasts in the television programs which they broadcast.[4] This new segment of the television industry is known as CATV (Community Antenna Television). In the course of arguing against a motion for a change in venue in a recent case,[5] the following statement was made:

[1] See Solinger, *Unauthorized Uses of TV Broadcasts*, 48 COLUM. L. REV. 848 (1948).

[2] *Id.* at 849.

[3] "As applied to programs already broadcast on standard television transmitters . . . it would seem that, legal technicalities aside, there should be no basic objection to such action." Kupferman, *Rights in New Media*, 19 LAW & CONTEMP. PROB. 180 (1954).

[4] Time, November 13, 1964, p. 110.

[5] United Artists Associated, Inc. v. NWL Corp., 198 F. Supp. 953 (S.D.N.Y. 1961).

The action and defenses herein do not concern localized controversies, but raise issues of nationwide interest and impact on the motion picture and television industries.[6]

This case is concerned with allegations of copyright infringement, unfair competition and unfair trade practices made with reference to the operations of a local CATV system.

It is the purpose of this paper briefly to explore some of the legal issues which have arisen as a result of CATV system operations. These issues pertain to the existence of certain proprietary interests in television broadcasts which are claimed by various parts of the television industry and to the availability of remedies for the protection of those interests if they do exist.

WHAT IS COMMUNITY ANTENNA TELEVISION (CATV)?

Generally speaking, CATV systems are installed in fringe areas of television broadcast reception to provide the individual television viewer with better program reception and with a wider range of choice in television programs than he could otherwise have without prohibitory expense.[7] A strategically located and highly efficient antenna system is installed by the CATV system to receive television broadcast signals from transmitting stations beyond the normal reception range of the usual home television antenna. The broadcast signals thus received are then transmitted over privately owned communication facilities, which often include microwave links, directly to television receivers in individual homes or places of business. An initial connection charge is made when a television receiver is first connected to the CATV system and a periodic service charge is made thereafter.

---

[6] *Id.* at 956.

[7] Time, *supra* note 4; see generally, Pollock, *Community Television and the Telephone Company*, Telephone Engineer and Management, Nov. 15, 1964; see also, Blain, *Television, A New Horizon in Communications, Part I*, Telephony, Jan. 30, 1965, at p. 22.

Is CATV Infringing Proprietary Rights? 155

Although CATV systems are most prevalent in rural and suburban areas where ordinary television broadcast reception is affected adversely by natural topographical difficulties or extreme remoteness from the transmitting stations, CATV systems are also used by hotels and multiple dwellings in urban areas to eliminate the expense and the unsightly appearance of separate antenna installations for each room or apartment.[8] In 1961, approximately 700 communities in 40 different states were served by CATV systems.[9] Presently, there are approximately 1,400 CATV systems in operation serving well over one million viewers.[10] Annual revenue is now estimated to be $750,000,000.[11]

IMPACT OF CATV ON THE TELEVISION INDUSTRY

Although it is manifestly clear that CATV is now firmly established as a link in the chain of program transmission from the television broadcaster to the individual television receiver,[12] the complete legal posture of CATV operations within the television industry has yet to be fully determined.[13] Consider the operation of a local retail merchant who sells commercial goods directly to the consumer public. The merchant purchases his stock in trade either directly from a manufacturer or by way of a wholesale distributor in his area. The position of a CATV system in the television industry is somewhat analogous to the retail merchant if a television network is considered as a manufacturer of television programs and if a television broadcasting station is considered

---
[8] *Ibid.*
[9] See Blain, *Television, A New Horizon in Communications, Part II*, Telephony, Feb. 6, 1965, at 17; see also Intermountain Broadcasting Corp. v. Idaho Microwave, Inc., 196 F. Supp. 315, 317 (D. Idaho 1961).
[10] See Pollock, *supra* note 7.
[11] See Blain, *supra* note 9; see also Time, *supra* note 4.
[12] See generally, Blain, *Television, A New Horizon in Communications, Parts I, II and III*, Telephony, Jan. 30, 1965, Feb. 6, 1965 and Feb. 13, 1965.
[13] See United Artists Associated, Inc. v. NWL Corp., *supra* note 5, which is still pending decision on the merits.

as a local distributor. However, the analogy fails when the cost of the commercial product to a retail merchant is compared with the cost of television programs to a CATV system. The usual CATV system proprietor pays nothing for the television programs he receives and distributes for profit to his consumer public.[14] This situation may be particularly obnoxious to a local television station which has secured a license for exclusive broadcast of certain programs within its community, only to find a CATV system distributing the same programs in that community with different sponsors even before the programs are broadcast by the television station.

A recent series of cases [15] arose from a single fact situation which is particularly illustrative of the impact of CATV on the television industry as a whole. Twin Falls, Idaho, which is topographically isolated from television broadcasts originated by stations in Boise, Idaho and Salt Lake City, Utah, is served by a single local television station. The Twin Falls station contracted with the three major nationwide television networks for exclusive rights to the first run of network programs in the Twin Falls community. Since the common carrier facilities, by means of which network television programs are made available to the stations in Boise and Salt Lake City, are not accessible to the Twin Falls television station, the Twin Falls station contracted with the three network affiliated television stations in Salt Lake City for the right to rebroadcast their programs. A large antenna was erected to receive the television broadcasts from the Salt Lake City stations. Only one television program at a time could be rebroadcast "live" by the Twin Falls station. However, the received programs which were not immediately

---

[14] "Defendants deny any obligation on their part to obtain the consent of, or to account to, the plaintiffs for picking up and so distributing plaintiffs' broadcasts in this manner." Intermountain Broadcasting Corp. v. Idaho Microwave, Inc., 196 F. Supp. 315, 319 (D. Idaho 1961).

[15] Intermountain Broadcasting Corp. v. Idaho Microwave, Inc., *supra* note 14; Cable Vision, Inc. v. KUTV, Inc., 211 F. Supp. 47 (D. Idaho 1962), *vacated*, 335 F.2d 348 (9th Cir. 1964), *cert. denied*, 379 U.S. 989 (1965).

Is CATV Infringing Proprietary Rights? 157

rebroadcast were taped by the Twin Falls station for rebroadcast at a later time. A CATV system was then installed in Twin Falls which received and distributed network programs broadcast by the network affiliated stations in Boise. These programs were distributed in direct competition with those rebroadcast "live" by the Twin Falls station, and often were made available to the individual viewer before the taped programs were rebroadcast by the Twin Falls station.

The impact on the local television station in situations such as that described above is manifold. The very existence of a local station is threatened due to the depreciation in the value of advertising time on locally broadcast programs.[16] The practical value of exclusive contract agreements between television networks and local television stations becomes nebulous.[17] Common law and statutory copyright infringement by CATV system operations and those of its customers becomes an issue.[18]

REACTION TO CATV BY GOVERNMENTAL AGENCIES

The rapid increase in the number of CATV operations has led to recent predictions concerning the inevitability of governmental control of CATV.[19] Under the present law,[20] the

---

[16] "It is a matter of judicial notice, amply shown by the record here, that under our present national policy of free radio and television reception through a system of commercially competitive broadcasting stations, a television broadcast station, being unable to charge the public for reception of its programs, must necessarily maintain itself through revenues from sponsors willing to buy time intervals allowed before, during and after programs for commercial advertising purposes. The ability of a broadcasting station to attract and maintain such commercial advertising revenue depends upon the extent to which it can assure sponsors that its programs, and the spotted commercials presented therewith, are being viewed by the television public." Cable Vision, Inc. v. KUTV, Inc., 211 F. Supp. 47, 52 (D. Idaho 1962).

[17] See Intermountain Broadcasting Corp. v. Idaho Microwave, Inc., *supra* note 14, at 321.

[18] *Id.* at 320.

[19] Time, *supra* note 4; see also Telephone Engineer and Management, Jan. 15, 1965, p. 86, wherein possible regulation of CATV by the F.C.C. is mentioned.

[20] Federal Communications Act, 48 Stat. 1064, 47 U.S.C. §§ 151-744 (1964).

Federal Communications Commission disclaims any power to control CATV in its reception and distribution of broadcast television programs [21] since such activities do not constitute a "rebroadcast" within the meaning of the appropriate statute.[22] The only present vestige of Federal control is the licensing power of the Federal Communications Commission for the microwave systems,[23] which are often included in the private distribution facilities of CATV systems. The Federal Communications Commission has recently requested that its jurisdiction be extended to include CATV systems,[24] although in the past Congress has explicitly refused to do so.[25] The concern of the Federal Communications Commission regarding the situation as it presently exists is illustrated by its refusal, in one case, to grant a microwave system license to a CATV system until it was shown that the CATV system would not competitively duplicate programs broadcast by the local television broadcasting station.[26] In view of the demonstrated past reluctance of Congress to extend the jurisdiction of the Federal Commications Commission to this area, it seems doubtful at best that authority for direct Federal control over locally franchised CATV systems will be legislated in the immediate future.*

Another area of possible indirect governmental control over

[21] See Report and Order in Docket No. 12443, *Inquiry Into the Impact of Community Antenna Systems, TV Translations, TV "Satellite" Stations and TV "Repeaters" on the Orderly Development of Broadcasting*, 18 PIKE & FISCHER, RADIO REGULATION, 1573, 1600–01, ¶¶ 62–65 (1959).

[22] Broadcasting is "the dissemination of radio communications intended to be received by the public, directly or by the intermediary of relay stations." 48 Stat. 1064, 47 U.S.C. § 153(o). (1964).

[23] 47 U.S.C. §§ 201–23. (1964).

[24] F.C.C. Public Notice B, February 23, 1962.

[25] See SENATE COMM. ON INTERSTATE AND FOREIGN COMMERCE, 86TH CONG., 1ST SESS., REPORT NO. 923, p. 11 (Comm. Print 1959).

[26] Cable Vision, Inc. v. KUTV, Inc., 211 F. Supp. 47, 55 (D. Idaho 1962), citing, F.C.C., Carter Mountain Transmission, Docket No. 12931, Feb. 16, 1962.

* Editor's Note: On February 15, 1966, FCC Chairman E. William Henry announced the Commission's intention to assert jurisdiction over all CATV operations. For the seven points of regulation, and reaction of industry, Congress and the public, see Broadcasting Magazine, Feb. 21, 1966, pp. 25, 30.

Is CATV Infringing Proprietary Rights? 159

CATV, which has not presently been explored to any extent, is the regulatory power of a state over the operations of its public utilities. Often, the facilities of a local public utility are utilized by a CATV system either to transmit the actual television program signals or to support privately owned cables over which the signals are transmitted.[27] As evidenced in the recent setback to CATV's sister industry of pay television in California,[28] enforced withdrawal of public utility facilities from a CATV system might very well make the enterprise economically unsound.

REACTION TO CATV BY THE TELEVISION INDUSTRY

Reaction by the television industry to the impact of CATV has taken several courses. Some television networks and stations, recognizing the growth potential in CATV, have themselves acquired interests in CATV systems.[29] Other members of the industry have refused to acknowledge CATV's right of free access to broadcast television programs and have sought, in the courts, to define and protect the broadcaster's alleged proprietary interests in television programs.[30] Among the several property rights in television programs claimed by television broadcasters and other affected parties are: rights arising from common law copyright,[31] rights arising from exclusive contracts,[32] rights arising from nonexclusive con-

[27] Pollock, *Community Television and the Telephone Company*, Telephone Engineer and Management, Nov. 15, 1964.
[28] Time, *op. cit. supra* note 4, p. 72.
[29] See generally, Blain, *supra* note 12.
[30] *E.g.*, Z Bar Net v. Helena Television, Inc., 125 U.S.P.Q. 595 (Mont. Dist. Ct. 1960); United Artists Associated, Inc. v. NWL Corp., 198 F. Supp. 953 (S.D.N.Y. 1961); Intermountain Broadcasting Corp. v. Idaho Microwave, Inc., 196 F. Supp. 315 (D. Idaho 1961); Cable Vision, Inc. v. KUTV, Inc., 211 F. Supp. 47 (D. Idaho 1962), *vacated*, 335 F.2d 348 (9th Cir. 1964), *cert. denied*, 379 U.S. 989 (1965).
[31] See Z Bar Net v. Helena Television, Inc., *supra* note 30, concerning an action for infringement of common law copyright against a CATV system which resulted in a holding that the television broadcaster has no common law copyright interests in his broadcasts.
[32] See Cable Vision, Inc. v. KUTV, Inc., *supra* note 30, wherein an exclusive

tracts,[33] rights protected under the Federal Communications Act,[34] rights arising from unfair competition [35] and rights arising from statutory copyright.[36] All of these alleged proprietary interests, save the last, have been repudiated by the courts,[37] and the last, namely statutory copyright interests, have yet to be judicially determined in a definitive manner.[38]

STATUTORY COPYRIGHT—THE ONLY PROTECTABLE INTEREST?

One of the earlier efforts by a television broadcaster to curtail nonlicensed activities of a CATV system concerned an action for common law copyright infringement brought in 1960 by the owner of two television broadcasting stations against a competing CATV system.[39] A third television station was rebroadcasting, with appropriate consent, the television programs originated from one of the plaintiff's two stations. The rebroadcast programs were picked up and distributed by the CATV system in the same community covered by the other of the plaintiff's two stations. The state court indicated that the original broadcast coupled with the consent for rebroadcast of the programs placed the programs in the public domain within the meaning of the applicable state statute.[40]

---

contract for rights to the first showing of network originated television programs was held not to give rise to protectable proprietary interests in the programs; *but cf.*, Mutual Broadcasting Sys., Inc. v. Muzak Corp., 177 Misc. 489, 30 N.Y.S.2d 419 (Sup. Ct. 1941).

[33] See, *e.g.*, Intermountain Broadcasting Corp. v. Idaho Microwave, Inc., *supra* note 30, wherein a contract between television broadcasters for the rebroadcast of programs was held not to preclude competitive rebroadcast of the same programs by a CATV system.

[34] *Id.* at 324, noting that the prohibition against nonpermissive rebroadcast of radio and television transmissions provided by the Federal Communications Act is not presently applicable to CATV systems.

[35] *Ibid.*, holding that the doctrine of unfair competition does not apply absent misappropriation of profits from a common source.

[36] See, *e.g.*, United Artists Associated, Inc. v. NWL Corp., *supra* note 30.

[37] See Cable Vision, Inc. v. KUTV, Inc., 335 F.2d 348, 354 (9th Cir. 1964), cert. denied, 379 U.S. 989 (1965).

[38] *Ibid.*   [39] Z Bar Net v. Helena Television, Inc., *supra* note 30.

[40] "If the owner of a product of mind intentionally makes it public, a copy

Is CATV Infringing Proprietary Rights? 161

It was held that a television broadcasting station has no property interest, copyright or otherwise, in the programs it broadcasts or in the signals it transmits.[41]

Subsequently, in 1961, it was held by a Federal Court that, apart from copyright or exclusive license rights, a television station has no property rights in its broadcasts sufficient to support a requirement of consent by the broadcaster before a rebroadcast may be made by another party.[42] This case arose from the fact situation in Twin Falls, Idaho already described.[43] The Salt Lake City television stations sought a declaratory judgment as to their interests in broadcast programs in view of the manifested intent of the CATV system in Twin Falls to extend their services to include distribution in Twin Falls of programs received from the Salt Lake City stations. The District Court distinguished the business situation confronting the television stations from that encountered in *International News Service v. Associated Press*,[44] upon whose doctrine the Salt Lake City stations relied. The court held that the proper test for application of the doctrine of unfair competition enunciated in the *International News* case[45] was not met, since there was no misrepresentation by the CATV system as to its product or its product's source and since the source of profit to the CATV system (the television viewing public) differed from the source of profit to the Salt Lake City television stations (advertising sponsors).[46] It was suggested, in dicta, that only those interests arising from

---

or reproduction may be made public by any person, without responsibility to the owner, so far as the law of this state is concerned." MONT. REV. CODES § 67-1107.

[41] Z Bar Net v. Helena Television, Inc., *supra* note 30, at 596.

[42] Intermountain Broadcasting Corp. v. Idaho Microwave, Inc., *supra* note 30, at 328.

[43] *Supra* note 15.   [44] 248 U.S. 215 (1918).

[45] ". . . whether any such profit is one which under the circumstances rightfully belongs to plaintiffs so as to make it a misappropriation by defendants." Intermountain Broadcasting Corp. v. Idaho Microwave, Inc., 196 F. Supp. 315, 328 (D. Idaho 1961).

[46] *Id.* at 326, 130 U.S.P.Q. at 135.

exclusive contract or from copyright were protectable by the broadcaster.[47]

In a subsequent case,[48] arising in 1962 from the same set of facts,[49] on a crossclaim to an antitrust action by the CATV system, the local Twin Falls station alleged unfair competition by the CATV system in view of the television station's rights under its exclusive contract with the television networks. Here, the same Federal District Court held that such an exclusive contract did create valuable property rights in the first run of network programs and that these rights were subject to judicial protection under the unfair competition doctrine of the *International News Case*.[50] Subsequently, the U.S. Supreme Court handed down their landmark decisions in *Sears, Roebuck & Co. v. Stiffel Co.*,[51] and *Compco Corporation v. Day-Brite Lighting, Inc.*,[52] which severely limited the areas to which the law of unfair competition may be applied.[53] On the basis of its interpretation of the doctrine established in these two cases the Court of Appeals vacated the lower court decision, holding that:

Save for the limited protection accorded the creator of literary and intellectual works under the Copyright Act or its exceptions . . . anyone may freely and with impunity avail himself of such works to any extent he may desire and for any purpose whatever subject only to the qualification that he does not steal good will, or . . . deceive others in thinking the creations represent his own work.

. . . Parties by the mere expedient of an exclusive contract cannot

[47] *Id.* at 327–28.
[48] Cable Vision, Inc. v. KUTV, Inc., 211 F. Supp. 47 (D. Idaho 1962).
[49] *Supra* note 43.
[50] ". . . Such rights of exclusive first run as a broadcaster can validly obtain for its programs have commercial significance and value." Cable Vision, Inc. v. KUTV, Inc., *supra* n.48, at 52; and see *id.* at 55.
[51] 376 U.S. 225 (1964). [52] 376 U.S. 234 (1964).
[53] "The federal policy found in Art. 1, Sec. 8, Cl. 8 of the Constitution is to allow 'free access to copy whatever the federal patent and copyright laws leave in the public domain.'. . . That which is either not copyrighted, not copyrightable or on which the copyright has expired is in the public domain. . . ." Cable Vision, Inc. v. KUTV, Inc., 335 F.2d 348, 350 (9th Cir. 1964), *cert. denied*, 379 U.S. 989 (1965).

Is CATV Infringing Proprietary Rights? 163

'bootstrap' into existence rights from subject matter which at their source lie in the public domain.[54]

In arriving at the above-quoted interpretation of the *Sears* and *Compco* cases, supra, the court quoted liberally and with approval from the dissent of Mr. Justice Brandeis in the *International News* case, supra.[55] Again, in dicta, the Court of Appeals suggested that copyright interests should provide the basis for any action taken in the future, and this avenue was specifically left open by the court as a basis for future action when the case was remanded to the lower court.[56]

If the decisions discussed above withstand the tests of time and appeal, it would appear that only copyright infringement litigation remains as a judicially recognized means for protecting television networks and local television stations from unauthorized use of their broadcasts.[57]

SOME COPYRIGHT ASPECTS OF CATV OPERATIONS

It is assumed ab initio, for purposes of this discussion, that the program content of the television broadcasts considered herein is fully protected by statutory copyright. This assumption avoids the problem of establishing when common law copyright interests are divested by "publication"[58] and also avoids the problems encountered where broadcasts include "live" coverage of news events.[59]

---

[54] Cable Vision, Inc. v. KUTV, Inc., *supra* note 53, at 351; *but cf.* Mutual Broadcasting Sys. v. Muzak Corp., *supra* note 32.
[55] *Id.* at 352.   [56] *Id.* at 354.   [57] *Cf.* cases cited *supra* note 30.
[58] See Shapiro, Bernstein & Co. v. Miracle Record Co., 91 F. Supp. 473, rehearing, 86 U.S.P.Q. 193 (N.D. Ill. 1950); see also Metropolitan Opera Ass'n v. Wagner Nichols Recorder Corp., 199 Misc. 787, 101 N.Y.S.2d 483 (Sup. Ct. 1950), *aff'd*, 279 App. Div. 632, 107 N.Y.S.2d 795 (1st Dep't 1951); see generally SUBCOMM. ON PATENTS, TRADEMARKS AND COPYRIGHTS, SENATE COMM. ON THE JUDICIARY, 86TH CONG., 2D SESS., COPYRIGHT LAW REVISION STUDIES, Strauss, *Study No. 29, Protection of Unpublished Works* (Comm. Print 1961).
[59] See, *e.g.*, Davies v. Bowes, 209 Fed. 53 (S.D.N.Y. 1913); see also International News Serv. v. Associated Press, 248 U.S. 215 (1918).

CAPACITY TO SUE FOR INFRINGEMENT—
DIVISIBILITY OF COPYRIGHT

The first problem confronting a television station seeking to protect its interests in broadcasts made under copyright license concerns its capacity, as a licensee, to bring suit. Where copyright infringement is the basis for the requested relief, the indispensability of the copyright owner as a party may present difficulties.[60] Historically, only the owner or assignee of a copyright could enforce any claim of copyright infringement.[61] This rather inflexible rule was relaxed by the courts to permit an exclusive licensee of a copyright to sue on his own behalf for copyright infringement if the copyright owner joined as a party.[62] However, difficulties arose where the copyright owner was himself infringing the rights of his exclusive licensee and where the copyright owner refused to be a party to an infringement action.[63] Procedural reform in the context of more liberal rules on joinder of parties has somewhat eased this problem.[64] The non-exclusive licensee of a copyright still has no interest in the licensed copyright which he can enforce either with or without joinder of the copyright owner in an infringement action.[65]

The physical boundaries of exclusive contracts between television networks and television stations are controlled by the Federal Communications Commission.[66] At present, ex-

[60] See SUBCOMM. ON PATENTS, TRADEMARKS AND COPYRIGHTS, SENATE COMM. ON THE JUDICIARY, 86TH CONG., 2D SESS., COPYRIGHT LAW REVISION STUDIES, Kaminstein, *Study No. 11, Divisibility of Copyrights* (Comm. Print 1960).
[61] See Waterman v. Mackenzie, 138 U.S. 252 (1891); see generally Kaminstein, *supra*, at 13.
[62] See, *e.g.*, Field v. True Comics, Inc., 89 F. Supp. 611 (S.D.N.Y. 1950).
[63] *Cf.* Pratt and Whitney v. United States, 153 F. Supp. 409 (Ct. Cl. 1957); see generally Kaminstein, *supra* note 60.
[64] FED. R. CIV. P. 19; *cf.* Buck v. Kloeppel, 10 F. Supp. 345 (S.D. Fla. 1935).
[65] See Ilyin v. Avon Publications, Inc., 110 U.S.P.Q. 356 (S.D.N.Y. 1956); *cf.* Western Elec. Co. v. Pacent Reproducer Corp., 42 F.2d 116 (2d Cir. 1930), *cert. denied*, 282 U.S. 893 (1930); see generally Kaminstein, *supra* note 60.
[66] See, *e.g.*, National Broadcasting Co. v. United States, 319 U.S. 190 (1942); see generally 47 C.F.R. § 73.132.

clusivity is limited to the "community" specified in the contract as the location of the licensee.[67] The validity of an exclusive license under these rules might be a major factor in determining the capacity of the licensee to bring suit for infringement of the licensed copyright.[68] However, as suggested by judicial dicta, so long as television stations conform to current federal regulations in contracting with television networks for exclusive rights to network programs, they would appear to have the capacity to sue in their own behalf for copyright infringement if the copyright owner is joined.[69]

A number of proposed changes in the present copyright law are under consideration by the U.S. Congress.[70] One area being studied includes the problems inherent in our present law regarding divisibility of copyright and possible solutions thereto.[71] However, even under existing law, it seems that an exclusively licensed television station can seek protection of copyright interests arising from its exclusive license.[72]

CATV OPERATIONS AS A "PUBLIC PERFORMANCE"

The Copyright Act of 1909 granted a copyright proprietor the exclusive right "to perform or represent the copyrighted work publicly if it be a drama."[73] The term "drama" has been interpreted so as to encompass much of the material of which television programs are comprised, including: dramatico-musical works,[74] motion picture photoplays,[75] and,

[67] See Cable Vision, Inc. v. KUTV, Inc., 211 F. Supp. 47, 53, citing F.C.C., Regulations, § 3.568 (B).
[68] "Any exclusivity agreement broader than that would be not only in conflict with, but in violation of the national television policy as declared by the regulations of the Federal Communications Commission." *Ibid.*
[69] Cable Vision, Inc. v. KUTV, Inc., *supra* notes 53, 54.
[70] See generally SUBCOMM. ON PATENTS, TRADEMARKS AND COPYRIGHTS, HOUSE COMM. ON THE JUDICIARY, 88TH CONG., 2D SESS., COPYRIGHT LAW REVISION, PART 3, PRELIMINARY DRAFT FOR REVISED U.S. COPYRIGHT LAW AND DISCUSSIONS AND COMMENTS ON THE DRAFT (Comm. Print 1964).
[71] See Kaminstein, *supra* note 60.
[72] See Cable Vision, Inc. v. KUTV, Inc., *supra* notes 55, 56.
[73] 35 Stat. 1075, 17 U.S.C., § 1(d).
[74] See, e.g. Herbert v. Shanley Co., 229 Fed. 340 (2d Cir. 1916).
[75] See, e.g., Tiffany Prods. v. Dewing, 50 F.2d 911 (D. Md. 1931).

of course, dramatic plays.[76] This right is violated when the protected work is performed "publicly," whether or not commercial benefit or monetary gain is achieved by the performance.[77]

Early in the history of radio broadcasting it was held that a radio broadcast itself constituted a public performance within the meaning of the Copyright Act.[78] Television broadcasts rely on the same medium of program transmission utilized for radio broadcasts, namely, electrically polarized high frequency waves transmitted through the atmosphere. Although somewhat more sophisticated, the reception and utilization of television signals through conversion to electrical voltage impulses is analogous to the reception and utilization of radio signals. In view of these technical similarities and the similarity of prospective audiences, it is submitted that the legal reasoning previously applied to the copyright aspects of radio broadcasting should apply equally well to those of television broadcasting.[79]

It was subsequently held in *Buck v. Jewell-LaSalle Realty Co.*[80] that the reception and redistribution of radio broadcasts containing copyrighted material to both public and private rooms in a hotel was, in effect, a performance of the original radio program which infringed the rights in the copyrighted material.[81] In this case, the proprietor of a hotel utilized a master radio receiver for receiving standard radio broadcasts and distributed the received programs via amplifiers and private wiring to loudspeakers in each of the hotel's private guest rooms and in each of the hotel's public areas.[82]

A still later case, *Society of European Stage Authors & Composers v. New York Hotel Statler Co.*,[83] indicated that the rebroadcast by a hotel of radio programs only to private

---

[76] See, *e.g.*, Herbert v. Shanley Co., *supra* note 74.
[77] HOWELL, COPYRIGHT LAW, 138 (4th Ed. Latman rev. 1962).
[78] See, *e.g.*, Witmark v. Bamberger, 291 Fed. 776 (D.N.J. 1923).
[79] *Cf.* cases cited *supra* note 30.   [80] 283 U.S. 191 (1931).
[81] *Ibid.*   [82] *Ibid.*   [83] 19 F. Supp. 1 (S.D.N.Y. 1937).

Is CATV Infringing Proprietary Rights? 167

guest rooms was a public performance. Here, the hotel utilized two master radio receivers which were wired through amplifiers to loudspeakers so as to offer alternative radio programs to its guests. Each guest room was equipped with a loudspeaker and a switch by means of which a guest could select either of two radio programs. Even though these radio programs were not available in the public areas of the hotel and the ultimate program reception was controlled by the individual guest, the court held that a public performance was rendered. In the words of the court:

> [T]he defendant's hypothesis that individual reception is an alibi to a claim that its performance was public seems to me to be entirely destroyed . . . Consequently, I hold that the reproduction by the Hotel's master receiving sets of the electric impulses of the broadcast and their distribution among its rooms so that all who wish may, by turning a knob, listen to the broadcast, is a public performance . . .[84]

It would appear that the characterization of a performance as public or private depends primarily upon the degree to which the potential audience is restricted and the nature of the restriction imposed.[85] Where the only restriction on audience membership is the payment of an admission or service charge, the performance is obviously public.[86]

The operation of CATV is particularly analogous to the *Hotel Statler* case, supra. Programs are received and redistributed by CATV systems through private communication channels to receivers in return for a service charge. No other restriction is placed on audience membership. Accordingly, the redistribution of television programs by a CATV system

---

[84] *Id.* at 5, 6.
[85] *Cf.* Lerner v. Club Wander In, Inc., 174 F. Supp. 731 (D. Mass. 1959), indicating that a performance given at a club may be public even if the club can exclude those members of the public who do not meet standards set by the club; but *cf.* Metro-Goldwyn-Mayer v. Wyatt & Maryland Yacht Club, 21 BULL. CR. OFF. 203 (D. Md. 1932), holding that a performance given at a yacht club to which members invite guests is similar to a performance at a private home and therefore not public.
[86] *Cf.* Tiffany Prods, v. Dewing, *supra* note 75.

to paying customers should be considered a "public performance" within the meaning of the Copyright Act.[87] If any of the CATV system's customers are places of business where the redistributed television programs may be seen by the general public, the performance is public in nature under the principles of the *Jewell-LaSalle* case, supra.

CATV OPERATIONS AS A "PERFORMANCE FOR PROFIT"

Under the Copyright Act of 1909, the proprietor of a copyrighted work is granted the exclusive right "to perform the copyrighted work publicly for profit if it be a musical composition."[88] Originally, this protection was accorded only to dramatic and musical works.[89] However, in 1952, the Copyright Act was amended and the monopoly over public performance for profit of a copyrighted work was extended to nondramatic works such as books and poems.[90]

The landmark case of *Herbert v. Shanley Co.*[91] established the principle that direct pecuniary benefit is not a requisite for classifying a performance as one "for profit." In that case, a live performance by an orchestra given for the listening pleasure of those present in a hotel dining room was held to be a performance for profit even though no direct monetary charge was attributable to the privilege of listening to the performance. The indirect commercial benefit accrued through the attraction of customers to the restaurant was held sufficient to constitute a "profit" within the statutory meaning.[92] Similar holdings were made in the *Jewell-LaSalle*[93] and *Hotel Statler*[94] cases with regard to radio broadcasts made available for the convenience of hotel guests without specific monetary charges therefor.[95]

---

[87] Annot., *Legal Aspects of Radio Communications and Broadcasting*, 124 A.L.R. 982, 995 (1940).
[88] 17 U.S.C., § 1(d).   [89] 35 Stat. 1075
[90] 66 Stat. 752 (eff. Jan. 1, 1953).   [91] 242 U.S. 591 (1917).
[92] *Id.* at 595.   [93] *Supra* note 80.   [94] *Supra* note 83.
[95] "The reproduction . . . of the electric impulses of the broadcast and their distribution among its rooms so that all who wish may . . . listen to the

Is CATV Infringing Proprietary Rights? 169

The provision of CATV systems by proprietors of hotels and multiple dwellings for the convenience of guests and tenants is directly analogous to the fact situation in the *Hotel Statler* case. The indirect commercial benefit received through the attraction of guests and tenants by provision of CATV services should be sufficient to characterize the operation as a performance for profit within the principles of the *Hotel Statler* case.[96]

CATV systems serving private homes and places of business should also be considered within the scope of the *Hotel Statler* case.[97] The private nature of individual receivers in private homes appears directly analogous to the repudiated argument in that case regarding the private nature of the individual loudspeakers in the private guest rooms. The provision by a hotel of individual radio receivers unconnected to any master receiver for each of its guest rooms does not seem to constitute a performance for profit within the *Hotel Statler* case. It was the use of a master receiver for receiving and redistributing radio programs to loudspeakers over private communication channels that constituted the performance. The same distinction exists between the mere presence of individual television receivers in private homes and the connection of those television receivers to a CATV system. The CATV system, like the hotel's master receivers, receives and redistributes television programs over private communication channels to a plurality of television sets. The element of profit to the CATV system is obviously supplied by the connection and service charges made for use of the system. Where a business establishment is served by a CATV system, the viewing of television programs distributed by the CATV

---

broadcast, is a public performance for profit of the broadcast program, and is made at the Hotel's risk insofar as copyrighted musical compositions are concerned." Society of European Stage Authors & Composers v. New York Hotel Statler Co., *supra* note 83.

[96] Annot., *Legal Aspects of Radio Communications and Broadcasting*, *supra* note 87.

[97] *Supra* note 83.

system in the business establishment should be construed as a further infringing performance for profit of the copyrighted material included in the television programs.[98]

CONCLUSIONS

The policy of protecting the proprietary interest of a creator in his inventive or artistic creation is fundamental to our economic structure. This policy and its underlying principle of encouraging creative endeavor is undermined whenever any particular business or class of persons is privileged with immunity from liability to the owner of a patent or copyright when profitable use is made of the subject of the patent or copyright. Accordingly, CATV systems have an obligation, as a part of the broadcasting industry, to assume the same responsibility as other members of the industry in maintaining a climate which promotes creative activity by financially contributing to the creators and suppliers of the product in which they trade. It is in the best interests of the television industry as a whole, including CATV systems, that television broadcasters should seek to protect the interests of those who create the program material on which the entire industry relies for its very existence.[99]

Television broadcasters who find themselves in competition with CATV operations must resort to their position as an exclusive copyright licensee to protect their interests if the present trend of cases continues. Interests protected by statutory copyright appear to be the only protectable propri-

---

[98] *Cf.* Harms, Inc. v. Sansom House Enterprises, Inc., 162 F. Supp. 129 (E.D. Pa. 1958), *aff'd sub. nom.* Leo Feist, Inc. v. Lew Tendler Tavern, Inc., 267 F.2d 494 (3d Cir. 1959), indicating that the distribution of copyrighted music to a place of business by private communications channel for the listening pleasure of customers is a performance for profit; see also Annot., *Legal Aspects of Radio Communications and Broadcasting, supra* note 87.

[99] See Finkelstein, *Memorandum to Register of Copyrights,* Preliminary Draft for Revised U.S. Copyright Law and Discussions and Comments on the Draft, *supra* note 70, at 365.

Is CATV Infringing Proprietary Rights? 171

etary rights in broadcast television programs. If the apparent similarity between the radio and television industries is judicially recognized, CATV system operation should be construed a public performance for profit within the meaning of present copyright law. Accordingly, any unlicensed redistribution of television programs which include copyrighted material would be an infringement of the rights of the copyright owner and his exclusive licensees.

HONORABLE MENTION, 1965

Choreography and Copyright

By GARY D. ORDWAY
DRAKE UNIVERSITY SCHOOL OF LAW

THE DANCE is an expression of long standing in the history of man. It originated primarily as a means by which emotions could be expressed through spontaneous bodily movements. As society developed, dancing did also, resulting in organized patterns of dance, such as ritual and folk dances. In recent years, the dance has developed into an art form commonly known as choreography. This art form consists of a specific pattern of body movements, performed by dancers in theatrical presentations, which conveys thought, drama, or emotion to an audience. Through the media of television, theater, and motion pictures, choreography has become an integral and valuable part of the entertainment industry.[1]

A choreographic work created for theatrical performance is comparable to a play or musical composition since each is an art form by which thought, feeling, or emotion is conveyed to an audience. A dance may be an integral part of a drama or a separate independent production involving the use of dance, music, scenery, costumes, sound effects, and lighting. This points up an essential distinction between simple dances, such as ballroom and social dances, devised and performed primarily for the enjoyment of the dancers themselves, and those more complex and intricate dances, such as ballet,

---

[1] SACHS, WORLD HISTORY OF THE DANCE Chs. 6, 7; Koner & Doner, *Technological Progress and the Dance*, in THE DANCE HAS MANY FACES 111 (Sorell ed. 1951).

Choreography and Copyright

which are devised and performed by skilled artists for the entertainment of an audience. "Choreographic work," in the context of copyright, refers to the latter and relates to both the dance itself as conceived by the author and performed for an audience, and the graphic representation of the dance as recorded in some concrete form.

The choreographer, as author of an intricate dance, creates an artistic and intellectual product which should be afforded legal protection as a literary property right.[2] However, the legal protection afforded choreography has been slow in development. This article, therefore, will examine the nature and scope of the development of legal protection afforded choreography under the Federal Copyright Act.[3]

Unquestionably the most significant factor restricting development of copyright protection for choreography has been the lack of a sound dance notation system. Attempts to reduce dance movements to a tangible form through systems of notation extend back as far as the fifteenth century. However, it was not until 1928, when Rudolf Laban first published his system, that a sound and practical method was developed.[4] The Laban system is now widely used by choreographers and consists of scoring the dance in a manner similar to that used for music through the use of symbols and lines. Another recent development, the motion picture, represents yet another means for recording a dance in graphic form, although this

---

[2] The choreographer's intellectual product would seem to be equal in merit to that of music composers, literary writers, dramatic writers, and creators of works of art which are allowed copyright registration under 17 U.S.C. § 4 (1958). The creative genius of such great choreographers as Kurt Jooss, Sigurd Leeder, Albrecht Knust, Dussia Bereska, Rudolf Laban and George Balanchine cannot be questioned. The music critic B. H. Haggin once wrote of George Balanchine as "an artist of the same magnitude as Picasso, and the only one I can think of now working in any of the arts. . . . He is, it seems to me, even more disciplined in the exercise of his powers than Picasso: the originality, no matter how astounding, always remains part of the continuous development." TAPER, BALANCHINE 8 (1963).

[3] 17 U.S.C. §§ 1–215 (1964).

[4] Hutchinson, *The Preservation of the Dance Score through Notation*, in THE DANCE HAS MANY FACES, *supra* note 1, at 49.

system is little used because of cost and other practical limitations.[5]

Previous to these developments, the creations of a choreographer were preserved largely through the memory of the author. This lack of notation caused the loss of many great choreographic works when either the author died or his memory failed without the works having been passed on to another by word of mouth and by demonstration.

Attempts were made at describing dances in written text or in pictures, but these usually proved unsatisfactory because the process was laborious and the resulting descriptions inaccurate. In view of the absence of a concrete record of the dance movements, it became practically impossible to determine and prove whether a choreographer's works were being pirated by others.

These considerations highlight the value of motion pictures and the Laban system of dance notation to the choreographer. It is largely because of these innovations that copyright protection may now be afforded to choreographic works. Such protection seems proper in view of the increasing importance of the dance as a medium of public entertainment and artistic expression.

COMMON-LAW COPYRIGHT

A review of the concept of common-law copyright indicates that its principles could be used to protect intellectual property rights in unpublished choreographic works.[6] No case has been found that rules directly on this point,[7] but the

---

[5] For discussion of the limitations see Hutchinson, *id.* at 57.

[6] For an excellent discussion of common law property rights as applied to choreographic works see Mirell, *Legal Protection for Choreography*, 27 N.Y.U.L. REV. 792, 794 (1952).

[7] Literary property rights in a dance were asserted by the plaintiff in Savage v. Hoffman, 159 Fed. 584 (C.C.S.D.N.Y. 1908), but the court failed to answer the question and held that even if such rights existed they did not belong to the plaintiff.

absence of case law can be attributed to the fact that, until recently, no practical method existed for reducing choreographic works to tangible form. Protection in the United States for common-law rights in intellectual property is evidenced by Section 2 of the Copyright Act.[8]

It has been held that Section 2 preserves not only the legal and equitable rights at common law of printing and publishing but also the right to "use" unpublished works.[9] This presumably includes the right to exhibit, represent, dramatize, or otherwise use and control the work. As to the rights recognized at common law, the Supreme Court of Illinois held in *Ferris v. Frohman:*

At common law the author of a literary composition has an absolute property right in his production, which he could not be deprived of so long as it remained unpublished, nor could he be compelled to publish it. This right of property exists at common law in all productions of literature, the drama, music, art, etc.[10]

It should be noted that common-law property rights may exist in forms of intellectual creations which are not copyrightable under the Copyright Act.[11] In *White v. Kimmel,* the court said:

The common law has long recognized a property right in the products of man's creative mind, regardless of the form in which they took expression.[12]

---

[8] 17 U.S.C. § 2 (1964) states: "Nothing in this title shall be construed to annul or limit the right of the author or proprietor of an unpublished work, at common law or in equity, to prevent the copying, publication, or use of such unpublished work without his consent, and to obtain damages therefor."
[9] Harper Bros. v. Donohue, 144 F. 491 (C.C.N.D. Ill. 1905).
[10] 238 Ill. 430, 87 N.E. 327 (1909), *aff'd,* 223 U.S. 424 (1912).
[11] Common law protection has been held to exist in recordings, Granz v. Harris, 198 F.2d 585 (2d Cir. 1952); in a color chart, Ketcham v. N.Y. World's Fair 1939, 34 F. Supp. 657 (E.D.N.Y. 1940), *aff'd,* 119 F.2d 422 (2d Cir. 1941); and in slogans, Healey v. Macy & Co., 251 App. Div. 440, 297 N.Y.S. 165 (1st Dep't 1937).
[12] 94 F. Supp. 502, 504 (S.D. Cal. 1950), *rev'd on the facts,* 193 F.2d 744 (9th Cir. 1952), *cert. denied,* 343 U.S. 957 (1952).

There are four basic requirements which must be satisfied before common-law protection can be afforded intellectual creations such as choreography: (a) The work must be an original product of the mind; [13] (b) The author's labors must be reduced to tangible form; [14] (c) The work must not be immoral, licentious or generally against public policy; [15] (d) The work must be unpublished.[16]

Thus, there would seem to be no reason why the common-law protection generally accorded unpublished works of authorship would not extend to an unpublished choreographic work which satisfies the above requirements.

STATUTORY COPYRIGHT

CHOREOGRAPHY AS A DRAMATIC COMPOSITION

Since the primitive beginning of artistic and literary creations, it has been necessary for the author of intellectual productions to be entitled "to reap the fruits of his labor in every field where he has contributed to the enlightenment

---

[13] Brightly v. Littleton, 37 Fed. 103 (C.C.E.D. Pa. 1888); Schwarg v. Universal Pictures Co., 85 F. Supp. 270 (S.D. Cal. 1945). It should be noted that the work need not be original in its entirety. Aronson v. Baker, 43 N.J. Eq. 365, 12 Atl. 177 (Ch. Div. 1888). The choreographer uses dance steps and techniques just as a composer uses notes and scales: none of these elements are original creations of the mind in their own right, but when they are arranged and constructed into an intricate dance pattern, the result is an original mental product.

[14] Palmer v. DeWitt, 47 N.Y. 532 (1872). A choreographic work may be reduced to tangible form by use of the Laban system of dance notation.

[15] Chicago Bd. of Trade v. L. A. Kinsey Co., 125 Fed. 72 (C.C.D. Ind. 1903), rev'd on other grounds, 130 Fed. 507 (7th Cir. 1904), aff'd, 198 U.S. 236 (1905); Broder v. Zeno Mauvais Music Co., 88 Fed. 74 (C.C.N.D. Cal. 1898); Keene v. Kimball, 16 Gray 545 (Mass. 1860).

[16] Atlantic Monthly Co. v. Post Publishing Co., 27 F.2d 556 (D. Mass. 1928); Black v. Plaut, 87 F. Supp. 49 (D. Ill. 1949). It should be noted that public presentation of a dramatic composition does not constitute publication. Ferris v. Frohman, 223 U.S. 424 (1912); Palmer v. DeWitt, 47 N.Y. 532 (N.Y. 1870). An attempt to define the term "publication" with reference to copyright law is beyond the scope of this work. It will suffice to say that publication means dedication of the author's works to the public domain by openly disseminating copies thereof or by abandonment.

and the rational enjoyment of mankind."[17] It was for this reason, primarily, that the Federal Copyright Act[18] was enacted.

Of all arts—architecture, sculpture, painting, literature, music, and dance—the latter is the most intangible. The first three can be recognized through visible, solid objects, while the latter three exist as thoughts which can be recognized only when transmitted from mind to mind. Literature can express concrete ideas whereas choreography or dance is usually limited to the expression of feelings and emotions through rhythmic bodily movements. A particular dance may convey such emotions by telling a story or developing a character, while other dances, such as most "modern dances," are devoid of any storyline.

The Copyright Act does not specifically mention choreographic works among the catagories of copyrightable works set out therein. However, "choreographic works" have been allowed registration under Section 5(d) as a species of "dramatic compositions." The Copyright Office Regulations authorize registration of copyright claims in choreographic works. Section 202.7 of the regulations states:

Choreographic works of a dramatic character, whether the story or theme be expressed by music and action combined or by actions alone, are subject to registration in Class D. However, descriptions of dance steps and other physical gestures, including ballroom and social dances or choreographic works which do not tell a story, develop a character or emotion, or otherwise convey a dramatic concept or idea are not subject to registration in Class D.[19]

This regulation indicates that the copyright office will allow copyright registration of a choreographic work, as a "dramatic composition," if it tells a story, develops a character or emotion, or otherwise conveys a dramatic concept or idea.[20]

[17] Carte v. Duff, 25 Fed. 183 (1885) ("Mikado Case").
[18] 17 U.S.C. §§ 1–215 (1964).   [19] 37 C.F.R. § 202.7 (1959).
[20] The Copyright Office has also stated in Information Circular No. 51, which provides general information with regard to registration of choreo-

It is important to note that, although the copyright office will allow registration of certain choreographic works, this does not guarantee that the courts will enforce protection against unauthorized use of such works.[21] Since the Copyright Act does not deal specifically with choreography, protection in each case is dependent upon what the court is willing to include within the purview of the statutory phrase "dramatic composition."

Three basic tests have evolved from the cases dealing with "dramatic compositions." The first test is evidenced by the early case of *Daly v. Palmer*,[22] where a federal court held that silent action in a theatrical performance may constitute a drama. The case is usually cited for the proposition that if the work has capacity for stage presentation or performance, it is a dramatic composition.[23]

The second and most widely accepted test is whether the

---

graphic works, as follows: "The copyright office, therefore, may consider in Class D claims to copyright in choreographic works of a dramatic character, whether the story or theme be expressed by music and actions combined or by actions alone. . . . Descriptions of dance steps and other physical gestures, including ballroom and other social dances or choreographic works which do not tell a story, develop a character or emotion, or otherwise convey a dramatic concept or idea are not subject to registration in Class D as dramatic or dramatico-musical composition."

[21] The Copyright Act presupposes an original intellectual creation of authorship. The courts determine, in each case, whether the work in question satisfies this prerequisite. Information Circular No. 51 of the Copyright Office states: "The registration by the Copyright Office of a choreographic work in Class D or any other class should not, particularly in the absence of a statutory provision dealing specifically with choreographic works, be taken as an expression of opinion by the Copyright Office as to whether the applicant will or will not be entitled to performance rights in the choreography. The Copyright Office does not undertake to decide questions of extent of rights in particular works, and therefore takes no position as to whether the courts will enforce protection against unauthorized performance of a given work."

[22] 6 Fed. Cas. 1132, No. 3,552 (C.C.S.D.N.Y. 1868). Judge Blatchford, speaking for the court, said, at p. 1136, "A written work, consisting wholly of directions, set in order for conveying the ideas of the author on a stage or public place, by means of characters who represent the narrative wholly by action, is as much a dramatic composition designed or suited for public representation as if language or dialogue was used in it to convey some of its ideas."

[23] SHAFTER, MUSICAL COPYRIGHT 55 (2d ed. 1939). See also Bell v. Mahn, 121 Pa. St. 225 (1888).

work, when presented, tells a story. In *Fuller v. Bemis*,[24] the plaintiff had filed a copyright claim in a written description of the movements of a dance to be performed on stage. She sued the defendant for copyright infringement on the grounds of unauthorized public performance of the so-called "umbrella or skirt dance." Plaintiff contended the dance was a "dramatic composition," but the court in denying relief said:

> An examination of the description of complainants dance as filed for copyright, shows that the end sought for and accomplished was solely the devising of a series of graceful movements, combined with an attractive arrangement of drapery, lights, and shadows, *telling no story, portraying no character, depicting no emotion.*[25]

The court went on to say that the dance was devised to convey "no other idea than that a comely woman is illustrating the poetry of motion in a singularly graceful fashion." [26]

In *Kalem Co. v. Harper Bros.*,[27] the Court held that the action in a silent motion picture was a dramatization of the novel "Ben Hur" and subject to legal protection. Justice Holmes for the Court said:

> [D]rama may be achieved by action as well as by speech. Action can tell a story, display all the most vivid relations between men, and depict every kind of human emotion, without the aid of a word. It would be impossible to deny the title of drama to pantomime as played by masters of the art.[28]

The third and least accepted test is whether the work arouses the emotions. In *Russell v. Smith*,[29] an English case,

---

[24] 50 Fed. 926 (C.C.S.D.N.Y. 1892). See also WEIL, COPYRIGHT LAW 76 (1917); BALL, LAW OF COPYRIGHT AND LITERARY PROPERTY 363 (1944).
[25] Fuller v. Bemis, 50 Fed. 926, at 929. (Emphasis added.)
[26] *Ibid.* Mirell, *supra* note 7, at 808, criticizes the decision in Fuller v. Bemis, and states: "It is submitted that the court, rather than deny protection to this work on the ground that it had little merit, or that it was immoral, matters for value judgment, adopted a narrow concept of drama and required that it tell a story." He suggests that the dance was "a risqué piece even for the 'gay nineties'" and that immorality is the true grounds for the court's holding.
[27] 222 U.S. 55 (1911).   [28] *Id.* at 61.
[29] 12 Q.B. 267 (1848). See also Clark v. Bishop, 25 L.T. 908 (1872) and Green v. Luby, 177 Fed. 287 (C.C.S.D.N.Y. 1909).

it was held that a song performed by a singer while accompanying himself on the piano is a dramatic composition since it arouses the emotions. Although this test may have merit, it has been rejected by the American courts.[30]

A review of the foregoing tests indicates that a choreographic work which is suited for theatrical performances and which tells a story is clearly subject to copyright protection as a "dramatic composition." However, not all works suited for theatrical performance will qualify as such.

In *Martinetti v. Maguire*,[31] the court denied copyright protection to a stage production consisting of scant dialogue accompanied by unconnected ballet and tableaux. It was held that "an exhibition of women lying about loose or otherwise, is not a dramatic composition, and, therefore, not entitled to the protection of the copyright act." [32]

In *Barns v. Miner*,[33] the court held that a stage production consisting of a woman singing songs and reciting dialogue in costume together with a motion picture showing the woman changing costume during scene changes was not a proper subject for copyright protection.

The two cases most relevant to the question of what constitutes a dramatic dance are *Fuller v. Bemis* [34] and *Kalem Co. v. Harper Bros.*[35] The *Kalem* decision indicates that action alone, if it portrays a character or depicts an emotion, may qualify as a dramatic composition. There is language in the

---

[30] Nichols v. Universal Pictures Corp., 45 F.2d 119 (2d Cir. 1930), cert. denied, 282 U.S. 902 (1931). See also MALEVINSKY, SCIENCE OF PLAYWRITING 50 (1925).

[31] 16 Fed. Cas. 920, No. 9,173 (S.D. Cal. 1938). The court described the production as "a mere spectacle. The dialogue is very scant and meaningless, and appears to be mere accessory to the action of the piece—a sort of verbal machinery tacked on to a succession of ballet and tableaux. The principal part of the attraction of the spectacle seems to be an exhibition of women in novel dress or no dress, and in attractive attitudes or action." *Id.* at 922.

[32] The holding seems to have been prompted by the questionable moral values implicit in the work, but even so the case may be distinguished on the ground that this was not an original creation of intellectual authorship.

[33] 122 Fed. 480 (C.C.S.D.N.Y. 1903).

[34] *Cf.* text accompanying note 26 *supra*.

[35] *Cf.* text accompanying note 29 *supra*.

Fuller decision which seems to require a storyline before a dance may qualify as a dramatic composition, and this case is usually cited as so holding. But a careful reading of the opinion indicates that this is an unduly restricted construction of the court's holding. The opinion implies that if a dance portrays a character or depicts an emotion it may also be considered a dramatic composition.[36] It seems proper, therefore, to conclude that a choreographic work which constitutes an original creation of dance movements, to be performed before an audience, conveying some story or depicting a character or emotional concept, would qualify as a dramatic composition.[37]

But even though some choreography may qualify as dramatic composition, it is equally obvious from the foregoing that not all dance is embraced within that concept. The traditional ballets which are commonly noted for conveying a storyline would obviously qualify. It is in the area of the "modern and abstract" dances, where the dramatic content is questionable, that the real problem lies. There is little doubt that many such dances constitute creative works of authorship. The bodily movements in such dances, however, are primarily intended to convey some esthetic or emotional concept to the audience, although no storyline is readily apparent in their composition. In *Fuller v. Bemis,* the court implied that, if a

[36] The court said: "It is essential to such a composition that it should tell some story. The plot may be simple. It may be but the narrative or representation of a single transaction; but it must repeat or mimic some action, speech, emotion, passion, or character, real or imaginary. And when it does, it is the ideas thus expressed which become subject of copyright." Fuller v. Bemis, 50 Fed. 926, at 929. See also text accompanying note 26, *supra.*

[37] Mirell, *supra* note 7, at 804, expresses the fear that in order for a work to be a dramatic composition, it must tell a story. He states further: "A reevaluation of *Fuller v. Bemis* is called for the next time the question of statutory rights in a dance is before the court. The case is contrary to the mainstream of opinion as represented by *Daly v. Palmer,* it is questionable law on its own facts, and it is contrary to current expanded views as to what constitutes intellectual property and its protection. If the copyright laws of this country are to perform their constitutional function, that is, promote the arts by giving the author a limited monopoly in his works, they cannot rationally be denied efficability in achieving this for the creative art of choreography." *Id.* at 809.

dance conveyed an emotional concept to the audience, it may qualify as a dramatic composition. Although this conclusion can be reached only by a liberal construction of that case, such a conclusion appears proper in view of the artistic and creative merit inherent in many modern and abstract dances.

Mention has been made of the distinction between social or ballroom dances, which are intended to be executed for the personal enjoyment of the dancer, and theatrical or dramatic dances, which are intended to be performed on the stage by skilled or professional dancers. The former would generally be considered too simple to qualify as a creative work of authorship and it would be baseless to contend that such dances are dramatic in any sense of the term. Social or ballroom dances should therefore not qualify as dramatic compositions and copyright protection should be restricted to theatrical or dramatic dances which are intended for performance before an audience.

Even though certain dances are intended for theatrical performance, they may fail to qualify for copyright protection because the sequence of bodily movements is so simple or stereotyped as to possess no substantial element of creative authorship. Ordinary "dance routines" and variety show dances, in which the originality is negligible, would be examples of such stereotyped dances. It must always be remembered that copyright presupposes originality and creative authorship. Therefore, even though a choreographic work may qualify as dramatic in character, it must also constitute an original sequence or series of bodily movements sufficient to merit its being considered as a work of creative authorship.

FIXATION OF CHOREOGRAPHIC WORKS

The United States Constitution [38] empowers Congress to enact copyright legislation to protect the "writings" of au-

[38] Art. 1, § 8, cl. 8: "The Congress shall have power . . . To promote the Progress of Science and Useful Arts by securing for limited times to Authors and Inventors the exclusive Right to their respective Writings and Discoveries."

Choreography and Copyright 183

thors. As at common law, before copyright protection will be afforded an original creation of authorship, the intellectual product must be reduced to some tangible form. Taken literally, the above constitutional provision would require tangible form to mean written script. However, the term "writing" has been liberally construed and even includes three-dimensional objects [39] and motion pictures.

The necessity for fixation in choreographic works is of prime importance, since in the absence of some tangible record of the original dance movements it would be practically impossible to determine if the dance were being pirated. For a choreographic work to be entitled to copyright protection under the federal statute, either a copy of the work in unpublished form must be deposited in the Copyright Office [40] or two copies in published form with notice of copyright must be deposited.[41]

Information Circular 51 of the Copyright Office states, with reference to fixation, that "the copy or copies must constitute the acting form of the work fixed in writing or other conventional signs." The use of the term "acting form" indicates

[39] See Mazer v. Stein, 347 U.S. 201 (1954), where the court held that statuettes of Bali dancers, which had been registered for copyright, were entitled to copyright protection.

[40] 17 U.S.C. § 12 (1964) states in part: "Copyright may also be had of the works of an author, of which copies are not reproduced for sale, by the deposit, with claim of copyright, of one complete copy of such work if it be a lecture or similar production or a dramatic, musical, or dramatico-musical composition. . . . But the privilege of registration of copyright secured hereunder shall not exempt the copyright proprietor from the deposit of copies, under sections 13 and 14 of this title, where the work is later reproduced in copies for sale." It is submitted that most choreographic works would be registered in unpublished form since there is little market for the commercial selling of such works. The primary interest is performance from the copy rather than sale of such copies.

[41] 17 U.S.C. § 10 (1964) states in part: "Any person entitled thereto by this title may secure copyright for his work by publication thereof with notice of copyright required by this title; and such notice shall be affixed to each copy thereof published or offered for sale in the United States by authority of the copyright proprietor. . . ." Publication, within the meaning of this section, means the sale or distribution of copies of the work to the public in such a manner as to destroy the common-law rights in the work. The manner for giving proper notice of copyright is set out in 17 U.S.C. § 19 (1964).

that the fixation must reveal the movements of the dance in sufficient detail to enable performance therefrom. Moreover, a written description of the story or theme of the work, in sufficient detail to demonstrate that the work is a dramatic compositon, must also be submitted.[42]

Fixation of choreographic works may generally be achieved in three ways: (a) by a detailed textual description of the dance movements, (b) by making a motion picture of the dance as performed, (c) by dance notation such as the Laban system. As discussed previously, textual descriptions of dance movements have proved to be a poor method for recording choreographic works. They are uneconomical and fail in most cases accurately to describe the dance as initially created by the author.

The motion picture has proved to be a more accurate method for recording dance movements than textual description, but this method also has serious defects. A motion picture can only record the choreographic work as interpreted by the dancer. This allows the insertion of the dancer's style and defects into the original creation as conceived by the choreographer. This method has also proved uneconomical

[42] Information Circular No. 51 states: "In addition, whenever the copy or copies submitted are merely diagrammatic of the actions performed, whether in writing or otherwise, there shall also be deposited a description, in writing, of the production as a whole. The story or theme to be performed should be described with sufficient completeness to demonstrate that the work properly falls within the category of a dramatic or dramatico-musical composition." The Circular goes on to say that "text matter concerning choreography or describing a choreographic work, when published with appropriate statutory notice" may be registered in Class A as a published book; and that "motion pictures which depict ballets and other dance forms may be deposited in Class L or M." It should be noted with reference to the last mentioned classes of registration that the rights accruing therefrom are quite different from the rights in dramatic works. Dramatic compositions are protected from unauthorized public performance, while no such right inheres in nondramatic literary works. (See 17 U.S.C. § 1(a)–(d).) Thus, a textual description of the history of dancing or a critical analysis of a particular choreographic work would be restricted to the protection accorded nondramatic literary works when registered in Class A.

Choreography and Copyright 185

and its usefulness is generally restricted to recording the overall style of the work and its staging.[43]

Kinetography Laban (the Laban system of dance notation) is unquestionably the most accurate method for recording choreographic works. This system of dance notation can accurately depict all elements of space, time, and bodily motions through the use of symbols and lines which can be easily read by skilled dance notators and reinterpreted into dance movements.[44]

Although the system may appear complex and vague to the ordinary person, its principles may be readily understood through diligent study. In fact, the Laban system of dance notation is now commonly taught in most large dance schools as a result of the efforts of the Dance Notation Bureau in New York City.[45]

It is therefore submitted that the Laban system of dance notation should be used to record all choreographic works which are registered for copyright. Moreover, the use of this

---

[43] Balanchine has said: "While some people advocate the use of films to record ballet, I have found them useful only in indicating the style of the finished product and in suggesting the general over-all visual picture and staging. A film cannot reproduce a dance, step by step, since the lens shoots from but one angle and there is a general confusion of blurred impressions which even constant re-showing can never eliminate." *Preface* to HUTCHINSON, LABANOTATION (1954). "A frequent suggestion in our day is to record a dance or ballet by means of filming it, but it would be impossible to reconstruct a ballet from a film; just as impossible as it would be for a conductor without a musical score to rehearse even a simple piece of music with his orchestra from a gramophone record." COTON, THE NEW BALLET 80 (1946).

[44] Mitell, *supra* note 7, at 793, describes the Laban system as follows: "There is a basic staff which is divided vertically by a center line and then into vertical columns. This staff represents the body; all columns right of the center line are for the use of the right side of the body, and those to the left are for the left side. Each part of the body has its column. The symbols of direction are placed in the appropriate columns. These direction symbols show by their shape the direction, by their shading the level, and by their length the time value of the movement. The Laban notation alphabet includes symbols for the joints (shoulders, knees, elbow, etc.), for various surfaces of the body (palm, face, chest, etc.), signs for touching, clapping, sliding, turning, floor patterns, dynamics, and so on."

[45] HUTCHINSON, LABANOTATION 4 (1954).

accurate system will undoubtedly preclude a court from denying copyright protection on the grounds that the work is not sufficiently fixed in tangible form.

RIGHTS IN CHOREOGRAPHIC WORKS

Although choreographic works are not specifically named in the Copyright Act, it would appear that, since they are allowed registration as a species of dramatic works, they should be accorded the same statutory protection provided for dramatic compositions.

Copyright owners of all classes of registered works are accorded the exclusive right "to print, reprint, publish, copy, and vend" their works.[46] This right would enable the copyright owner of a choreographic work to have exclusive control over the reproduction of his writing [47] and to prohibit others from copying it without his consent.[48]

Unquestionably the most important right, as far as choreographic works and dramatic compositions are concerned, is the exclusive right "to perform or represent the copyrighted work publicly." [49] This right extends to *all* public performances, whereas copyright owners of nondramatic musical works [50] and nondramatic literary works [51] have only the exclusive right to public performance "for profit" and public delivery "for profit" respectively.[52] As indicated pre-

---

[46] 17 U.S.C. § 1(a) (1964).

[47] The term "writing" used in this context refers to the tangible form in which the author's creation is recorded; *e.g.* written text, motion pictures, notated text.

[48] Jeweler's Circular Publishing Co. v. Keystone Publishing Co., 281 Fed. 83 (2d Cir. 1922).

[49] 17 U.S.C. § 1(d) (1964).   [50] 17 U.S.C. § 1(e) (1964).

[51] 17 U.S.C. § 1(c) (1964).

[52] The reason additional protection is accorded dramatic compositions has been amply stated by Stephen P. Ladas in his work on international copyright. "The law considers that persons attending a performance of a dramatic work will not ordinarily attend a second performance of the same work and therefore an unauthorized performance, though gratuitous, will cause the author a monetary loss, by depriving him of a potential audience." LADAS, THE INTERNATIONAL PROTECTION OF LITERARY AND ARTISTIC PROPERTY 783 (1938).

Choreography and Copyright

viously, a choreographic work must be recorded in a fixed form sufficient to enable performance therefrom. If this requirement is not complied with, the work will qualify only as a nondramatic literary work. Copyright in this form of work will protect it against public delivery "for profit," but this refers only to the public reading or recitation of the text where some fee is paid by the audience.

Another important right accorded dramatic choreographic works is "to make or to procure the making of any transcription or record thereof by or from which, in whole or in part, it may in any manner or by any method be exhibited, performed, represented, produced, or reproduced.[53] This right would entitle the copyright owner to make motion pictures or video tapes of the choreographic work which could be publicly presented in theaters or on television. This right may prove to be of great value in the future in view of the recent increase in television presentation of choreographic material.

Also important for works of choreography is the right "to vend any manuscript or record" of an unpublished dramatic work.[54] Rudolf Laban has said: "the endeavor to describe the movements of dance in special symbols has one main purpose. This is the creation of a literature of movement and dance." [55] He indicates that script-dance literature has potential for being utilized in the training of young dancers just as sheet-music is used in the training of musicians. This prediction will undoubtedly manifest itself in the near future in view of the rapid growth in the use of the Laban system of dance notation. When it does, the value of the right to vend a choreographic manuscript will be greatly enhanced.

[53] 17 U.S.C. § 1(d) (1964).
[54] 17 U.S.C. § 1(d) (1964). This right accrues to unpublished choreographic works which have been registered under 17 U.S.C. § 12 (1964) as works not reproduced for sale. If the work has been registered as published, then the same rights accrue to the copyright owner under section 1(a).
[55] *Foreword* to HUTCHINSON, LABANOTATION (1954). Mr. Laban states further that "The manifestation of human spirituality which has made dance a sister art of poetry and music can survive only if its products are written, printed, and read by a large circle of laymen and performers."

Of minor importance to works of choreography is the right "to convert it into a novel or other nondramatic work." [56] This right would appear to have little use as far as choreographic works are concerned since these generally have minor or elementary storylines.

SUMMARY AND CONCLUSIONS

A review of the foregoing discussion indicates that choreographic works which constitute original creations of authorship should be afforded copyright protection. Such protection probably may be secured through common-law copyright in unpublished works, although no case precedent has been found in support of this view. This is subject to the major disadvantage that dissemination of this material, even if only for the purpose of teaching, would constitute publication and would thus defeat the copyrights.

Copyright protection may also be secured for published or unpublished choreographic works by registering copies thereof in the Copyright Office as a species of "dramatic composition" in Class 5(d) of the Federal Copyright Act. Copies registered for copyright must depict the choreographic work in sufficient detail to enable performance therefrom. The most accurate method for fixing such works in "acting form" is the Laban system of dance notation; however, written textual descriptions or motion pictures may also be used.

The treatment of choreographic works as a species of dramatic composition has served to define and delimit the types of dances which may be registered for copyright. It has also served to define the rights to which a copyright owner of a choreographic work is entitled. However, a serious disadvantage exists in treating choreographic works in this class of composition.

Case precedent indicates that in order to qualify as a

[56] 17 U.S.C. § 1(b) (1964).

dramatic composition a work must convey some storyline or theme to the audience. Most "modern and abstract" dances lack any storyline or theme. The bodily movements in such dances are primarily intended to convey some aesthetic or emotional concept to the audience. Although many of these dances constitute original creations of authorship, their qualification as a dramatic composition is uncertain.

In the interest of clarifying this uncertainty it is submitted that the Copyright Act be amended to reflect the following proposals:

1. Section 5 should be amended by adding choreographic compositions as a separate class of copyrightable works.

2. Copyrightable choreographic compositions should be limited to those which constitute an original creation of authorship intended for public performance.

3. These choreographic compositions should be accorded the same rights and protection as those presently accorded dramatic compositions.

Panels of Judges

SYMPOSIUM NUMBER ONE (1939)
  Edward A. Sargoy, Stephen P. Ladas, Edward S. Rogers, Dr. Louis Charles Smith, the late John H. Wigmore, members of a Committee of the American Bar Association appointed by Thomas E. Robertson, Chairman of the Section of Patent, Trade-Mark and Copyright Law

SYMPOSIUM NUMBER TWO (1940)
  Herman Finkelstein, General Attorney, American Society of Composers, Authors and Publishers

SYMPOSIUM NUMBER THREE (1940)
  The late John H. Wigmore, Dean of Northwestern University School of Law

SYMPOSIUM NUMBER FOUR (1952)
  The late Judge Herbert F. Goodrich, of the United States Court of Appeals for the Third Circuit
  Justice Roger J. Traynor, of the Supreme Court of the State of California
  Judge George T. Washington, of the Court of Appeals for the District of Columbia Circuit

SYMPOSIUM NUMBER FIVE (1954)
  Judge Stanley H. Fuld, of the Court of Appeals of the State of New York
  Chief Judge Leon R. Yankwich, of the United States District Court for the Southern District of California

SYMPOSIUM NUMBER SIX (1955)
  The late Chief Judge Sam Driver, of the United States District Court for the Eastern District of Washington
  The late Dean Wesley A. Sturges, President of the American Association of Law Schools

SYMPOSIUM NUMBER SEVEN (1956)
  Justice George Rossman, of the Supreme Court of Oregon
  Loyd Wright, President of the American Bar Association
  Edward A. Sargoy, former Chairman of the Copyright Subsection of the Patent, Trade-Mark and Copyright Section of the American Bar Association
  The late Louis E. Swarts, former Chairman of the above Subsection

SYMPOSIUM NUMBER EIGHT (1957)
> The late Chief Judge Charles E. Clark, of the United States Court of Appeals for the Second Circuit
> The late Chief Justice A. Cecil Snyder, of the Supreme Court of Puerto Rico

SYMPOSIUM NUMBER NINE (1958)
> Chief Judge John Biggs, Jr., of the United States Court of Appeals for the Third Circuit
> Chief Judge Simon E. Soboloff, of the United States Court of Appeals for the Fourth Circuit
> Judge William H. Hastie, of the United States Court of Appeals for the Third Circuit

SYMPOSIUM NUMBER TEN (1959)
> Chief Justice Frank R. Kenison, of the Supreme Court of New Hampshire
> Chief Judge Alfred P. Murrah, of the United States Court of Appeals for the Tenth Circuit

SYMPOSIUM NUMBER ELEVEN (1962)
> *Panel for 1959 National Competition*
> Chief Judge Charles S. Desmond, of the New York Court of Appeals
> Judge David T. Lewis, of the United States Court of Appeals for the Tenth Circuit
> *Panel for 1960 National Competition*
> Justice Tom C. Clark, of the United States Supreme Court
> Chief Justice Paul Reardon, of the Superior Court of Massachusetts
> Judge Elbert P. Tuttle, of the United States Court of Appeals for the Fifth Circuit

SYMPOSIUM NUMBER TWELVE (1963)
> *Panel for 1961 National Competition*
> Justice Walter V. Schaefer, of the Illinois Supreme Court
> Judge Sterry R. Waterman, of the United States Court of Appeals for the Second Circuit
> *Panel for 1962 National Competition*
> Judge Frederick G. Hamley, of the United States Court of Appeals for the Ninth Circuit
> Judge John Minor Wisdom, of the United States Court of Appeals for the Fifth Circuit

SYMPOSIUM NUMBER THIRTEEN (1964)
> Justice Leonard v. B. Sutton, of the Supreme Court of Colorado
> Justice Samuel Freedman, of the Court of Appeal of Manitoba
> Justice James L. McLennan, of the Supreme Court of Ontario

Panels of Judges

SYMPOSIUM NUMBER FOURTEEN (1966)
  Judge Carl McGowan, of the United States Court of Appeals for the District of Columbia
  Judge Charles M. Merrill, of the United States Court of Appeals for the Ninth Circuit
  Justice Haydn Proctor, of the Supreme Court of New Jersey
SYMPOSIUM NUMBER FIFTEEN (1966)
  Judge Roger J. Kiley, of the United States Court of Appeals for the Seventh Circuit
  Judge Francis Bergan, of the New York Court of Appeals

Papers Appearing in Copyright Law Symposia Numbers One through Fourteen

SYMPOSIUM NUMBER ONE (1939)

Page

Walter L. Pforzheimer, YALE UNIVERSITY SCHOOL OF LAW
Copyright Protection for the Performing Artist in His Interpretive Rendition   9

Paul Gitlin, HARVARD UNIVERSITY LAW SCHOOL
Radio Infringement of Music Copyright   61

Nathan Cohen, UNIVERSITY OF OREGON SCHOOL OF LAW
State Regulation of Musical Copyright   91

E. DeMatt Henderson, UNIVERSITY OF ARKANSAS SCHOOL OF LAW
The Law of Copyright, Especially Musical   125

Thomas O. Shelton, UNIVERSITY OF TEXAS SCHOOL OF LAW
The Protection of the Interpretative Rights of a Musical Artist Afforded by the Law of Literary Property, or the Doctrine of Unfair Competition   173

SYMPOSIUM NUMBER TWO (1940)

Paul P. Lipton, UNIVERSITY OF WISCONSIN LAW SCHOOL
The Extent of Copyright Protection for Law Books   11

Charles W. Joiner, STATE UNIVERSITY OF IOWA COLLEGE OF LAW
Analysis, Criticism, Comparison and Suggested Corrections of the Copyright Law of the U.S. Relative to Mechanical Reproduction of Music   43

George W. Botsford, UNIVERSITY OF ARIZONA COLLEGE OF LAW
Some Copyright Problems of Radio Broadcasters and Receivers of Musical Compositions   71

Irving E. Bernstein, YALE UNIVERSITY SCHOOL OF LAW
The Motion Picture Distributor and the Copyright Law   119

W. Marion Page, UNIVERSITY OF GEORGIA SCHOOL OF LAW
Copyright Laws in Georgia History   151

Papers in Copyright Law Symposia

SYMPOSIUM NUMBER THREE (1940)
  Frank R. Miller, STATE UNIVERSITY OF IOWA COLLEGE OF LAW
    A Re-Examination of Literary Piracy   2
  Frank D. Emerson, WESTERN RESERVE UNIVERSITY SCHOOL OF LAW
    Public Performance for Profit, Past and Present   52
  Calvin Welker Evans, UNIVERSITY OF ARIZONA COLLEGE OF LAW
    The Law of Copyright and the Right of Mechanical Reproduction of Musical Compositions   112
  Irving Propper, BROOKLYN LAW SCHOOL OF ST. LAWRENCE UNIVERSITY
    American "Popular" Music and the Copyright Law   164
  Robert W. Bergstrom, CHICAGO-KENT COLLEGE OF LAW
    The Businessman Deals with Copyright   248
  Howard B. Pickard, UNIVERSITY OF OKLAHOMA SCHOOL OF LAW
    Common-Law Rights before Publication   298
  Milton H. Aronson, WASHINGTON UNIVERSITY OF ST. LOUIS SCHOOL OF LAW
    The Development of Motion Picture Copyright   338

SYMPOSIUM NUMBER FOUR (1952)
  Melville B. Nimmer, HARVARD UNIVERSITY LAW SCHOOL
    Inroads on Copyright Protection   2
  Clinton R. Ashford, UNIVERSITY OF MICHIGAN LAW SCHOOL
    The Compulsory Manufacturing Provision: An Anachronism in the Copyright Act   48
  Franklin Feldman, COLUMBIA UNIVERSITY SCHOOL OF LAW
    The Manufacturing Clause: Copyright Protection to the Foreign Author   76
  Arthur S. Katz, NEW YORK UNIVERSITY SCHOOL OF LAW
    The Doctrine of Moral Right and American Copyright Law: A Proposal   78
  Charles O. Whitley, WAKE FOREST COLLEGE SCHOOL OF LAW
    Copyrights and the Income Tax Problem   158

SYMPOSIUM NUMBER FIVE (1954)
  Reginald Ray Reeves, UNIVERSITY OF IDAHO COLLEGE OF LAW
    Superman v. Captain Marvel: or, Loss of Literary Property in Comic Strips   3
  Russell H. Schlattman, ST. LOUIS UNIVERSITY SCHOOL OF LAW
    The Doctrine of Limited Publication in the Law of Literary

Papers in Copyright Law Symposia 197

Property Compared with the Doctrine of Experimental Use in the Law of Patents 37
Gilbert K. Bovard, STATE UNIVERSITY OF IOWA COLLEGE OF LAW
Copyright Protection in the Area of Scientific and Technical Works 68
William T. Birmingham, UNIVERSITY OF ARIZONA COLLEGE OF LAW
A Critical Analysis of the Infringement of Ideas 107
William F. Burbank, UNIVERSITY OF LOUISVILLE SCHOOL OF LAW
Television—a Public Performance for Profit? 133
James A. Webster, Jr., WAKE FOREST COLLEGE SCHOOL OF LAW
Protecting Things Valuable—Ideas 158
C. Harold Herr, TEMPLE UNIVERSITY SCHOOL OF LAW
The Patentee v. the Copyrightee 185
Sheldon M. Young, OHIO STATE UNIVERSITY COLLEGE OF LAW
Plagiarism, Piracy, and the Common Law Copyright 205
Ted Fair, BAYLOR UNIVERSITY SCHOOL OF LAW
Publication of Immoral and Indecent Works, with Regard to the Constitutional and Copyright Effects 230
Robert L. Wyckoff, UNIVERSITY OF COLORADO SCHOOL OF LAW
Defenses Peculiar to Actions Based on Infringement of Musical Copyrights 256

SYMPOSIUM NUMBER SIX (1955)
Richard W. Pogue, UNIVERSITY OF MICHIGAN LAW SCHOOL
Borderland—Where Copyright and Design Patent Meet 3
Saul Cohen, STANFORD UNIVERSITY SCHOOL OF LAW
Fair Use in the Law of Copyright 43
Richard C. Seither, TULANE UNIVERSITY SCHOOL OF LAW
UNESCO: New Hope for International Copyright? 74
Arthur L. Stevenson, Jr., HARVARD UNIVERSITY LAW SCHOOL
Moral Right and the Common Law: A Proposal 89
John J. DeMarines, DICKINSON SCHOOL OF LAW
State Regulation of Musical Copyright 118
Frank L. Bixby, UNIVERSITY OF WISCONSIN LAW SCHOOL
Hurn v. Oursler after Twenty Years 140

SYMPOSIUM NUMBER SEVEN (1956)
Raya S. Dreben, HARVARD UNIVERSITY LAW SCHOOL
Publication and the British Copyright Law 3

Papers in Copyright Law Symposia

J. Roger Shull, DUKE UNIVERSITY SCHOOL OF LAW
Collecting Collectively: ASCAP's Perennial Dilemma — 35

Ronald Cracas, HARVARD UNIVERSITY LAW SCHOOL
Judge Learned Hand and the Law of Copyright — 55

Franklin T. Laskin, YALE UNIVERSITY SCHOOL OF LAW
All Rights Unreserved: The Author's Lost Property in Publishing and Entertainment — 91

Robert E. Young, COLUMBIA UNIVERSITY SCHOOL OF LAW
The Copyright Term — 139

Daniel M. Singer, YALE UNIVERSITY SCHOOL OF LAW
International Copyright Protection and the United States: The Impact of the Universal Copyright Convention on Existing Law — 176

SYMPOSIUM NUMBER EIGHT (1957)

Maurice B. Stiefel, GEORGE WASHINGTON UNIVERSITY LAW SCHOOL
Piracy in High Places—Government Publications and Copyright Law — 3

Nathan Newbury III, HARVARD UNIVERSITY LAW SCHOOL
Protection of Comic Strips — 37

William G. Wells, UNIVERSITY OF ILLINOIS COLLEGE OF LAW
The Universal Copyright Convention and the United States: A Study of Conflict and Compromise — 69

Stephen E. Strom, UNIVERSITY OF MISSOURI SCHOOL OF LAW
Depreciation and Income Aspects of Copyright under the Internal Revenue Code of 1954 — 103

SYMPOSIUM NUMBER NINE (1958)

Arthur Rosett, COLUMBIA UNIVERSITY SCHOOL OF LAW
Burlesque as Copyright Infringement — 1

G. T. McConnell, HARVARD UNIVERSITY LAW SCHOOL
The Effect of the Universal Copyright Convention on Other International Conventions and Arrangements — 32

Stuart Jay Young, COLUMBIA UNIVERSITY SCHOOL OF LAW
Freebooters in Fashions: The Need for a Copyright in Textile and Garment Designs — 76

Richard W. Roberts, UNIVERSITY OF VIRGINIA LAW SCHOOL
Publication in the Law of Copyright — 111

Edward Silber, UNIVERSITY OF WISCONSIN LAW SCHOOL
Use of the Expert in Literary Piracy: A Proposal — 149

SYMPOSIUM NUMBER TEN (1959)

Samuel A. Olevson, HARVARD UNIVERSITY LAW SCHOOL

Papers in Copyright Law Symposia

English Experience with Registration and Deposit	1
Roger Needham, UNIVERSITY OF MICHIGAN LAW SCHOOL	
Tape Recording, Photocopying, and Fair Use	75
John L. Wilson, UNIVERSITY OF MICHIGAN LAW SCHOOL	
The Scholar and the Copyright Law	104
Arthur R. Miller, HARVARD UNIVERSITY LAW SCHOOL	
Problems in the Transfer of Interests in a Copyright	131
Eugene Mooney, UNIVERSITY OF ARKANSAS SCHOOL OF LAW	
The Jukebox Exemption	194
L. Lee Phillips, CORNELL UNIVERSITY LAW SCHOOL	
Related Rights and American Copyright Law: Compatible or Incompatible?	219
Martin Leach-Cross Feldman, TULANE UNIVERSITY SCHOOL OF LAW	
The Relationship between Copyright and Unfair Competition Principles	266
William F. Swindler, UNIVERSITY OF NEBRASKA COLLEGE OF LAW	
News: Public Right v. Property Right	285
Dino Joseph Caterini, NEW YORK UNIVERSITY SCHOOL OF LAW	
Contributions to Periodicals	321
Peter H. Morrison, COLUMBIA UNIVERSITY SCHOOL OF LAW	
Copyright Publication: The Sale and Distribution of Phonograph Records	387

SYMPOSIUM NUMBER ELEVEN (1962)

Rita E. Hauser, NEW YORK UNIVERSITY SCHOOL OF LAW	
The French Droit de Suite: The Problem of Protection for the Underprivileged Artist under the Copyright Law	1
William B. Colsey III, VILLANOVA UNIVERSITY SCHOOL OF LAW	
The Protection of Advertising and the Law of Copyright	28
Alan T. Dworkin, BOSTON UNIVERSITY SCHOOL OF LAW	
Originality in the Law of Copyright	60
William H. Garland, UNIVERSITY OF FLORIDA LAW SCHOOL	
Our Copyright Law—Growing Pains in International Society	82
John E. Harrington, UNIVERSITY OF DENVER COLLEGE OF LAW	
Copyright Duration	96
John Rittenhouse, Jr., UNIVERSITY OF DENVER COLLEGE OF LAW	
Section 24—Renewal Rights, Survivors, and Confusion: A Case Study	113

Donald L. Gunnels, WASHINGTON UNIVERSITY SCHOOL OF LAW
Copyright Protection for Writers Employed by the Federal Government   138

Richard P. Crowley, NEW YORK LAW SCHOOL
The Register of Copyrights as an Art Critic   155

SYMPOSIUM NUMBER TWELVE (1963)

Roger M. Milgrim, NEW YORK UNIVERSITY SCHOOL OF LAW
Territoriality of Copyright: An Analysis of Assignability under the Universal Copyright Convention   1

Robert A. Gorman, HARVARD UNIVERSITY LAW SCHOOL
Copyright Protection for the Collection and Representation of Facts   30

Donald L. A. Kerson, UNIVERSITY OF CALIFORNIA SCHOOL OF LAW AT BERKELEY
Sequel Rights in the Law of Literary Property   76

Don Metz, INDIANA UNIVERSITY SCHOOL OF LAW
Rights of Federal Government Personnel under the Copyright Act   96

Milton D. Andrews, UNIVERSITY OF OKLAHOMA COLLEGE OF LAW
Copyrighting Reproductions of Physical Objects   123

Arnold B. Silverman, UNIVERSITY OF PITTSBURGH SCHOOL OF LAW
The Scope of Protection of Copyrights and Design Patents in the United States   152

Juan G. Burciaga, UNIVERSITY OF NEW MEXICO SCHOOL OF LAW
Divestative Publication—Two-Century Dilemma   201

Thomas B. Morris, Jr., HARVARD UNIVERSITY LAW SCHOOL
The Origins of the Statute of Anne   222

Elery Wilmarth, UNIVERSITY OF COLORADO SCHOOL OF LAW
Statutory Remedies for Record Piracy   261

SYMPOSIUM NUMBER THIRTEEN (1964)

Elizabeth Heazlett Kury, UNIVERSITY OF PITTSBURGH SCHOOL OF LAW
Protection for Creators in the United States and Abroad   1

Charles S. McGuire, SUFFOLK UNIVERSITY LAW SCHOOL
Common-Law Overtones of Statutory Copyright: An Inquiry into the Status of a Federal Common Law of Unfair Competition   33

Joseph G. Cook, UNIVERSITY OF ALABAMA SCHOOL OF LAW
The Fine Arts: What Constitutes Infringement   65

Papers in Copyright Law Symposia

Bruce E. Fritch, YALE UNIVERSITY SCHOOL OF LAW
Some Copyright Implications of Videotapes (Suggesting the Need for Statutory Revision) — 87
Robert Stephen Savelson, COLUMBIA UNIVERSITY SCHOOL OF LAW
Electronic Music and the Copyright Law — 133
John M. Moellenberg, ST. LOUIS UNIVERSITY SCHOOL OF LAW
The Question of Choice Between Copyrighting or Patenting a Design — 165

SYMPOSIUM NUMBER FOURTEEN (1966)
Marion Lozier Woltmann, COLUMBIA UNIVERSITY SCHOOL OF LAW
The Author and the State: An Analysis of Soviet Copyright Law — 1
S. Paul Posner, HARVARD UNIVERSITY LAW SCHOOL
State and Federal Power in Patent and Copyright — 51
Monroe E. Price, YALE UNIVERSITY SCHOOL OF LAW
The Moral Judge and the Copyright Statute: The Problem of Stiffel and Compco — 90
John F. Banzhaf III, COLUMBIA UNIVERSITY SCHOOL OF LAW
Copyright Protection for Computer Programs — 118
David C. Petre, NOTRE DAME LAW SCHOOL
Statutory Copyright Protection for Books and Magazines Against Machine Copying — 180
Robert Shaye, COLUMBIA UNIVERSITY SCHOOL OF LAW
Piracy Within the Law: A Consideration of the Copyright Protection Afforded Foreign Authors in the United States and the Soviet Union — 226
D. E. Harding, UNIVERSITY OF CALIFORNIA SCHOOL OF LAW AT BERKELEY
Copyright in Lectures, Sermons, and Speeches — 272

Law Schools Contributing Papers to Previous Copyright Law Symposia

UNIVERSITY OF ALABAMA SCHOOL OF LAW
Joseph G. Cook, *The Fine Arts: What Constitutes Infringement*, SYMPOSIUM NUMBER THIRTEEN 65 (1964).

UNIVERSITY OF ARIZONA COLLEGE OF LAW
George W. Botsford, *Some Copyright Problems of Radio Broadcasters and Receivers of Musical Compositions*, SYMPOSIUM NUMBER TWO 71 (1940).
Calvin Welker Evans, *The Law of Copyright and the Right of Mechanical Reproduction of Musical Compositions*, SYMPOSIUM NUMBER THREE 112 (1940).
William T. Birmingham, *A Critical Analysis of the Infringement of Ideas*, SYMPOSIUM NUMBER FIVE 107 (1954).

UNIVERSITY OF ARKANSAS SCHOOL OF LAW
E. DeMatt Henderson, *The Law of Copyright, Especially Musical*, SYMPOSIUM NUMBER ONE 125 (1939).
Eugene Mooney, *The Jukebox Exemption*, SYMPOSIUM NUMBER TEN 194 (1959).

BAYLOR UNIVERSITY SCHOOL OF LAW
Ted Fair, *Publication of Immoral and Indecent Works, with Regard to the Constitutional and Copyright Effects*, SYMPOSIUM NUMBER FIVE 230 (1954).

BOSTON UNIVERSITY SCHOOL OF LAW
Alan T. Dworkin, *Originality in the Law of Copyright*, SYMPOSIUM NUMBER ELEVEN 60 (1962).

BROOKLYN LAW SCHOOL OF ST. LAWRENCE UNIVERSITY
Irving Propper, *American "Popular" Music and the Copyright Law*, SYMPOSIUM NUMBER THREE 164 (1940).

UNIVERSITY OF CALIFORNIA SCHOOL OF LAW AT BERKELEY
Donald L. A. Kerson, *Sequel Rights in the Law of Literary Property*, SYMPOSIUM NUMBER TWELVE 76 (1963).
D. E. Harding, *Copyright in Lectures, Sermons, and Speeches*, SYMPOSIUM NUMBER FOURTEEN 272 (1966).

204 Law Schools Contributing to Previous Symposia

CHICAGO-KENT COLLEGE OF LAW
>Robert W. Bergstrom, *The Businessman Deals with Copyright*, SYMPOSIUM NUMBER THREE 248 (1940).

UNIVERSITY OF COLORADO SCHOOL OF LAW
>Robert L. Wyckoff, *Defenses Peculiar to Actions Based on Infringement of Musical Copyrights*, SYMPOSIUM NUMBER FIVE 256 (1954).
>
>Elery Wilmarth, *Statutory Remedies for Record Piracy*, SYMPOSIUM NUMBER TWELVE 261 (1963).

COLUMBIA UNIVERSITY SCHOOL OF LAW
>Franklin Feldman, *The Manufacturing Clause: Copyright Protection to the Foreign Author*, SYMPOSIUM NUMBER FOUR 76 (1952).
>
>Robert E. Young, *The Copyright Term*, SYMPOSIUM NUMBER SEVEN 139 (1956).
>
>Arthur Rosett, *Burlesque as Copyright Infringement*, SYMPOSIUM NUMBER NINE 1 (1958).
>
>Stuart Jay Young, *Freebooters in Fashions: The Need for a Copyright in Textile and Garment Designs*, SYMPOSIUM NUMBER NINE 76 (1958).
>
>Peter H. Morrison, *Copyright Publication: The Sale and Distribution of Phonograph Records*, SYMPOSIUM NUMBER TEN 387 (1959).
>
>Robert Stephen Savelson, *Electronic Music and the Copyright Law*, SYMPOSIUM NUMBER THIRTEEN 133 (1964).
>
>Marion Lozier Woltmann, *The Author and the State: An Analysis of Soviet Copyright Law*, SYMPOSIUM NUMBER FOURTEEN 1 (1966).
>
>John F. Banzhaf III, *Copyright Protection for Computer Programs*, SYMPOSIUM NUMBER FOURTEEN 118 (1966).
>
>Robert Shaye, *Piracy Within the Law: A Consideration of the Copyright Protection Afforded Foreign Authors in the United States and the Soviet Union*, SYMPOSIUM NUMBER FOURTEEN 226 (1966).

CORNELL UNIVERSITY LAW SCHOOL
>L. Lee Phillips, *Related Rights and American Copyright Law: Compatible or Incompatible?* SYMPOSIUM NUMBER TEN 219 (1959).

UNIVERSITY OF DENVER COLLEGE OF LAW
>John E. Harrington, *Copyright Duration*, SYMPOSIUM NUMBER ELEVEN 96 (1962).
>
>John Rittenhouse, Jr., *Section 24—Renewal Rights, Survivors, and Confusion: A Case Study*, SYMPOSIUM NUMBER ELEVEN 113 (1962).

Law Schools Contributing to Previous Symposia 205

DICKINSON SCHOOL OF LAW
John J. DeMarines, *State Regulation of Musical Copyright*, SYMPOSIUM NUMBER SIX 118 (1955).

DUKE UNIVERSITY SCHOOL OF LAW
J. Roger Shull, *Collecting Collectively: ASCAP's Perennial Dilemma*, SYMPOSIUM NUMBER SEVEN 35 (1956).

UNIVERSITY OF FLORIDA LAW SCHOOL
William H. Garland, *Our Copyright Law: Growing Pains in International Society*, SYMPOSIUM NUMBER ELEVEN 82 (1962).

GEORGE WASHINGTON UNIVERSITY LAW SCHOOL
Maurice B. Stiefel, *Piracy in High Places—Government Publications and Copyright Law*, SYMPOSIUM NUMBER EIGHT 3 (1957).

UNIVERSITY OF GEORGIA SCHOOL OF LAW
W. Marion Page, *Copyright Laws in Georgia History*, SYMPOSIUM NUMBER TWO 151 (1940).

HARVARD UNIVERSITY LAW SCHOOL
Paul Gitlin, *Radio Infringement of Music Copyright*, SYMPOSIUM NUMBER ONE 61 (1939).

Melville B. Nimmer, *Inroads on Copyright Protection*, SYMPOSIUM NUMBER FOUR 2 (1952).

Arthur L. Stevenson, Jr., *Moral Right and the Common Law: A Proposal*, SYMPOSIUM NUMBER SIX 89 (1955).

Ronald Cracas, *Judge Learned Hand and the Law of Copyright*, SYMPOSIUM NUMBER SEVEN 55 (1956).

Raya S. Dreben, *Publication and the British Copyright Law*, SYMPOSIUM NUMBER SEVEN 3 (1956).

Nathan Newbury III, *Protection of Comic Strips*, SYMPOSIUM NUMBER EIGHT 37 (1957).

G. T. McConnell, *The Effect of the Universal Copyright Convention on Other International Conventions and Arrangements*, SYMPOSIUM NUMBER NINE 32 (1958).

Samuel A. Olevson, *English Experience with Registration and Deposit*, SYMPOSIUM NUMBER TEN 1 (1959).

Arthur R. Miller, *Problems in the Transfer of Interests in a Copyright*, SYMPOSIUM NUMBER TEN 131 (1959).

Robert A. Gorman, *Copyright Protection for the Collection and Representation of Ideas*, SYMPOSIUM NUMBER TWELVE 30 (1963).

Thomas B. Morris, Jr., *The Origins of the Statute of Anne*, SYMPOSIUM NUMBER TWELVE 222 (1963).

S. Paul Posner, *State and Federal Power in Patent and Copyright*, SYMPOSIUM NUMBER FOURTEEN 51 (1966).

UNIVERSITY OF IDAHO COLLEGE OF LAW
Reginald Ray Reeves, *Superman v. Captain Marvel: or, Loss of*

206 Law Schools Contributing to Previous Symposia

Literary Property in Comic Strips, SYMPOSIUM NUMBER FIVE 3 (1954).

UNIVERSITY OF ILLINOIS COLLEGE OF LAW

William G. Wells, The Universal Copyright Convention and the United States: A Study of Conflict and Compromise, SYMPOSIUM NUMBER EIGHT 69 (1957).

INDIANA UNIVERSITY SCHOOL OF LAW

Don Metz, Rights of Federal Government Personnel under the Copyright Act, SYMPOSIUM NUMBER TWELVE 96 (1963).

STATE UNIVERSITY OF IOWA COLLEGE OF LAW

Charles W. Joiner, Analysis, Criticism, Comparison and Suggested Corrections of the Copyright Law of the U.S. Relative to Mechanical Reproduction of Music, SYMPOSIUM NUMBER TWO 43 (1940).

Frank R. Miller, A Re-Examination of Literary Piracy, SYMPOSIUM NUMBER THREE 2 (1940).

Gilbert K. Bovard, Copyright Protection in the Area of Scientific and Technical Works, SYMPOSIUM NUMBER FIVE 68 (1954).

UNIVERSITY OF LOUISVILLE SCHOOL OF LAW

William F. Burbank, Television—a Public Performance for Profit? SYMPOSIUM NUMBER FIVE 133 (1954).

UNIVERSITY OF MICHIGAN LAW SCHOOL

Clinton R. Ashford, The Compulsory Manufacturing Provision: An Anachronism in the Copyright Act, SYMPOSIUM NUMBER FOUR 48 (1952).

Richard W. Pogue, Borderland—Where Copyright and Design Patent Meet, SYMPOSIUM NUMBER SIX 3 (1955).

Roger Needham, Tape Recording, Photocopying, and Fair Use, SYMPOSIUM NUMBER TEN 75 (1959).

John L. Wilson, The Scholar and the Copyright Law, SYMPOSIUM NUMBER TEN 104 (1959).

UNIVERSITY OF MISSOURI SCHOOL OF LAW

Stephen E. Strom, Depreciation and Income Aspects of Copyright Under the Internal Revenue Code of 1954, SYMPOSIUM NUMBER EIGHT 103 (1957).

UNIVERSITY OF NEBRASKA COLLEGE OF LAW

William F. Swindler, News: Public Right v. Property Right, SYMPOSIUM NUMBER TEN 285 (1959).

UNIVERSITY OF NEW MEXICO SCHOOL OF LAW

Juan G. Burciaga, Divestative Publication—A Two-Century Dilemma, SYMPOSIUM NUMBER TWELVE 201 (1963).

NEW YORK UNIVERSITY SCHOOL OF LAW

Arthur S. Katz, The Doctrine of Moral Right and American Copy-

Law Schools Contributing to Previous Symposia 207

right Law: A Proposal, SYMPOSIUM NUMBER FOUR 78 (1952).
Dino Joseph Caterini, *Contributions to Periodicals*, SYMPOSIUM NUMBER TEN 321 (1959).
Rita E. Hauser, *The French Droit de Suite: The Problem of Protection for the Under-privileged Artist under the Copyright Law*, SYMPOSIUM NUMBER ELEVEN 1 (1962).
Roger M. Milgrim, *Territoriality of Copyright: An Analysis of Assignability under the Universal Copyright Convention*, SYMPOSIUM NUMBER TWELVE 1 (1963).

NOTRE DAME LAW SCHOOL
David C. Petre, *Statutory Copyright Protection for Books and Magazines Against Machine Copying*, SYMPOSIUM NUMBER FOURTEEN 180 (1966).

OHIO STATE UNIVERSITY COLLEGE OF LAW
Sheldon M. Young, *Plagiarism, Piracy, and the Common Law Copyright*, SYMPOSIUM NUMBER FIVE 205 (1954).

UNIVERSITY OF OKLAHOMA SCHOOL OF LAW
Howard B. Pickard, *Common-Law Rights Before Publication*, SYMPOSIUM NUMBER THREE 298 (1940).
Milton D. Andrews, *Copyrighting Reproductions of Physical Objects*, SYMPOSIUM NUMBER TWELVE 123 (1963).

UNIVERSITY OF OREGON SCHOOL OF LAW
Nathan Cohen, *State Regulation of Musical Copyright*, SYMPOSIUM NUMBER ONE 91 (1939).

UNIVERSITY OF PITTSBURGH SCHOOL OF LAW
Elizabeth Heazlett Kury, *Protection for Creators in the United States and Abroad*, SYMPOSIUM NUMBER THIRTEEN 1 (1964).
Arnold B. Silverman, *The Scope of Protection of Copyrights and Design Patents in the United States*, SYMPOSIUM NUMBER TWELVE 152 (1963).

ST. LOUIS UNIVERSITY SCHOOL OF LAW
John M. Moellenberg, *The Question of Choice between Copyrighting or Patenting a Design*, SYMPOSIUM NUMBER THIRTEEN 165 (1964).
Russell H. Schlattman, *The Doctrine of Limited Publication in the Law of Literary Property Compared with the Doctrine of Experimental Use in the Law of Patents*, SYMPOSIUM NUMBER FIVE 37 (1954).

STANFORD UNIVERSITY SCHOOL OF LAW
Saul Cohen, *Fair Use in the Law of Copyright*, SYMPOSIUM NUMBER SIX 43 (1955).

SUFFOLK UNIVERSITY LAW SCHOOL
Charles S. McGuire, *Common-Law Overtones of Statutory Copy-*

208 Law Schools Contributing to Previous Symposia

right: An Inquiry into the Status of a Federal Common Law of Unfair Competition, Symposium Number Thirteen 33 (1964).

TEMPLE UNIVERSITY SCHOOL OF LAW
C. Harold Herr, *The Patentee v. the Copyrightee,* Symposium Number Five 185 (1954).

UNIVERSITY OF TEXAS SCHOOL OF LAW
Thomas O. Shelton, *The Protection of the Interpretative Rights of a Musical Artist Afforded by the Law of Literary Property, or the Doctrine of Unfair Competition,* Symposium Number One 173 (1939).

TULANE UNIVERSITY SCHOOL OF LAW
Richard C. Seither, *UNESCO: New Hope for International Copyright?* Symposium Number Six 74 (1955).
Martin Leach-Cross Feldman, *The Relationship between Copyright and Unfair Competition Principles,* Symposium Number Ten 266 (1959).

VILLANOVA UNIVERSITY SCHOOL OF LAW
William B. Colsey III, *The Protection of Advertising and the Law of Copyright,* Symposium Number Eleven 28 (1962).

UNIVERSITY OF VIRGINIA LAW SCHOOL
Richard W. Roberts, *Publication in the Law of Copyright,* Symposium Number Nine 111 (1958).

WAKE FOREST COLLEGE SCHOOL OF LAW
Charles O. Whitley, *Copyrights and the Income Tax Problem,* Symposium Number Four 158 (1952).
James A. Webster, Jr., *Protecting Things Valuable—Ideas,* Symposium Number Five 158 (1954).

WASHINGTON UNIVERSITY SCHOOL OF LAW
Donald L. Gunnels, *Copyright Protection for Writers Employed by the Federal Government,* Symposium Number Eleven 138 (1962).

WASHINGTON UNIVERSITY OF ST. LOUIS SCHOOL OF LAW
Milton H. Aronson, *The Development of Motion Picture Copyright,* Symposium Number Three 338 (1940).

WESTERN RESERVE UNIVERSITY SCHOOL OF LAW
Frank D. Emerson, *Public Performance for Profit, Past and Present,* Symposium Number Three 52 (1940).

UNIVERSITY OF WISCONSIN LAW SCHOOL
Paul P. Lipton, *The Extent of Copyright Protection for Law Books,* Symposium Number Two 11 (1940).
Frank L. Bixby, *Hurn v. Oursler after Twenty Years,* Symposium Number Six 140 (1955).
Edward Silber, *Use of the Expert in Literary Piracy: A Proposal,* Symposium Number Nine 149 (1958).

Law Schools Contributing to Previous Symposia

YALE UNIVERSITY SCHOOL OF LAW

Walter L. Pforzheimer, *Copyright Protection for the Performing Artist in his Interpretive Rendition*, SYMPOSIUM NUMBER ONE 9 (1939).

Irving E. Bernstein, *The Motion Picture Distributor and the Copyright Law*, SYMPOSIUM NUMBER TWO 119 (1940).

Bruce E. Fritch, *Some Copyright Implications of Videotapes (Suggesting the Need for Statutory Revision)*, SYMPOSIUM NUMBER THIRTEEN 87 (1964).

Franklin T. Laskin, *All Rights Unreserved: The Author's Lost Property in Publishing and Entertainment*, SYMPOSIUM NUMBER SEVEN 91 (1956).

Daniel M. Singer, *International Copyright Protection and the United States: The Impact of the Universal Copyright Convention on Existing Law*, SYMPOSIUM NUMBER SEVEN 176 (1956).

Monroe E. Price, *The Moral Judge and the Copyright Statute: The Problem of* Stiffel *and* Compco, SYMPOSIUM NUMBER FOURTEEN 90 (1966).

Statutes and Cases

STATUTES

UNITED STATES

U.S. Const., art. 1, § 8, 2n14; 10n58; 52n227; 93n58; 134n3; 162n53; 182n38
15 U.S.C. §§ 1051, 1052, 1057, 1091 (1958), 46n195; 47nn200,202; 51n222
15 U.S.C. §§ 1051–127 (1964), 51n222; 88n32; 89nn38,39
17 U.S.C. §§ 1 et seq. (1958), 2n8; 10n58; 33n150; 53nn230,234; 57n250; 62n274
17 U.S.C. §§ 1 et seq. (1964), 82n10; 83n12; 87n27; 134n1; 136n7; 138n25; 139n26; 148nn69,72,73; 165n73; 168n88; 173n3; 175n8; 177n18; 183nn40,41; 184n42; 186nn46,49–51; 187nn53,54; 188n56
35 U.S.C. §§ 1 et seq. (1958), 1n1; 10n58; 37n166; 39n173
35 U.S.C. §§ 1 et seq. (1964), 80n1; 81n3; 82n10; 87n27; 121n135
47 U.S.C. §§ 1 et seq. (1964), 157n20; 158nn22,23
1 Stat. 124 (1790), 83n12
2 Stat. 171 (1802), 83n12
4 Stat. 436 (1831), 83n12
5 Stat. 543 (1842), 80n1
11 Stat. 138 (1856), 83n12
12 Stat. 246 (1861), 80n1
13 Stat. 540 (1865), 83n12
16 Stat. 198 (1870), 80n1
32 Stat. 193 (1902), 80n1
35 Stat. 1075 (1909), 165n73; 168n89
48 Stat. 1064 (1934), 157n20; 158n22
60 Stat. 427 (1946), 51n222; 88n32
60 Stat. 428 (1946), 89n39
60 Stat. 429 (1946), 47n200
60 Stat. 430 (1946), 47n202
60 Stat. 435 (1946), 46n195; 89n38
66 Stat. 752 (1952), 168n90
66 Stat. 805 (1952), 80n1

76 Stat. 769 (1962), 89n39
Rev. Stat. (1870), §§ 4948-71, 83n12
37 C.F.R. § 202 (Regs. Copyright Office) (1960), 85n23; 86n25; 148nn70,71; 177n19
47 C.F.R. § 73.132, 164n66
19 Fed. R. Civ. P., 164n64
Mont. Rev. Codes, §§ 67-1107, 161n40

GREAT BRITAIN
12, 13, 14 Geo. 6, c. 88 (1949), 131n169
4 & 5 Eliz. 2, c. 74 (1956), 131n169
Copyright Act of November 5, 1956, 131n169
Registered Design Act of 1949, 131n169

CASES

Ex parte Adams, 1898 C.D. 115 (Comm'r of Patents), 118n127
Aerosol Research Co. v. Scovill Mfg. Co., 334 F.2d 751 (7th Cir. 1964), 13n70; 20n107
American Chicle Co. v. Topps Chewing Gum, Inc., 208 F.2d 560 (2d Cir. 1953), 17nn88,91
American Luggage Works, Inc. v. United States Trunk Co., 158 F. Supp. 50 (D. Mass. 1957), *aff'd sub nom.* Hawley Prods. Co. v. United States Trunk Co., 259 F.2d 69 (1st Cir. 1958), 21n114
American-Marietta Co. v. Krigsman, 275 F.2d 287, 289 (2d Cir. 1960), 5n35
American Safety Table Co. v. Schreiber, 269 F.2d 255, 271-72, 274-75, 277 (2d Cir.), *cert. denied*, 361 U.S. 915 (1959), 3n20; 4n24; 11n65; 15n79
American Tobacco Co. v. Werckmeister, 207 U.S. 284 (1907), 70n310
American Visuals Corp. v. Holland, 239 F.2d 740, 744 (2d Cir. 1956), 63n277
Amerock Corp. v. Aubrey Hardware Mfg., Inc., 273 F.2d 346, 349 (7th Cir. 1960), 126n160
Application of Bigelow, 194 F.2d 545 (C.C.P.A. 1952), 116n118
Application of Johnson, 175 F.2d 791 (C.C.P.A. 1949), 118n126
Application of Mogen David Wine Corp., 328 F.2d 925, 932 (C.C.P.A. 1964) (patents), reversing 134 U.S.P.Q. 576 (Patent Office Trademark Trial & Appeal Board 1962), 145 U.S.P.Q. 58 (Patent Office

Statutes and Cases 213

Trademark Trial and Appeal Board 1965), 44n193; 49n216; 50n221; 89n41; 91n51
Application of Oglesby, 3 O.G. Pat. Off. 211 (Feb. 24, 1873), reprinted in SIMONDS, THE LAW OF DESIGN PATENTS 121 (1874), 115n116.
Application of Park, 181 F.2d 155 (C.C.P.A. 1950), 126n161
Aro Mfg. Co. v. Convertible Top Replacement Co., 377 U.S. 476, 522 (1964), 57n249; 94n60
Aronson v. Baker, 43 N.J. Eq. 365, 12 Atl. 177 (Ch. Div. 1888), 176n13
Art Metal Works, Inc. v. Cunningham Prods. Corp., 137 Misc. 429, 242 N.Y. Supp. 294 (Sup. Ct. 1930), 25n125
Art Metal Works, Inc. v. Gibson Lighter Mfg. Co., 205 Misc. 155, 127 N.Y.S.2d 786 (Sup. Ct. 1953), modified per curiam, 283 App. Div. 937, 130 N.Y.S.2d 814 (1st Dept), aff'd mem., 283 App. Div. 1050, 131 N.Y.S.2d 891 (1st Dept. 1954), 25n125; 31n144
Atlantic Monthly Co. v. Post Publishing Co., 27 F.2d 556 (D. Mass. 1928), 62n275; 65n286; 176n16
Atlantic Works v. Brady, 107 U.S. 192, 199 (1882), 99n71
Audio Fidelity, Inc. v. High Fidelity Recordings, Inc., 283 F.2d 551 (9th Cir. 1960), 7nn42,44

Barns v. Miner, 122 Fed. 480 (C.C.S.D.N.Y. 1903), 180n33
Bell v. Mahn, 121 Pa. St. 225 (1888), 178n23
Berlinger v. Bush Jewelry Co., 48 F.2d 812 (2d Cir. 1931), 125n154
Birmingham Broadcasting Co. v. Bell, 259 Ala. 656, 68 So. 2d 314 (1953), 74n325
Black v. Plaut, 87 F. Supp. 49 (D. Ill. 1949), 176n16
Blanc v. Lantz, 83 U.S.P.Q. 137 (Cal. Super. Ct. 1949), 62n275
Bleistein v. Donaldson Lithographing Co., 188 U.S. 239 (1903), 83n14
Bobbs-Merrill Co. v. Straus, 210 U.S. 339, 346–47 (1908), 54n235; 57n253
Charles Boldt Co. v. Turner Bros. Co., 199 Fed. 139, 143 (7th Cir. 1912), 104n87; 127n162
Bolte & Weyer Co. v. Knight Light Co., 180 Fed. 412, 415 (7th Cir. 1910), 105nn88,89
Booth v. Garelly, 1 Blatch. 247 (S.D.N.Y. 1847), reprinted in SIMONDS, THE LAW OF DESIGN PATENTS (1874), 122n138
Bostitch, Inc. v. King Fastener Co., 87 R.I. 274, 286, 288, 140 A.2d 274, 280, 282 (1958), 17nn88,90; 19n102; 40n184
In re Bourns, 45 C.C.P.A (Patents) 821, 252 F.2d 582 (1958), 47n204
Chas. D. Briddell, Inc. v. Alglobe Trading Corp., 194 F.2d 416 (2d Cir. 1952), 3n15; 21n115

Statutes and Cases

Brightly v. Littleton, 37 Fed. 103 (C.C.E.D. Pa. 1888), 176n13
Broder v. Zeno Mauvais Music Co., 88 Fed. 74 (C.C.N.D. Cal. 1898), 176n15
Buck v. Kloeppel, 10 F. Supp. 345 (S.D. Fla. 1935), 164n64
Buck v. Jewell-LaSalle Realty Co., 283 U.S. 191 (1931), 166nn80,81, 82; 168n93
Burrow-Giles Lithograph Co. v. Sarony, 111 U.S. 53 (1884), 83n14

Cable Vision, Inc. v. KUTV, Inc., 211 F. Supp. 47, 52–55 (D.Idaho 1962), *vacated*, 335 F.2d 348, 350–52, 354 (9th Cir. 1964), *cert. denied*, 379 U.S. 989 (1965), 61n271; 62n273; 71n315; 156n15; 157n16; 158n26; 159nn30,32; 160nn37,38; 161n43; 162nn48,49, 50,53; 163nn54,55,56; 165nn67,69
William Calk Co. v. Neverslip Mfg. Co. 136 Fed. 210, 215 (M.D. Pa. 1905), *aff'd*, 145 Fed. 928 (1906), 117n120
Campbell Soup Co. v. Armour & Co., 175 F.2d 795 (3d Cir. 1949), 18n93
Capex Co. v. Swartz, 166 F.2d 5 (7th Cir. 1948), 127n166
Capitol Records, Inc. v. Greatest Records, Inc., 43 Misc. 2d 878, 252 N.Y.S.2d 553 (Sup. Ct. 1964), 24n122; 61n271; 68n303; 70n313
Capitol Records, Inc. v. Mercury Records Corp., 221 F.2d 657, 664, 667 (2d Cir. 1955), 11n64; 53nn231,232; 59n266; 64nn281,282; 68nn301,303; 70n312; 77n329
Cardinal Film Corp. v. Beck, 248 Fed. 368 (S.D.N.Y. 1918), 63nn276, 278
Ex parte Caron Corp., 100 U.S.P.Q. 356 (Comm'r 1954), 46nn197, 199
Caron Corp. v. Vivaudou, Inc., 4 F.2d 995 (2d Cir. 1925), 34n153
Carte v. Duff, 25 Fed. 183 (1885), 177n17
Chandler Adjustable Chair & Desk Co. v. Heywood Bros. & Wakefield Co., 91 Fed. 163 (D. Mass. 1898), 118n127
Cheney Bros. v. Doris Silk Corp., 35 F.2d 279–81 (2d Cir. 1929), *cert. denied*, 281 U.S. 728 (1930), 3nn16,18; 10n62; 11n63; 55n240; 59n266; 93n56; 97n65
Chesebrough Mfg. Co. v. Old Gold Chemical Co., 70 F.2d 383 (6th Cir.), *cert. denied*, 293 U.S. 599 (1934), 18n95
Chicago Board of Trade v. L. A. Kinsey Co., 125 Fed. 72 (C.C.D. Ind. 1903), *rev'd on other grounds*, 130 Fed. 507 (7th Cir. 1904), *aff'd*, 198 U.S. 236 (1905), 176n15
Circle S Prods. Co. v. Powell Prods., Inc., 174 F.2d 562 (7th Cir. 1949), 118n128
Clark v. Bishop, 25 L.T. 908 (1872), 179n29

Statutes and Cases 215

Coca-Cola Co. v. Glee-Nol Bottling Co., 221 Fed. 61 (5th Cir. 1915), 43n188

Richard J. Cole, Inc. v. Manhattan Modes Co., 2 App. Div. 2d 593, 159 N.Y.S.2d 259 (1956), 87n30

Colgate-Palmolive Co. v. North American Chem. Corp., 238 F. Supp. 81 (S.D.N.Y. 1964), 16n85

J. N. Collins Co. v. F. M. Paist Co., 14 F.2d 614 (E.D. Pa. 1926), 18nn96,100

Columbia Broadcasting Sys., Inc. v. Documentaries Unlimited, Inc., 42 Misc. 2d 723, 248 N.Y.S.2d 809 (Sup. Ct. 1964), 61n271; 68n300; 70n314

Compco Corp. v. Day-Brite Lighting, Inc., 376 U.S. 231, 234, 236–39 (1964), 7n47; 8n49; 9nn55,56; 11n65; 19n104; 38n170; 49n213; 51n224; 52n226; 60n269; 84n19; 93n58; 95n64; 162n52

Continental Casualty Co. v. Beardsley, 253 F.2d 702, 707 (2d Cir.), *cert. denied*, 358 U.S. 816 (1958), 63n279

Cook & Bernheimer Co. v. Ross, 73 Fed. 203 (C.C.S.D.N.Y. 1896), 37n164

Ex parte Crane, 1869 C.D. 7 (Comm'r of Patents), 117–18; 117n122

Crescent Tool Co. v. Kilborn & Bishop Co., 247 Fed. 299 (2d Cir. 1917), 6n38

Cuno Eng'r Corp. v. Automatic Devices Corp., 314 U.S. 84, 89 (1941), 126n158

Daly v. Palmer, 6 Fed. Cas. 1132, No. 3,552 (C.C.S.D.N.Y. 1868), 178n22; 181n37

Davies v. Bowes, 209 Fed. 53 (S.D.N.Y. 1913), 163n59

Day-Brite Lighting, Inc. v. Compco Corp., 311 F.2d 26, 27–28 (7th Cir. 1962), 8nn50,51

In re Deister Concentrator Co., 48 C.C.P.A. (patents) 952, 961, 966, 289 F.2d 496, 501, 504, 506 (1961), 44n189; 47n206; 48n207; 50; 50n220; 61n270; 91n48

De Jonge & Co. v. Breuker & Kessler Co., 181 Fed. 150 (E.D. Pa. 1910), 82n21

DeSilva Constr. Corp. v. Herrald, 213 F. Supp. 184 (M.D. Fla. 1962), 68n304

R. E. Dietz Co. v. Burr & Starkweather Co., 243 Fed. 592 (2d Cir. 1917), 115–16; 115nn114,115

Dior v. Milton, 9 Misc. 2d 425, 438, 155 N.Y.S.2d 443, 458 (Sup. Ct.), *aff'd mem.*, 2 App. Div. 2d 878, 156 N.Y.S.2d 996 (1st Dept. 1956), 58n255; 59nn262,265; 65n288; 93n55

Dobson v. Dornan, 118 U.S. 10 (1886), 123; 123nn140,141

Dominick & Haff v. R. Wallace & Sons Mfg. Co., 209 Fed. 223–24 (2d Cir. 1913), 39n176; 124nn148,149

Duplex Straw Dispenser Co. v. Harold Leonard & Co., 229 F. Supp. 401 (S.D. Cal. 1964), 13n70

Eastern Wine Corp. v. Winslow-Warren, Ltd., 137 F.2d 955, 957, 958 (2d Cir.), *cert. denied*, 320 U.S. 758 (1943), 3n17; 22n117

Eastman Kodak Co. v. Royal-Pioneer Paper Box Mfg. Co., 197 F. Supp. 132 (E.D. Pa. 1961), 21n114

Electric Storage Battery Co. v. Mine Safety Appliances Co., 143 U.S.P.Q. 163, 166, 168 (Patent Office Trademark Trial & Appeal Board 1964), 49–50; 49n214; 50n219

Jacob Elishewitz & Sons Co. v. Bronston Bros. & Co., 40 F.2d 434 (2d Cir. 1930), 39n175

Estate Stove Co. v. Gray & Dudley, 41 F.2d 462 (6th Cir. 1930), *vacated on other grounds*, 50 F.2d 413 (1931), 15n80

Ettore v. Philco Television Broadcasting Corp., 229 F.2d 481 (3d Cir.), *cert. denied*, 351 U.S. 926 (1956), 55n241; 64n281

William Faehndrich, Inc. v. Wheeler Riddle Cheese Co., 34 F.2d 43 (E.D.N.Y. 1929), 43n189

N. K. Fairbank Co. v. R. W. Bell Mfg. Co., 77 Fed. 869 (2d Cir. 1896), 17n92; 19n101; 34n159

Fashion Originators Guild of America, Inc. v. FTC, 114 F.2d 80, 84 (2d Cir. 1940), *aff'd on other grounds*, 312 U.S. 457 (1941), 11n64; 55n239; 60n267; 97n66

Feathercombs, Inc. v. Solo Prods. Corp., 306 F.2d 251 (2d Cir. 1962), 32n147

Leo Feist, Inc. v. Lew Tendler Tavern, Inc., 267 F.2d 494 (3d Cir. 1959), 170n98

Ferris v. Frohman, 238 Ill. 430, 87 N.E. 327 (1909), *aff'd* 223 U.S. 424 (1912), 67n297; 175n10; 176n16

Field v. True Comics, Inc., 89 F. Supp. 611 (S.D.N.Y. 1950), 164n62

Fisher v. Blank, 138 N.Y. 244, 33 N.E. 1040 (1893), 34n158

Fisher v. Star Co., 231 N.Y. 414, 435, 132 N.E. 133, 140, *cert. denied*, 257 U.S. 654 (1921), 55nn241, 242

F. W. Fitch Co. v. Camille, Inc., 106 F.2d 635 (8th Cir. 1939), 16n82

Flagg Mfg. Co. v. Holway, 178 Mass. 83, 59 N.E. 667 (1901), 4n26; 14nn73,74

Flamingo Telefilm Sales, Inc. v. United Artists Corp., 141 U.S.P.Q. 461 (N.Y. Sup. Ct. 1964), *rev'd on other grounds*, 22 App. Div. 2d 778, 254 N.Y.S.2d 36 (1st Dept. 1964), 71n316; 74n324

Statutes and Cases 217

Flexitized, Inc. v. National Flexitized Corp., 335 F.2d 744 (2d Cir. 1964), *cert. denied*, 380 U.S. 913 (1965), 60n268

Flint v. Oleet Jewelry Mfg. Co., 133 F. Supp. 459 (S.D.N.Y. 1955), 6n40

Florence Mfg. Co. v. J. C. Dowd & Co., 178 Fed. 73 (2d Cir. 1910), 18n99; 34n157

Folsom v. Marsh, 9 Fed. Cas. 342, 348 (No. 4901) (C.C.D. Mass. 1841), 142–43n47

Forestek Plating & Mfg. Co. v. Knapp-Monarch Co., 106 F.2d 554 (6th Cir. 1939), 112n106

Franklin Lamp Mfg. Co. v. Albe Lamp & Shade Co., 26 F. Supp. 960, 962 (E.D. Pa. 1939), 82n7; 114n111

Fuller v. Bemis, 50 Fed. 926, 929 (C.C.S.D.N.Y. 1892), 179nn24,25, 26; 180n34; 181nn36,37

Fulmer v. United States, 103 F. Supp. 1021 (Ct. Cl. 1952), 87n31

General Time Instruments Corp. v. United States Time Corp., 165 F.2d 853 (2d Cir.), *cert. denied*, 334 U.S. 846 (1948), 21n115

A. C. Gilbert Co. v. Shemitz, 45 F.2d 98 (2d Cir. 1930), 113n108

Glenn Raven Knitting Mills, Inc. v. Sanson Hosiery Mills, Inc., 189 F.2d 845 (4th Cir. 1951), 126n161; 127n164

Gold Seal Importers, Inc. v. Morris White Fashions, Inc. 124 F.2d 141, 142 (2d Cir. 1941), 126n157

Gorham Co. v. White, 81 U.S. (14 Wall.) 511, 528 (1871), 39n177; 81nn4,5; 123n139

Graff, Washbourne & Dunn v. Webster, 195 Fed. 522, 524 (2d Cir. 1912), 112n104

Graham v. John Deere Co., 383 U.S. 1 (1966), 121n135

Grant v. California Bench Co., 76 Cal. App. 2d 706, 173 P.2d 818 (Dist. Ct. App. 1956), 7n42

Granz v. Harris, 198 F.2d 585 (2d Cir. 1952), 175n11

Great Atlantic & Pacific Tea Co. v. Supermarket Equipment Corp., 340 U.S. 147, 152 (1950), 10n59

Green v. Luby, 177 Fed. 287 (C.C.S.D.N.Y. 1909), 179n29

Haeger Potteries v. Gilner Potteries, 123 F. Supp. 261 (S.D. Cal. 1954), 5n31

Ex parte Haig & Haig, Ltd., 118 U.S.P.Q. 229 (Comm'r 1958), 36n162; 89; 89n40

Hammond v. Stockton Combined Harvester & Agricultural Works, 70 Fed. 716 (9th Cir. 1895), 118n125

C. S. Hammond & Co. v. International College Globe, Inc., 210 F. Supp. 206, 219 (S.D.N.Y. 1962), 21n116; 25n125

Harms, Inc. v. Sansom House Enterprises, Inc., 162 F. Supp. 129 (E.D. Pa. 1958), *aff'd sub. nom*, 170n98

Harper Bros. v. Donohue, 144 F. 491 (C.C.N.D. Ill. 1905), 175n9

Hawley Prods Co. v. United States Trunk Co., 259 F.2d 69 (1st Cir. 1958), 21n114

Healey v. Macy & Co., 251 App. Div. 440, 297 N.Y.S. 165 (1st Dept. 1937), 175n11

Herbert v. Shanley Co., 229 Fed. 340 (2d Cir. 1916), 242 U.S. 591, 595 (1917), 165n74; 166n76; 168n91

Hesse v. Grossman, 152 Cal. App. 2d 536, 313 P.2d 625 (Dist. Ct. App. 1957), 58n258

Hi-Land Dairyman's Assn. v. Cloverleaf Dairy, 107 Utah 68, 151 P.2d 710 (1944), 18nn96,97; 34n157

In re Hillerich & Bradsby Co., 40 C.C.P.A. (Patents) 990, 204 F.2d 287 (1953), 36n161

Charles E. Hires Co. v. Consumers' Co., 100 Fed. 809 (7th Cir. 1900), 36n162

H. P. Hood & Sons, Inc. v. Du Mond, 336 U.S. 525 (1949), 57n251

In re Horne, 83 F.2d 692 (C.C.P.A. 1936), 119n128

Howard Dustless Duster Co. v. Carleton, 219 Fed. 913 (D. Conn. 1915), 34n158

Hueter v. Compco Corp., 179 F.2d 416 (7th Cir. 1950), 118n128

Huston v. Buckeye Bait Corp., 145 F. Supp. 600 (S.D. Ohio 1956), 4n27

Ilyin v. Avon Publications, Inc., 110 U.S.P.Q. 356 (S.D.N.Y. 1956), 164n65

Imperial Glass Co. v. A. H. Heisey & Co., 294 Fed. 267 (6th Cir. 1923), 127n165

Industrial Rayon Corp. v. Dutchess Underwear Corp., 17 F. Supp. 783 (S.D.N.Y.), *rev'd on other grounds*, 92 F.2d 33 (2d Cir. 1937), 43n188

Insect-O-Lite Co. v. Hagemeyer, 151 F. Supp. 829, 833 (E.D. Ky. 1957), 3n21

Intermountain Broadcasting Corp. v. Idaho Microwave, Inc., 196 F. Supp. 315, 317, 320–21, 324, 326–28 (D. Idaho 1961), 130 U.S.P.Q. 135, 155n9; 156nn14,15; 157nn17,18; 159n30; 160nn33,34,35; 161nn42, 43, 45; 162nn47, 49

International Business Mach. Corp. v. United States, 298 U.S. 131 (1936), 95n62

Statutes and Cases 219

International Latex Corp. v. Flexees, Inc., App. Div. 363, 119 N.Y.S.2d 409 (1st Dept. 1953), 43n186; 44n189

International News Service v. Associated Press, 248 U.S. 215, 239–40, 245 (1918), 3n18; 56n246; 58n259; 59nn260,264; 92n54; 111n103; 161n44; 162n50; 163n59

Jeweler's Circular Publishing Co. v. Keystone Publishing Co., 281 Fed. 83 (2d Cir. 1922), 168n48

Jones Bros. v. Underkoffler, 16 F. Supp. 729, 731 (M.D. Pa. 1936), 85n21; 87n31

Kalem Co. v. Harper Bros., 222 U.S. 55 (1911), 179nn27,28; 180n35

Dan Kasoff Inc. v. Novelty Jewelry Co., 209 F.2d 745, 746 (2d. Cir. 1962), 84n18

Keene v. Kimball, 16 Gray 545 (Mass. 1860), 176n15

Kellogg Co. v. National Biscuit Co., 305 U.S. 111 (1938), 10n60

Ketcham v. N.Y. World's Fair 1939, 34 F. Supp. 657 (E.D.N.Y. 1940), aff'd, 119 F.2d 422 (2d Cir. 1941), 175n11

King v. Mister Maestro Inc., 224 F. Supp. 101 (S.D.N.Y. 1963), 67; 67n292

King Features Syndicate v. Fleischer, 299 Fed. 533, 535 (2d Cir. 1924), 87n31

Kingsway, Inc. v. Werner, 233 F. Supp. 102 (E.D. Mo. 1964), 13n70; 20n106

Kitchens of Sara Lee, Inc., v. Nifty Foods Corp., 266 F.2d 541 (2d Cir. 1959), 16n85; 33n151

Knapp v. Will & Baumer Co., 273 Fed. 380 (2d Cir. 1921), 125n154

In re Koehring, 37 F.2d 421 (C.C.P.A. 1930), 118, 118nn123,124

H. H. Kolbe Co. v. Armgus Textile Co., 315 F.2d 70 (2d Cir. 1963), 87n28

Kono Mfg. Co. v. Vogue Optical Mfg. Co., 94 F. Supp. 251 (S.D.N.Y. 1950), 126n159

Korzybski v. Underwood & Underwood, Inc., 36 F.2d 727 (2d Cir. 1929), 85nn22,23

Krem-Ko Co. v. R. G. Miller & Sons, 68 F.2d 872, 873 (2d Cir. 1934), 37n167

Lucien Lelong, Inc. v. George W. Button Corp., 50 F. Supp. 708 (S.D.N.Y. 1943), 37n165

Lucien Lelong, Inc. v. Lander Co., 164 F.2d 395 (2d Cir. 1947), 38nn168,171

Lucien Lelong Inc. v. Lenel, Inc., 181 F.2d 3 (5th Cir. 1950), 89n36
Lerner v. Club Wander In, Inc., 174 F. Supp. 731 (D. Mass. 1959), 167n85
Nat Lewis Purses, Inc. v. Carole Bags, Inc., 83 F.2d 475 (2d Cir. 1936), 108n97; 125; 125n155
In re Lobl, 75 F.2d 219 (C.C.P.A. 1935), 119; 119n129
Loomskill, Inc. v. Puritan Dress Co., 134 U.S.P.Q. 20 (S.D.N.Y. 1962), 86n24

R. H. Macy Co. v. Colorado Clothing Mfg. Co., 68 F.2d 690 (10th Cir. 1934), 30n142
Man-Sew Pinking Attachment Corp. v. Chandler Mach. Co., 33 F. Supp. 950, 954–55 (D. Mass. 1940), 39n177
Ex parte Mars Signal-Light Co., 85 U.S.P.Q. 173 (Ass't Comm'r of Patents 1950), 89nn36,37
James P. Marsh Corp. v. United States Gauge Co., 129 F.2d 161, 165 (7th Cir. 1942), 9n56
Martinetti v. Maguire, 16 Fed. Cas. 920, 922, No. 9, 173 (S.D. Cal. 1938), 180n31
Martini & Rossi, Societa Anonima v. Consumers'-People's Products, 57 F.2d 599 (E.D.N.Y. 1931), *aff'd*, 57 F.2d 600 (2d Cir. 1932), 18n94
Marx v. United States, 96 F.2d 204 (9th Cir. 1938), 56n248
Mastercrafters Clock & Radio Co. v. Vacheron & Constantin-Le Coultre Watches, Inc., 221 F.2d 464 (2d Cir.), *cert. denied*, 350 U.S. 832 (1955), 92n55
Mazer v. Stein, 347 U.S. 201, 217, 221 (1954), 53n231; 83nn15,16; 85n20; 183n39
McCord Co. v. Plotnick, 108 Cal. App. 2d 392, 239 P.2d 32 (Dist. Ct. App. 1951), 58n257
William A. Meier Glass Co. v. Anchor Hocking Glass Corp., 95 F. Supp. 264 (W.D. Pa. 1951), 67n295; 70n310
Mercoid Corp. v. Mid-Continent Inv. Co., 320 U.S. 661 (1944), 95n62
G. & C. Merriam Co. v. Saalfield, 198 Fed. 369, 378 (6th Cir. 1912), 31n145
Ex parte Metals & Controls Corp., 110 U.S.P.Q. 62, 64 (Comm'r 1956), 38n172
Metro-Goldwyn-Mayer v. Wyatt & Maryland Yacht Club, 21 BULL. CR. OFF. 203 (D. Md. 1932), 167n85
Metropolitan Opera Assn., Inc. v. Wagner-Nichols Recorder Corp., 199 Misc. 786, 101 N.Y.S.2d 483 (Sup. Ct. 1950), *aff'd mem.*, 279

Statutes and Cases 221

App. Div. 632, 107 N.Y.S.2d 795 (1st Dept. 1951), 59n263; 69n307; 163n58
H. A. Metz Labs., Inc. v. Blackman, 153 Misc. 171, 275 N.Y. Supp. 407 (Sup. Ct. 1934), 18n100; 34n157
Dr. Miles Medical Co. v. John D. Park & Sons Co., 220 U.S. 373 (1911), 110n102
Ex parte Minnesota Mining & Mfg. Co., 92 U.S.P.Q. 74 (Patent Office Examiner-in-Chief 1952), 89n36
Ex parte Minnesota Mining & Mfg. Co., 335 F.2d 836, 839–40 (C.C.P.A. 1964) (Patents), 49n215; 50n218
Monroe v. Anderson, 58 Fed. 398 (3d Cir. 1893), 82n6
Moxie Co. v. Daoust, 206 Fed. 434 (1st Cir. 1913), 36n162
C. F. Mueller Co. v. A. Zeregas Sons, 12 F.2d 517 (2d Cir. 1926), 105n90
In re Muldoon, 56 F.2d 894 (C.C.P.A. 1932), 119n128
Murray v. Miller, 3 App. Div. 2d 1008, 164 N.Y.S.2d 257 (1st Dept. 1957), 27n132
Mutual Broadcasting Sys., Inc. v. Muzak Corp., 177 Misc. 489, 30 N.Y.S.2d 419 (Sup. Ct. 1941), 58n256; 160n32; 163n54
My-T-Fine Corp. v. Samuels, 69 F.2d 76 (2d Cir. 1934), 17n90

National Biscuit Co. v. Pacific Coast Biscuit Co., 83 N.J. Eq. 369, 91 Atl. 126 (1914), 34n159; 43n187; 44n191
National Broadcasting Co. v. United States, 319 U.S. 190 (1942), 164n66
National Comics Publications, Inc. v. Fawcett Publications, Inc., 191 F.2d 594, 598 (2d Cir. 1951), 55n239; 58n253
Neely v. Boland Mfg. Co., 274 F.2d 195 (8th Cir. 1960), 14n76
Neufeld-Furst & Co. v. Jay-Day Frocks, Inc., 112 F.2d 715 (2d Cir. 1940), 126n56
New York World's Fair 1964–1965 Corp. v. Colourpicture Publishers, Inc., 141 U.S.P.Q. 939, 941–42 (N.Y. Sup. Ct. 1964), aff'd mem., 21 App. Div. 2d 896, 251 N.Y.S.2d 885 (2d Dept. 1964), 61n271; 69nn306,308,309; 70n311
Nichols v. Universal Pictures Corp., 45 F.2d 119 (2d Cir. 1930), cert. denied, 282 U.S. 902 (1931), 180n30
North British Rubber Co. v. Racine Rubber Tire Co., 271 Fed. 936, 939 (2d Cir. 1921), 116n118
Northern Pacific Ry. v. United States, 356 U.S. 1, 4 (1958), 10n56
Northrup v. Adams, 18 Fed. Cas. No. 10,328 (E.D. Mich. 1877), 123n143
Norwich Pharmacal Co. v. Sterling Drug, Inc., 271 F.2d 569, 570–

71 (2d Cir. 1959), *cert. denied,* 362 U.S. 919 (1960), 3n19; 21n116
Nutt v. National Institute, Inc., 31 F.2d 236 (2d Cir. 1929), 67n296

Oakite Prods., Inc. v. Boritz, 161 Misc. 807, 293 N.Y. Supp. 399 (Sup. Ct. 1936), 44n189
Oneida, Ltd. v. National Silver Co., 25 N.Y.S.2d 271, 276 (Sup. Ct. 1940), 7n45; 92n55
Osgood v. A. S. Aloe Instrument Co., 69 Fed. 291 (C.C.E.D. Mo. 1895), 63n276

Pagliero v. Wallace China Co., 198 F.2d 339 (9th Cir. 1952), 5n32
Palmer v. De Witt, 47 N.Y. 532 (1872), 176nn14,16
Parker Pen Co. v. Finstone, 7 F.2d 753 (S.D.N.Y. 1925), 25n123
Pavesich v. New England Life Ins. Co., 122 Ga. 190, 50 S.E. 68 (1905), 73n322
J.C. Penney Co. v. H. D. Lee Mercantile Co., 120 F.2d 949 (8th Cir. 1941), 15n78; 34n155
Peter Pan Fabrics, Inc. v. Brenda Fabrics, Inc., 169 F. Supp. 142 (S.D.N.Y. 1959), 2n12
Peter Pan Fabrics, Inc. v. Martin Weiner Corp., 274 F.2d 487 (2d Cir. 1960), 87n28
Pfeffer v. Western Doll Mfg. Co., 283 Fed. 966 (7th Cir. 1922), 127n163
Pharmaceuticals, Inc. v. United Whelan Corp., 197 N.Y.S.2d 22 (Sup. Ct. 1959), 18n94
Picard v. United Aircraft Corp., 128 F.2d 632, 640, 642 (2d Cir. 1942), 100nn74,76; 121n135; 126n158
Pierce & Bushnell Mfg. Co. v. Werckmeister, 72 Fed. 54 (1st Cir. 1896), 62n276
In re Pollack Steel Co., 50 C.C.P.A. (Patents) 1045, 314 F.2d 566 (1963), 48n211
Pratt & Whitney v. United States, 153 F. Supp. 409 (Ct. Cl. 1957), 164n63

RCA Mfg. Co. v. Whiteman, 114 F.2d 86, 88 (2d Cir.), *cert. denied,* 311 U.S. 712 (1940), 65n285; 68n302
G. Ricordi & Co. v. Haendler, 194 F.2d 914 (2d Cir. 1952), 10n58; 54n237; 65n284
Harold F. Ritchie, Inc. v. Chesebrough-Pond's, Inc., 281 F.2d 755, 760 (2d Cir. 1960), 4n28; 17n89
Ronson Art Metal Works, Inc. v. Gibson Lighter Mfg. Co., 205 Misc. 155, 127 N.Y.S.2d 786 (Sup. Ct. 1953), *modified per curiam,* 283

Statutes and Cases 223

App. Div. 937, 130 N.Y.S.2d 814 (1st Dept.), aff'd mem., 283 App.
Div. 1050, 131 N.Y.S.2d 891 (1st Dept. 1954), 30n143; 31n144
Ronson Art Metal Works, Inc. v. Gibson Lighter Mfg. Co., 3 App.
Div. 2d 227, 231–32, 159 N.Y.S.2d 606, 610–11 (1st Dept. 1957),
15n81; 33n149
Roseweb Frocks Inc. v. Moe Feinberg-Mor Wiesen, Inc., 40 F. Supp.
979 (S.D.N.Y. 1941), 126n159
Rowe v. Blodgett & Clapp Co., 103 Fed. 873, 874 (D. Conn. 1900),
117n119
Rushton v. Vitale, 218 F.2d 434 (2d Cir. 1955), 2n10
Russell v. Smith, 12 Q.B. 267 (1848), 179n29

Santa's Workshop, Inc. v. Sterling, 282 App. Div. 328, 122 N.Y.S.2d
(1957), aff'd, 3 N.Y.2d 757, 143 N.E.2d 529, 163 N.Y.S.2d 986
(1957), 7nn41,44
Savage v. Hoffman, 159 Fed. 584 (C.C.S.D.N.Y. 1908), 174n7
Schwarg v. Universal Pictures Co., 85 F. Supp. 270 (S.D. Cal. 1945),
176n13
Scott Paper Co. v. Marcalus Mfg. Co., 326 U.S. 249 (1945), 10n58
Sears, Roebuck & Co. v. Stiffel Co., 376 U.S. 225 (1964), 7nn46,47;
8n52; 13n71; 25n126; 26n127; 36n160; 55n244; 56n245; 61n272;
84n19; 91n44; 93n57; 162n51
Seven Up Co. v. Sheer Up Sales Co., 148 F.2d 909 (8th Cir.), cert.
denied, 326 U.S. 727 (1945), 43n188
Shapiro, Bernstein & Co. v. Miracle Record Co., 91 F. Supp. 473, re-
hearing, 86 U.S.P.Q. 193 (N.D. Ill. 1950), 163n58
In re Shenango Ceramics, Inc., 143 U.S.P.Q. 48 (Trademark Trial
& Appeal Board, Sept. 23, 1964), 47n206
Shilkret v. Musicraft Records, Inc., 131 F.2d 929 (2d Cir. 1942),
cert. denied, 319 U.S. 742 (1943), 56n248
Shredded Wheat Co. v. Humphrey Cornell Co., 250 Fed. 960, 967
(2d Cir. 1918), 4n26; 27n131; 28nn133,135
Singer Mfg. Co. v. June Mfg. Co., 163 U.S. 169 (1896), 54n238
Smith v. Paul, 174 Cal. App. 2d 744, 345 P.2d 546 (1959), 56n247
Smith v. Stewart, 55 Fed. 481, 483 (E.D. Pa. 1893), 124;
124nn146,147
Smith v. Whitman Saddle Co., 148 U.S. 674 (1893), 123nn143,144;
125; 125n152
Smith, Kline & French Labs. v. Clark & Clark, 157 F.2d 725 (3d Cir.
1946), 27n130; 29nn136,137
Society of European Stage Authors & Composers v. New York Hotel
Statler Co., 19 F. Supp. 1 (S.D.N.Y. 1937), 166n83; 167n84;
168nn94,95; 169n97

Socony-Vacuum Oil Co., Inc. v. Rosen, 108 F.2d 632 (6th Cir. 1940), 17*n*91; 19*n*103

Spangler Candy Co. v. Crystal Pure Candy Co., 235 F. Supp. 18 (N.D. Ill. 1964), aff'd, 147 U.S.P.Q. 434 (7th Cir. 1965), 353 F.2d 641 (7th Cir. 1965), 20*n*107; 40*n*183; 41*n*185

Spaulding v. Guardian Light Co., 267 F.2d 111 (7th Cir. 1959), 118*n*128

Standard Brands, Inc. v. Smidler, 151 F.2d 34, 37 (2d Cir. 1945), 3*n*17

Steffens v. Stevens, 232 Fed. 862, 865 (2d Cir. 1916), 125; 125*nn*150, 151

Stein v. Expert Lamp Co., 188 F.2d 611 (7th Cir. 1951), 83*n*15

Stein v. Rosenthal, 205 F.2d 633 (9th Cir. 1953), 83*n*15

Jerrold Stephens Co., Inc. v. Alladin Plastics, Inc., 229 F. Supp. 536 (S.D. Cal. 1964), 13*n*70

Stern v. Jerome H. Remick & Co., 175 Fed. 282 (S.D.N.Y. 1915), 62*n*276

Stiffel Co. v. Sears, Roebuck & Co., 313 F.2d 115, 116–17 (7th Cir. 1963), 8*nn*53,54

In re Stimpson, 24 F.2d 1012 (D.C. Cir. 1928), 119*n*128

Strause Gas Iron Co. v. William M. Crane Co., 235 Fed. 126, 131 (2d Cir. 1916), 125*n*153

Swanson Mfg. Co. v. Feinberg-Henry Mfg. Co., 54 F. Supp. 805 (S.D.N.Y. 1943), *modified*, 147 F.2d 500 (2d Cir. 1945), 30*n*141

Tas-T-Nut Co. v. Variety Nut & Date Co., 245 F.2d 3 (6th Cir. 1957), 18*n*97; 19*n*102; 34*n*156; 37*n*168

Taylor Instrument Co. v. Fawley-Brost Co., 139 F.2d 98 (7th Cir. 1943), 85*n*22

Tiffany Prods. v. Dewing, 50 F.2d 911 (D. Md. 1931), 165*n*75; 167*n*86

Trifari, Krussman & Fishel, Inc. v. Charel Co., 134 F. Supp. 551 (S.D.N.Y. 1955), 2*n*11

United Artists Associated, Inc. v. NWL Corp., 198 F. Supp. 953, 956 (S.D.N.Y. 1961), 153*n*5; 154*n*6; 155*n*13; 159*n*30; 160*n*36

United States v. United Shoe Mach. Co., 247 U.S. 32, 57–59 (1918), 95*n*62

United States Plywood Corp. v. Watson, 171 F. Supp. 193 (D.D.C. 1958), 91*n*46

United States Tobacco Co. v. McGreenery, 144 Fed. 531 (C.C. Mass.), aff'd per curiam, 144 Fed. 1022 (1st Cir. 1906), 43*n*188

Untermeyer v. Freund, 37 Fed. 342 (S.D.N.Y. 1889), 124*n*149

Statutes and Cases 225

Upjohn Co. v. Schwartz, 246 F.2d 254 (2d Cir. 1957), 30n140
Uproar Co. v. National Broadcasting Co., 8 F. Supp. 358 (D. Mass. 1934), *modified*, 81 F.2d 373 (1st Cir. 1936), 67n298

Vacheron & Constantin-LeCoultre Watches, Inc. v. Benrus Watch Co., 260 F.2d 637, 642–44 (2d Cir. 1958), 1n6; 131n168
Vaughan Novelty Mfg. Co. v. G. G. Greene Mfg. Corp., 202 F.2d 172 (3d Cir. 1953), 26n128

Walker Process Equip., Inc. v. Food Mach. & Chem. Corp., 382 U.S. 172 (1965), 95n62
Waring v. WOAS Broadcasting Station, Inc., 327 Pa. 433, 456, 194 Atl. 631, 642 (1937), 74n323
William R. Warner & Co. v. Eli Lilly & Co., 265 U.S. 526 (1924), 14n75; 29nn138,139; 30n140
Waterman v. Mackenzie, 138 U.S. 252 (1891), 164n61
Werckmeister v. American Lithograph Co., 134 Fed. 321 (2d Cir. 1904), 63n276
Wesson v. Galef, 286 Fed. 621 (S.D.N.Y. 1922), 14n27
West Point Mfg. Co. v. Detroit Stamping Co., 222 F.2d 581 (6th Cir.), *cert. denied*, 350 U.S. 840 (1955), 1n2; 5n33; 15n77; 18n98; 34n154
Western Electric Co. v. Pacent Reproducer Corp., 42 F.2d 116 (2d Cir. 1930), 164n65
White v. Kimmell, 94 F. Supp. 502, 504 (S.D. Cal. 1950), *rev'd on the facts*, 193 F.2d 744 (9th Cir.), *cert. denied*, 343 U.S. 957 (1952), 67n294; 175n12
White v. Leanore Frocks, Inc. 120 F.2d 113 (2d Cir. 1941), 97n65
White v. Lombardy Dresses, Inc., 40 F. Supp. 548 (S.D.N.Y. 1941), 97n65
H. C. White Co. v. Morton E. Converse & Sons Co., 20 F.2d 311, 312 (2d Cir. 1927), 114n110
Wilson v. Haber Bros., 275 Fed. 246 (2d Cir. 1921), 86n23
Winston & Newell Co. v. Piggly Wiggly Northwest, Inc., 221 Minn. 287, 22 N.W.2d 11 (1946), 15n78
H. E. Winterton Gum Co. v. Autosales Gum & Chocolate Co., 211 Fed. 612, 617 (6th Cir. 1914), 37n163
Wirtz v. Eagle Bottling Co., 50 N.J. Eq. 164, 24 Atl. 658 (1892), 16n86; 18n96
Witmark v. Bamberger, 291 Fed. 776 (D.N.J. 1923), 166n78
Wolf & Vine, Inc. v. Pioneer Display Fixture Co. 142 U.S.P.Q. 112 (N.Y. Sup. Ct. 1964), 13n70
Ex parte Alan Wood Steel Co., 101 U.S.P.Q. 209 (Examiner in Chief

1954), *aff'd,* Alan Wood Steel Co. v. Watson, 150 F. Supp. 861 (D.D.C. 1957), 47n205; 91n47

Edgar H. Wood Associates, Inc. v. Skene, 347 Mass. 351, 197 N.E.2d 886 (1964), 56n248; 61n271; 62n276; 68n305

Worcester v. Crane, 2 Fisher's Pat. Cases 583 (S.D.N.Y. 1865), reprinted in SIMONDS, THE LAW OF DESIGN PATENTS (1874), 122n138

Wm. Wrigley, Jr. Co. v. Colker, 245 Fed. 907 (E.D. Ky. 1914), 19n101

Z Bar Net v. Helena Television, Inc., 125 U.S.P.Q. 595, 596 (Mont. Dist. Ct. 1960), 159 nn30,31; 160n39; 161n41

Zippo Mfg. Co. v. Manners Jewelers, Inc., 180 F. Supp. 845 (E.D. La. 1960), 6n39; 15n78

Zippo Mfg. Co. v. Rogers Imports, Inc., 216 F. Supp. 670, 682–84 (S.D.N.Y. 1963), 5n32; 21n114; 25n124; 26n129; 28n134

Works Cited

Abramson, *The Economic Bases of Patent Reform*, 13 LAW & CONTEMP. PROB. 339, 341, 346–51 (1948), 98n70; 102n85

Allen, *Design Patentability*, 9 J. PAT. OFF. SOC'Y 298, 299 (1927), 113n107

Andrew, *Domestic Protection of Commercial Designs: The Federal-State Conflict*, 39 ST. JOHN's L. REV. 23, 29–38 (1964), 11n66; 46n194; 47n203; 50n218

Arnold, *A Philosophy on the Protection Afforded by Patent, Trademark, Copyright and Unfair Competition Law: The Sources and Nature of Product Simulation Law*, 54 TRADEMARK REP. 413 (1964), 48n210

BALL, LAW OF COPYRIGHT AND LITERARY PROPERTY (1944), 179n24

William N. Bartholomew, 1869 C.D. 103 (Comm'r of Patents), 120n130

Bender, in *Symposium—Product Simulation: A Right or a Wrong?*, 64 COLUM. L. REV. 1228 (1964), 12n67; 20n105; 55n243; 60n268

Blain, *Television, a New Horizon in Communications, Parts I, II and III*, TELEPHONY (Jan. 30, Feb. 6, and Feb. 13, 1965), 155n12; 159n29

Blain, *op. cit.*, Part I, TELEPHONY (Jan. 30, 1965), 154n7

Blain, *op. cit.*, Part II, TELEPHONY (Feb. 6, 1965), 155nn9,11

Bloustein, *Privacy as an Aspect of Human Dignity: An Answer to Dean Prosser*, 39 N.Y.U.L. REV. 962, 1000–7 (1964), 72n318; 73n321; 74n323

Bowen, *Design Patents and Modern Industrial Design*, 37 J. PAT. OFF. SOC'Y 744 (1955), 120n132

Broadcasting Magazine, February 21, 1966, 158n

Brown, in *Symposium—Product Simulation: A Right or a Wrong?*, 64 COLUM. L. REV. 1216, 1222 (1964), 11n65; 22n118; 24n121; 31n146; 32n148

Callmann, *He Who Reaps Where He Has Not Sown: Unjust Enrichment in the Law of Unfair Competition*, 55 HARV. L. REV. 595 (1942), 76n326

Callmann, *Style and Design Piracy*, 22 J. Pat. Off. Soc'y 557 (1940), 6n37
1 Callmann, Unfair Competition and Trade-Marks (2d ed. 1950), 1n5
3 Callmann, *op. cit.*, 6n40
4 Callmann, *op. cit.*, 47n201
Callmann, *What is Unfair Competition?*, 28 Geo. L.J. 585 (1940), 21nn112,113
Canadian Royal Commission on Patents, Copyright, Trade Marks and Industrial Designs, Report on Industrial Designs (1958), 90n42; 106n92; 108n96; 131n170
Chafee, *Unfair Competition*, 53 Harv. L. Rev. 1289, 1318 (1940), 10n61
Chamberlain, The Theory of Monopolistic Competition (7th ed. 1960), 4n24
Chapman, *The Supreme Court and Federal Law of Unfair Competition*, 54 Trademark Rep. 573 (1964), 11n66
Comment, 1957 U. Ill. L.F., 677, 13n72
Comment, 1959 Wis. L. Rev. 652, 2n13
Comment, 73 Yale L.J. 389 (1963), 10n61
Coton, The New Ballet (1946), 185n43

Dalsimer, *New Concepts of Design Protection* (Eighth Annual Public Conference of the Patent, Trademark & Copyright Institute), 8 Idea: The Patent, Trademark, & Copyright Journal of Research & Educ. 168 (1964), 105n91
Dance Has Many Faces, The (Sorell ed. 1951), 172n1; 173n4; 174n5
2 Deller, Walker on Patents (2d ed. 1964), 82n7; 114n113
Derenberg, *Copyright No-Man's Land: Fringe Rights in Literary and Artistic Property*, 35 J. Pat. Off. Soc'y 627, 646 (1953), 83n13; 131n168
Derenberg, *The Seventeenth Year of Administration of the Lanham Trademark Act of 1946*, 54 Trademark Rep. 655, 658–63, 699–706 (1964), 9n55; 11n66; 22n119; 39n179; 48n209
Derenberg, in *Symposium—Product Simulation: A Right or a Wrong?*, 64 Colum. L. Rev. 1192, 1206 (1964), 5n34; 48n208; 49n212; 50n218
De Wolf, An Outline of Copyright Law (1925), 57n248
Diamond, *The Proposed Federal Unfair Commercial Activities Act*, 23 Ohio St. L.J. 110 (1962), 77n332

Works Cited 229

Dienner, *Protection of Industrial Design*, 45 J. PAT. OFF. SOC'Y 673, 676 (1963), 121n136

EDWARDS, MAINTAINING COMPETITION: REQUISITES OF A GOVERNMENTAL POLICY (1949), 100nn75,76; 102nn84,85
Elman, *The Limits of State Jurisdiction in Affording Common Law Protection to Clothing Designs*, 11 VAND. L. REV. 501 (1958), 66n289

Federal Communications Commission, *Public Notice B*, February 1962, 158n24
Federal Communications Commission, *Regulations*, 165nn67,68
Finkelstein, *Memorandum to Register of Copyrights*, Preliminary Draft for Revised U.S. Copyright Law and Discussions and Comments on the Draft, 170n99
FROST, THE PATENT SYSTEM AND THE MODERN ECONOMY, STUDY NO. 2, PREPARED FOR THE SUBCOMMITTEE ON PATENTS, TRADEMARKS, AND COPYRIGHTS OF THE SENATE COMM. ON THE JUDICIARY, 84th Cong., 2d Sess. (1957), S. Doc. No. 22, 85th Cong., 1st Sess. (1957), 9n56; 10n58; 101n82; 121n135; 126n158; 131n168

GALBRAITH, AMERICAN CAPITALISM (1952), 4n24
Galbally, *Unfair Trade in the Simulation of Rival Goods—the Test of Commercial Necessity*, 3 VILL. L. REV. 333 (1958), 16n85; 20n108; 21n110
Gamboni, *Unfair Competition Protection after Sears and Compco*, 1–78, 90n43
GLOAG, INDUSTRIAL ART EXPLAINED (2d. ed. 1946), 120n133
GOTSHAL, TODAY'S FIGHT FOR DESIGN PROTECTION (1957), 1n4

Hamilton, in CANADIAN ROYAL COMMISSION ON PATENTS, COPYRIGHT, TRADE MARKS AND INDUSTRIAL DESIGNS, REPORT ON INDUSTRIAL DESIGNS (1958), 131n170
HAMILTON, PRICE AND PRICE POLICIES (1938), 106n93
Hamilton & Till, *What is a Patent?*, 13 LAW & CONTEMP. PROB. 245, 253–56 (1948), 102n85
Handler, in *Symposium—Product Simulation: A Right or a Wrong?*, 64 COLUM. L. REV. 1188–89 (1964), 94n61
Handler, *Unfair Competition*, 21 IOWA L. REV. 175, 189 (1936), 4n24
Harris, *Some Aspects of the Underlying Legislative Intent of the*

Works Cited

Patent Act of 1952, 23 GEO. WASH. L. REV. 658, 677–79 (1955), 126n58

Hearings Before Subcomm. on Patents, Trademarks & Copyright of the U.S. Senate Comm. on the Judiciary on the American Patent System, 84th Cong., 1st Sess. (1955), 83n11; 102n84; 131n168

Hearings Before Subcomm. on Patents, Trademarks and Copyrights of the Senate Comm. on the Judiciary on S. 1884, 87th Cong., 1st Sess. (1961), 87nn29,30; 107n95; 108nn98,99,100; 113n108

Hearings on H.R. 4651, 88th Cong., 2d Sess., 77n332

Hearings on H.R. 4651 Before the Subcommittee on Commerce and Finance of the House Committee on Interstate and Foreign Commerce, 88th Cong., 2d Sess. (1964), 11n66; 76n328; 77nn330,332, 333; 78nn335,336

HOUSE COMM. ON JUDICIARY, 87th CONG., 1st SESS., COPYRIGHT LAW REVISION, PART 1, REPORT OF THE REGISTER OF COPYRIGHTS ON THE GENERAL REVISION OF THE U.S. COPYRIGHT LAW (Comm. Print 1961), 135nn4,6; 139nn28,29,30; 141nn38,39; 142n47; 143n49; 148n73

HOUSE COMM. ON JUDICIARY, 88th CONG., 1st SESS., COPYRIGHT LAW REVISION, PART 2, DISCUSSION AND COMMENTS ON REPORT OF THE REGISTER OF COPYRIGHTS ON THE GENERAL REVISION OF THE U.S. COPYRIGHT LAW (Comm. Print 1963), 135n6; 139n31; 144nn52, 53,54; 148n73

HOUSE COMM. ON JUDICIARY, 88th CONG., 2d SESS., COPYRIGHT LAW REVISION, PART 3, PRELIMINARY DRAFT FOR REVISED U.S. COPYRIGHT LAW AND DISCUSSIONS AND COMMENTS ON THE DRAFT (Comm. Print 1964), 135n6; 138nn20,21,22; 143n51; 145n59; 151nn81,82; 165n70

HOUSE COMM. ON JUDICIARY, 88th CONG., 2d SESS., COPYRIGHT LAW REVISION, PART 4, FURTHER DISCUSSIONS AND COMMENTS ON PRELIMINARY DRAFT FOR REVISED U.S. COPYRIGHT LAW (Comm. Print 1964), 134n2; 135n6; 136nn11,12,13; 137n14; 148n73; 151n80

HOUSE COMM. ON JUDICIARY, 89th CONG., 1st SESS., COPYRIGHT LAW REVISION, PART 5, 1964 REVISION BILL WITH DISCUSSIONS AND COMMENTS (Comm. Print 1965), 135nn6,9,10; 138nn23,24; 139n27; 141nn40,41; 143n48; 144nn56,58; 151n80; 152n83

HOWELL, COPYRIGHT LAW (4th ed. Latman rev. 1962), 166n77

H.R. 4347, 89th Cong., 1st Sess. (1965), 139n32; 140nn34,35,36,37; 142n46; 145nn60,61,62; 146nn63,64; 147nn67,68; 149nn74, 75,76,77,78

H. R. 4651, 88th Cong., 1st Sess. (1963), reprint in 54 TRADEMARK REP. 781–84 (1964), 52n225; 77n331

Works Cited

H.R. 11947, 88th Cong., 2d Sess. (1964), 66n291
H.R. 12354, 88th Cong., 2d Sess. (1964), 66n291
H.R. Rep. No. 1758, 87th Cong., 2d Sess. (1962), 24n122; 66n290
Hudson, *A Brief History of the Development of Design Patent Protection in the United States*, 30 J. Pat. Off. Soc'y 380–81, 397 (1948), 1n3; 80nn1,2; 105n91
Hutchinson, *Design Piracy*, 18 Harv. Bus. Rev. 191 (1940), 3n16
Hutchinson, Labanotation (1954), 185nn43,45; 187n55
Hutchinson, *The Preservation of the Dance Score through Notation*, in The Dance Has Many Faces (Sorell ed., 1951), 173n4; 174n5

Inquiry Into the Impact of Community Antenna Systems, TV Translations, TV "Satellite" Stations and TV "Repeaters" on the Orderly Development of Broadcasting, Report and Order in Docket No. 12443, 18 Pike & Fischer, Radio Regulation (1959), 158n21

Jackson, *Industrial Designs in the United Kingdom*, 45 J. Pat. Off. Soc'y 488, 492–93 (1963), 108n98; 131n169

Kahn, *The Role of Patents*, in Miller, Competition, Cartels and Their Regulation 311–13, 317, 319 (1962), 98n67; 99n71,72,73; 101nn80,83; 102n85
Kalodner & Vance, *The Relation Between Federal and State Protection of Literary and Artistic Property*, 72 Harv. L. Rev. 1079, 1091–96 (1959), 62n275; 63n280; 65n287
Kaminstein, Divisibility of Copyrights, Study No. 11, Prepared for the Subcommittee on Patents, Trademarks, and Copyrights of the Senate Comm. on the Judiciary, 86th Cong., 2d Sess. (Comm. Print 1960), 164nn60,61; 165n71
Kaplan, *Performer's Right and Copyright: The Capitol Records Case*, 69 Harv. L. Rev. 409, 415–29 (1956), 57n252; 64n283; 66n290; 94n61
Kaplan, *Publication in Copyright Law: The Question of Phonograph Records*, 103 U. Pa. L. Rev. 469, 478–79, 487 (1955), 56n248; 68n299
William King, 1870 C.D. 109 (Comm'r of Patents), 88n34
Kunin, *The Lindsay Bill Before and After the Stiffel Case*, 54 Trademark Rep. 731 (1964), 11n66; 77n332
Kupferman, *Rights in the New Media*, 19 Law & Contemp. Prob. 180 (1954), 153n3

Ladas, The International Protection of Literary and Artistic Property (1938), 186n52

Latman, *The New Design Protection Proposals Before Congress*, 8 BULL. COPYRIGHT SOC'Y 356 (1961), 78n335

Law & Junkins, *Registrability of Packages and Configurations of Goods on the Supplemental Register: Design Patent vs. Trademark Registration*, 45 TRADEMARK REP. 22, 33–35 (1955), 39nn174,178; 40n182

Leeds, in *Symposium—Product Simulation: A Right or a Wrong?*, 64 COLUM. L. REV. 1179, 1182 (1964), 12nn67,68

Legal Aspects of Radio Communications and Broadcasting, 124 A.L.R. 982, 995 (1940), 168n87; 169n96; 170n98

MACHLUP, AN ECONOMIC REVIEW OF THE PATENT SYSTEM, STUDY NO. 15, PREPARED FOR THE SUBCOMMITTEE ON PATENTS, TRADEMARKS, AND COPYRIGHTS OF THE SENATE COMM. ON THE JUDICIARY, 85th Cong., 2d Sess. (Comm. Print 1958), 98nn69,70; 100nn77,78; 101nn79,80,81; 102n85

MALEVINSKY, SCIENCE OF PLAYWRITING (1925), 180n30

Marks, *Copying an Article of Commerce not Necessarily Unfair Competition*, 55 TRADEMARK REP. 47 (1965), 11n66

Meiklejohn, *Dresses—The Impact of Fashion on a Business*, in HAMILTON, PRICE AND PRICE POLICIES (1938), 106nn93,94; 112n105

MELMAN, THE IMPACT OF THE PATENT SYSTEM ON RESEARCH, STUDY NO. 11, PREPARED FOR THE SUBCOMMITTEE ON PATENTS, TRADEMARKS, AND COPYRIGHTS OF THE SENATE COMM. ON THE JUDICIARY, 85th Cong., 2d Sess. (Comm. Print 1958), 99n72; 100nn74,75

Michaelson, *The Nature of the Protection of Artistic and Industrial Design*, 37 J. PAT. OFF. SOC'Y 543, 553 (1955), 81n3; 82n9; 123nn138,142; 126n159

MILLER, COMPETITION, CARTELS AND THEIR REGULATION (1962), 98n67

Mirell, *Legal Protection for Choreography*, 27 N.Y.U.L. REV. 792–94, 804, 808 (1952), 174n6; 179n26; 181n37; 185n44

Nelson, *The Simple Economics of Basic Scientific Research*, 67 J. POL. ECON. 297, 304 (1959), 101n80

Netterville, *California Law of Unfair Competition: Unprivileged Imitation*, 28 SO. CAL. L. REV. 240, 277 (1955), 5n30; 20n109; 21n112

NIMMER, COPYRIGHT (1963), 52nn228,229; 53n232; 54n236; 148n71

NIMMER, *op. cit.* (1964), 84n17

Nimmer, *Copyright Publication*, 56 COLUM. L. REV. 185 (1956), 53n233; 58n254; 67n293

Nims, Unfair Competition and Trade-Marks (3d ed., 1929), 3n22
1 Nims, Unfair Competition and Trade-Marks (4th ed. 1947), 16nn83,84; 40n180
Note, 33 Cinn. L. Rev. 382, 400 (1964), 110n101
Note, 42 Colum. L. Rev. 290, 294–95 (1942), 86n23
Note, 64 Colum. L. Rev. 544, 551 (1964), 4n29
Note, 78 Harv. L. Rev. 1269 (1965), 89n41; 91n49
Note, 49 Yale L.J. 1290 (1940), 1n4
Note, *Competitive Torts*, 77 Harv. L. Rev. 888, 908, 913–16, 919–22, 932–47 (1964), 13n72; 21n114; 34n152; 59n261; 92nn52,53; 108n97; 116n117
Note, *Misrepresentation and the Lindsay Bill: A Stab at Uniformity in the Law of Unfair Competition*, 70 Yale L.J. 406 (1961), 10n59; 77n332
Note, *Principal Registration of Contours of Packages and Containers under the Trademark Act of 1946*, 27 Geo. Wash. L. Rev. 104, 120 (1958), 36n162; 39n174; 40n182
Note, *Protecting the Artistic Aspects of Articles of Utility: Copyright or Design Patent?*, 66 Harv. L. Rev. 877, 885 (1953), 2n7; 121n136
Note, *Protection of Styles and Designs in the Garment Industry*, 26 U. Cinc. L. Rev. 86 (1957), 76n327
Note, *Registrability of Package & Configuration of Goods on the Supplemental Register*, 23 Geo. Wash. L. Rev. 82 (1954), 89n36
Note, *Study of the Term "Writings" in the Copyright Clause of the Constitution*, 31 N.Y.U.L. Rev. 1263 (1956), 52n227; 84n17
Note, *The Supreme Court, 1963 Term*, 78 Harv. L. Rev. 143, 312 (1964), 57n249
Note, *Trade-Marks and Unfair Competition*, 68 Harv. L. Rev. 814, 856 (1955), 5n32
Note, *Unfair Competition and the Doctrine of Functionality*, 64 Colum. L. Rev. 544 (1964), 4n24
Note, *Unfair Competition Protection after Sears and Compco*, 40 N.Y.U.L. Rev. 101 (1965), 90n43; 94n59; *see also* Gamboni

Oppenheim, *The Public Interest in Legal Protection of Industrial and Intellectual Property*, 40 Trademark Rep. 613 (1950), 10n58

18 Pike & Fischer, Radio Regulation (1959), 158n21
Pogue, *Borderland—Where Copyright and Design Patent Meet*, 52 Mich. L. Rev. 33, 62 (1953), 80n2

Pollack, *Unfair Trading by Product Simulation: Rule or Rankle?*, 23 OHIO ST. L.J. 74 (1962), 4n25; 23n120

Pollock, *Community Television and the Telephone Company*, TELEPHONE ENGINEER AND MANAGEMENT, November 15, 1964, 154n7; 155n10; 159n27

Prosser, *Privacy*, 48 CALIF. L. REV. 383 (1960), 72n317

Report of the Attorney General's National Comm. to Study the Antitrust Laws: Chapter V—Patent-Antitrust Problems, in 37 J. PAT. OFF. SOC'Y 331 (1955), 95n62

RESTATEMENT (SECOND), TORTS (Tent. Draft No. 8, 1963), 17n89

Rich, *Trademark Problems As I See Them—Judiciary*, 52 TRADEMARK REP. 1183, 1188–89 (1962), 91n44

RINGER & GITLIN, COPYRIGHTS (1963), 148n71

Rogers, GOODWILL, TRADE-MARKS AND UNFAIR COMPETITION (1914), 17n87

SACHS, WORLD HISTORY OF THE DANCE (1937), 172n1

SAMUELSON, ECONOMICS (1961), 4n24

1 SEIDEL, DUBROFF & GONDA, TRADEMARK LAW AND PRACTICE (1963), 40n181; 46nn196,199

Sell, *The Doctrine of Misappropriation in Unfair Competition*, 11 VAND. L. REV. 483, 497 (1958), 3n15; 76n327; 78n337

Selvin, *Should Performance Dedicate?*, 42 CALIF. L. REV. 40, 50–51 (1954), 68n299

S. 776 (Design Protection Act), 88th Cong., 1st Sess. (1963), 77n334

S. 1006, 89th Cong., 1st Sess. (1965), 135n5; 139n32; 140nn34,35,36,37; 142n46; 145nn60,61,62; 146nn63,64; 147n67; 148n73; 149nn74,75,76,77,78

S. 1038, 88th Cong., 1st Sess. (1963), reprint in 54 TRADEMARK REP., 781–84 (1964), 77n331

S. 3008, 88th Cong., 2d Sess. (1964), 66n291

S. REP. No. 686, 88th Cong., 1st Sess. (1963), 78n334

SENATE COMM. ON INTERSTATE AND FOREIGN COMMERCE, 86th CONG., 1st SESS., REPORT 923 (Comm. Print 1959), 158n25

SHAFTER, MUSICAL COPYRIGHT (2d ed. 1939), 178n23

SHOEMAKER, PATENTS FOR DESIGNS (1929), 82nn6,7; 89n35; 114n112; 117nn118,121; 122n137

SIMONDS, THE LAW OF DESIGN PATENTS (1874), 115n116; 122n138; 123n145

Smith, *"In Vino (Mogen David Brand) Veritas"?*, 54 TRADEMARK REP. 581, 587 (1964), 12nn66,67; 38n169; 50n217

Works Cited 235

Solinger, *Unauthorized Uses of TV Broadcasts*, 48 COLUM. L. REV. 848 (1948), 153nn1,2

Stedman, *Invention and Public Policy*, 12 LAW & CONTEMP. PROB. 649, 653 (1947), 9n56

Stern & Hoffman, *Public Injury and the Public Interest: Secondary Meaning in the Law of Unfair Competition*, 110 U. PA. L. REV. 935, 940, 950 (1962), 6n36; 9n56; 23n120

STRAUSS, PROTECTION OF UNPUBLISHED WORKS, STUDY No. 29, PREPARED FOR THE SUBCOMMITTEE ON PATENTS, TRADEMARKS, AND COPYRIGHTS OF THE SENATE COMM. ON THE JUDICIARY, 86th CONG., 2d SESS. (Comm. Print 1961), 163n58

SUBCOMM. ON PATENTS, TRADEMARKS, AND COPYRIGHTS, SENATE COMM. ON THE JUDICIARY, 86th CONG., 1st & 2d SESS., COPYRIGHT LAW REVISION STUDIES, 135n6

Survey of Copyrighted Material Reproduction Practices in Scientific and Technical Fields, 11 BULL. COPYRIGHT SOC'Y 69, 71 (1963), 137nn18,19

SYMONS, THE LAW OF PATENTS FOR DESIGNS (1914), 88n33; 123n145

Symposium—*Product Simulation: A Right or a Wrong?*, 64 COLUM. L. REV. 1178–79, 1182, 1188–89, 1192, 1201–2, 1216, 1222, 1228, 1238, 1241 (1964), 5n34; 11n65; 12nn66,67; 20n105; 22n118; 24n121; 31n146; 32n148; 48n208; 55n243; 60n268; 93n59; 94n61

TAPER, BALANCHINE (1963), 173n2

TEAGUE, DESIGN THIS DAY (1949), 121n134

Telephone Engineer and Management, January 15, 1965, 157n19

Time, November 13, 1964, 153n4; 154n7; 155n11; 157n19; 159n28

Time, Feb. 19, 1965, 137nn15,16

Treece, *Copying Methods of Product Differentiation: Fair or Unfair Competition?*, 38 NOTRE DAME LAW. 244, 262 (1963), 40n184

Treece, *Patent Policy and Preemption: The Stiffel and Compco Cases*, 32 U. CHI. L. REV. 80, 89, 95 (1964), 12n66; 60n268; 65n284; 93n59

Treece, *Protectability of Product Differentiation: Is and Ought Compared*, 18 RUTGERS L. REV. 1019, 1059–68 (1964), 4n23; 7n48; 12nn66,69

UNAUTHORIZED DUPLICATION OF SOUND RECORDINGS, STUDY No. 26, PREPARED FOR THE SUBCOMMITTEE ON PATENTS, TRADEMARKS, AND COPYRIGHTS OF THE SENATE COMM. ON THE JUDICIARY, 86th CONG., 2d SESS. (Comm. Print 1960), 66n280

UNITED KINGDOM BOARD OF TRADE, DEPARTMENTAL COMMITTEE, SECOND INTERIM REPORT ON PATENTS AND DESIGNS ACT, Cmd. No. 6789 (1946), 98n68

United States Copyright Office *Circular No. 20* (June 1962), 141n42

United States Copyright Office *Information Circular No. 51*, 177n20; 178n21; 184n42

United States Patent Commissioner, *Report to 27th Cong., 2d Sess., Feb. 8, 1841, see* Hudson, *Brief History,* etc.

UNITED STATES PATENT OFFICE, ANNUAL REPORT 10 (1963), 82n8

VAN DOREN, INDUSTRIAL DESIGN (1954), 120n131

VARMER, LIMITATIONS ON PERFORMING RIGHTS, STUDY No. 16, COPYRIGHT LAW REVISION STUDIES (1960), 139n33; 142nn43,44

VAUGHAN, THE UNITED STATES PATENT SYSTEM (1956), 83n11; 102n85; 130n167

WALKER ON PATENTS, *see under* DELLER

Walter, *A Ten Year Survey of Design Litigation,* 35 J. PAT. OFF. SOC'Y 389 (1953), 2n6; 126n160

Warren & Brandeis, *The Right to Privacy,* 4 HARV. L. REV. 193 (1890), 72nn319,320

Wehringer, *Two for One: Trademarks and Design Patents,* 50 TRADEMARK REP. 1158, 1162–63 (1960), 46n198; 91nn45,50

WEIL, COPYRIGHT LAW (1917), 179n24

William Whyte, 1871 C.D. 304 (Comm'r of Patents), 88n34; 113n109

Index

American Textbook Publishers Institute, 138
Arnold, Thurman, quoted, 101–2
Art, *see* Works of art

Barns v. Miner, 180
Beatle record case, 68, 70, 71, 73
Black, Justice Hugo: opinions, 11n65, 57; opinions quoted, 12, 49, 55–56, 94, 95
Bottles, *see* Design patent
Brandeis, Justice Louis D., opinion quoted, 163
Broadcasting: use of coyright material by educators, 143–47; *see also* Television broadcasting
Buck v. Jewell-LaSalle Realty Co., 166, 168

Cable Vision, Inc. v. KUTV, Inc., 71, 156–57
Canadian Royal Commission on Patents, Copyright, Trademarks and Industrial Design, 105–6, 107–8
Capitol Records, Inc. v. Mercury Records Corp., 68
CATV, *see* Community Antenna Television
Choreographer, as author of dance, 173
Choreography: and copyright, 172–89; dance notation, 173–74, 184, 185
Clark, Justice Thomas C., opinions, 65n65
Common-law copyright, 52–75 *passim*, and choreography, 174–76
Community Antenna Television (CATV): and proprietary rights in broadcasts, 153–70; description of system, 154; and television industry, 155–57, 159–60; possibility of government control, 157–59; and statutory copyright, 160–70

Compco Corp. v. Day-Brite Lighting, Inc., 1–78 *passim*, 93, 162
Competition, free, *see* Free competition
Competition, unfair, *see* Unfair competition
Configuration, 17–18, 27, 34, 46–48, 49, 81–82, 88, 89–92, 117–18, 119
Constitution, U.S., 10n58, 51, 52, 53, 58, 85, 134, 182
Copying, 51, 58, 59; *see also* Photocopying
Copyright: statutory, 2, 52–75 *passim*, 176–88; works of art, 2, 52, 53, 83–86; of three-dimensional objects, 2, 53; trademarks, 16–17, 45–52; labels, 33–36; constitutional basis of, 51, 52, 53, 58, 85, 134, 182; common-law, 52–75 *passim*, 174–76; "writings," 53, 54–62, 83–84, 86; compared with design patent, 83–88; term of, 87; use of materials by educators in classrooms, 135–43; use of materials by educators over broadcasting media, 143–47; educators as authors, 147–50; and CATV, 160–70; infringement, 164–65; and choreography, 172–89
Copyright Act (17 U.S.C.), 53, 56–57, 61, 63–64, 70, 71, 76, 84, 136, 138–39, 148–49, 163; effect of revision on educators as users of copyright materials, 134–52; comparison with proposed revised act, 150–52; choreography and, 173, 175, 177, 188–89
Copyright Act of 1909 (35 Stat. 1075), 165, 168
Crane, Ex parte, 117–18

Daly v. Palmer, 178
Dance notation: Laban system, 173–74, 184, 185

Deister Concentrator Co., In re, 50
Design patent: *Sears* and *Compco* decisions, 1–78 *passim,* 93–94, 96, 132; lamps, 6, 8–9, 83–86, 93, 105; bottles, 37–40, 89–92; criteria for, 81–82; compared with copyright, 83–88; term of, 87; trademarks, 88–92; unfair competition, 92–97; economics of, 102–12, 129; dresses, 106–10; legal problems of, 112–21; requirement criteria of, 113–28
Design Patent Act (35 U.S.C.), 1, 37, 80nn1,2, 113
Design protection, 79–133; economics of, 97–102; conclusions on, 128–33; *see also* Design patent
Design Protection Act, 77–78
Dictionaries, *see* Subjects of copyright
Dietz, R. E. Co. v. Burr & Starkweather Co., 115
Dobson v. Dornan, 123
Douglas, Justice William O., opinions quoted, 83–84
Dress design, 106–10

Educators: use of copyrighted materials, effect of proposed revision of Copyright Act, 135–52
Electric Storage Battery Co. v. Mine Safety Appliances Co., 49

Fair use doctrine, 141–43
Federal Communications Act, 160
Federal Communications Commission, 158, 164–65
Federal power: U.S. federal preemption and state jurisdictions, 8–13
Ferris v. Frohman, 175
Frank, Judge J.: opinions, 22n; opinion quoted, 3n17
Free competition, 3–4, 7, 22–25, 28, 79
Fuller v. Bemis, 179, 180, 180–81
Functionality doctrine, 4–5, 8, 50, 113–21

Gorham v. White, 81–82, 123

Haig & Haig, Ltd., Ex parte, 89, 91
Hand, Judge Learned: opinions, 4n26, 10, 68, 77n329; opinions quoted, 3n16, 59–60, 64–65, 92–93, 113–14

Harlan, Justice John M., opinion quoted, 12
Herbert v. Shanley Co., 168
Holmes, Judge, opinion, 4n26
H.R. 4347 (proposed revision of Copyright Act), 135–52 *passim*

Intermountain Broadcasting Corp. v. Idaho Microwave, Inc., 156–57, 161
International News Serv. v. Associated Press, 56, 58–60, 69, 92–93, 161, 163
Invention, as design patent requirement, 121–28

Kalem Co. v. Harper Bros., 179, 180
King v. Mister Maestro, Inc., 67
Koehring, In re, 118
KUTV, Inc., see Cable Vision, Inc. v.

Laban, Rudolf, dance notation system, 173–74, 184, 185
Labeling, 13–19, 20, 24–28
Labels, copyright of, 33–36
Lamps, *see* Design patent
Lanham Trademark Act (1946), 45–46, 49
Lewis Purses, Inc. Nat v. Carole Bags, Inc., 125–26
Lobl, In re, 119

Martinetti v. Maguire, 180
Mazer v. Stein, 83–86, 132
Merriam, G. & C. Co., 31–32
Mine Safety Appliances Co., *see Electric Storage Battery v.*
Misappropriation, 59, 67, 68, 96
Mogen David Wine Corp., Application of, 50, 89–90, 91–92

National Education Association, 141, 150
Novelty, as design patent requirement, 120–21

Originality, requirement of in copyright, 1, 11, 16, 23
Ornamentation, as design patent requirement, 113–21

Packaging, 36–45
Patent, design, *see* Design patent

Index

Patent system, 98–102, 103–4; applications and grants, 82n8 (*table*)
Performing right, 138–41; CATV, 165–70; choreography, 186–88
Phonograph records, 67–68, 148
Photocopying, of copyrighted materials for classroom use, 136–38, 151
Product appearance: confusion among competing products, 7, 8, 17–18, 24–25, 28; configuration, 17–18, 27, 34, 46–48, 49, 81–82, 88, 89–92, 117–18, 119; *see also* Labeling
Publication, definition of, 62–70

Reed, Justice Stanley, opinion quoted, 84–85
Ronson Art Metal Works, Inc. v. Gibson Lighter Mfg. Co., 30–31, 32
Russell v. Smith, 179–80

Sears, Roebuck & Co. v. Stiffel Co., 1–78 *passim*, 93–94, 162
Smith v. Stewart, 124
Smith, Kline & French Labs. v. Clark & Clark, 29–30
Society of European Stage Authors and Composers v. New York Hotel Statler Co., 166–67, 168, 169
State laws, unfair competition, 6–7, 9, 12, 19, 23, 25, 26, 52, 55, 66–67, 70
Statutory copyright, 2, 52–75 *passim*; and choreography, 176–88
Steffens v. Stevens, 125
Subjects of copyright: works of art, 2, 52, 53, 83–86; dictionaries, 31, 32; writings, 53, 54–62, 83–84, 86; videotape, 148

Television broadcasting: rights of broadcasters, 61, 71; use of copyrighted material, 143–47, 151; CATV and, 153–70; impact of CATV on, 155–57; reaction of industry to CATV, 159–60
Three-dimensional objects, copyright of, 2, 53
Trade dress, 16–19, 36–45
Trademarks: copyright of, 16–17, 45–52; design patent of, 88–92

Unfair Commercial Activities Bill, proposed, 52, 77–78
Unfair competition: results of *Sears* and *Compco* decisions, 1–78 *passim*; doctrine of, 3–4, 7, 9, 21–23; lamps, 6, 8–9; labeling in, 13–19, 24–28; cigarette lighters, 25, 28, 30–31, 32; in drug industry, 28–30; dictionaries, 31–32; packaging (trade dress), 36–45; television, 61; design patents, 92–97
United States Supreme Court, cases: *Sears* and *Compco*, 1–78 *passim*, 9–11, 22–23, 46, 50, 52, 60; *International News Serv. v. Associated Press*, 56, 58–60, 69, 92–93, 161, 163; *Cable Vision, Inc. v. KUTV, Inc.*, 71, 156–57; *Gorham v. White*, 81–82, 123; *Mazer v. Stein*, 83–86, 132; *R. E. Dietz Co. v. Burr & Starkweather Co.*, 115; *Dobson v. Dornan*, 123; *Smith v. Stewart*, 124; *Buck v. Jewell-LaSalle Realty Co.*, 166, 168; *Herbert v. Shanley Co.*, 168

Videotape, *see* Subjects of copyright

White v. Kimmel, 175
Works of art, copyright of, *see* Subjects of copyright
Writings, copyright of, *see* Subjects of copyright

Zippo Mfg. Co. v. Rogers Imports, Inc., 25, 28

American Society of Composers Authors and Publishers

OFFICERS

STANLEY ADAMS, *Pres.*
ADOLPH VOGEL, *Vice-Pres.*
NED WASHINGTON, *Vice-Pres.*

PAUL CRESTON, *Secy.*
FRANK H. CONNOR, *Treas.*
MORTON GOULD, *Asst. Secy.*

J. J. BREGMAN, *Asst. Treas.*

BOARD OF DIRECTORS

STANLEY ADAMS
RICHARD ADLER
VICTOR BLAU
J. J. BREGMAN
LEON J. BRETTLER
IRVING CAESAR
CY COLEMAN
FRANK H. CONNOR
PAUL CRESTON
LOUIS DREYFUS
L. WOLFE GILBERT
MORTON GOULD

LOU LEVY
ARNOLD MAXIN
PETER MENNIN
JIMMY MCHUGH
EDWIN H. MORRIS
HOWARD S. RICHMOND
RICHARD RODGERS
ARTHUR SCHWARTZ
RUDOLPH TAUHERT
ADOLPH VOGEL
NED WASHINGTON
JACK YELLEN

Z
551
P
C78
#15

APR 7 1967